WILLIAM AND HARRY

WILLIAM
AND
HARRY

Ingrid Seward

Arcade Publishing • New York

FIRST U.S. EDITION

First published in Great Britain in 2003 by Headline Book Publishing

Every effort has been made to fulfill requirements with regard to reproducing
copyrighted material. The author and publisher will be glad to rectify any
omissions at the earliest opportunity.

Library of Congress Cataloging-in-Publication Data

Seward, Ingrid.
   William and Harry : a portrait of two princes / Ingrid Seward. —1st U.S. ed.
      p. cm.
   Includes index.
   ISBN 1-55970-690-2
      1. William, Prince, grandson of Elizabeth II, Queen of Great Britian,
   1982– 2. Henry, Prince, grandson of Elizabeth II, Queen of Great Britian,
   1984– 3. Princes—Great Britian—Biography. I. Title.
   DA591.A45W557 2003
   941.085'092'2—dc21   2002044057

Published in the United States by Arcade Publishing, Inc., New York
Distributed by AOL Time Warner Book Group

Visit our Web site at www.arcadepub.com

10 9 8 7 6 5 4 3 2 1

Designed by John Hawkins

EB

PRINTED IN THE UNITED STATES OF AMERICA

To Chloe, Daisy and Charlie Bunn
and the memory of their late mother, Lorna

WILLIAM AND HARRY

Introduction

R oyal princes are born, not elected. There is nothing democratic about their titles or position. These come from birth rather than ability.

That can be a weighty burden in an age when scepticism has replaced awe, the hereditary principle is being discarded in so many areas of public life, and the role of the Royal Family is under scrutiny as never before.

It is not a situation with which William and Harry are comfortable. William, in particular, has shown a noticeable reluctance to rise above the parapet of privilege and put himself on public show. He is embarrassed by royalty's display and prefers the peace of his cottage up an unmade road at Tam-na-Ghar on the Balmoral estate to the pomp of the castle. He dislikes being recognised; when a Japanese tourist asked him for his autograph after a polo match at Cirencester, he replied, 'I don't give autographs.'

And when the Prince of Wales suggested that he accompany him to Hong Kong for the handover in 1997, which marked the symbolic end of the Empire his forebears had once reigned over, he declined his father's invitation, explaining, 'I just don't feel ready.'

The time is fast approaching, however, when William and his brother will have to shoulder the responsibilities that go with their position. That is the duty they were born to. As their grandfather Prince Philip, in one of his more curmudgeonly moods, explained, 'Everyone has to have a sense of duty – a duty to society, to their family. If you haven't got a sense of duty you get the sort of community we have now.'

Like William, Prince Philip resents the extraordinary attention the Royal Family attracts and the way it is now focused, not on their good works or their constitutional tasks, but on their emotional and marital difficulties. In times past its members could take shelter behind the shield of deference, their failings and misdemeanours hidden from public view. The Duke of Windsor, as Prince of Wales, had a series of affairs with the wives of other men and his brother, the Duke of Kent, was a drug-taking homosexual, but only a very few people knew what was going on and they kept their silence. No longer. Who the Royal Family are is now as important as what they are – and perhaps even more so. The dry obsequiousness of the Court Circle has been overtaken by the lurid gossip of the front pages and hardly a day passes without some startling new 'revelation' that further erodes the mystique that has been royalty's traditional shroud.

It is not a change they relish but there is little point in complaining. As William's cousin, Prince Michael of Kent, once told me, 'Life isn't fair. Whoever said it would be? You have to accept the good with the bad. Obviously there are penalties. But there are also advantages. If you have privilege you have no option but to accept some kind of obligation. You can't have all the perks without pulling your weight.'

Prince Philip set out the guidelines that William and Harry must take into consideration. 'If you are really going to have a monarchy you have got to have a family – and the family has got to be in the public eye.'

How they cope with that imperative will give resonance to their lives and define the future of the British monarchy, with important consequences for those who live under its reign. It will be no easy task, as their parents readily acknowledged. I have discussed the matter at some length with the Prince of Wales and, shortly before her untimely and tragic death, with Diana, and those informal conversations, over cups of tea (with him) and coffee (with her), have given me an enlightening insight into their concerns. Both were very conscious of the pitfalls that lie ahead as the Royal Family faces up to the difficult task of adapting itself to the demands of a world which is very different from the one they were brought up in. But both were confident that the princes would rise to the challenge.

Diana told me, 'I'm sure they will deal with the problems. They will have to. William, being the intellectual one, finds it harder, but he is very aware of people and their feelings, which will be to his advantage. Harry is very artistic and sporty. He doesn't mind anything, which will help him, too.'

A good part of the difficulties they will face, it must be said, were of her own making. Before she burst on to the scene and into the public consciousness, the Royal Family was a dowdy and ageing anachronism whose major function was to serve up a little national colour with their births, weddings, funerals and occasional jubilees, old-fashioned signposts in the headlong rush into an uncertain future. Through the force of her personality and her beauty she made the institution she had married into the subject of worldwide and often intrusive interest. She frequently complained about the interest she aroused, yet was not averse to going out of her way to court it when it happened to suit her purposes. William saw what that did to his mother and, as she was honest enough to admit, his sometimes ambivalent attitude towards his position is a reaction to the stresses Diana endured.

One of the things Diana kept emphasising to me when we met that summer before her death was how she hoped that as time passed they would be able to do things together as a family once more. It was to have been her way of making amends. But death robbed her of that opportunity and it is their father who has had to steer them towards maturity.

The ghost of Diana was never far away, however. They could see it in their own faces and hear it in their voices.

William bears an uncanny physical resemblance to his mother. It is not something he appreciates. He likes to think he looks like himself. Harry, for his part, has the same breathy quality in his voice that Diana had. But he also likes to see himself as his own man. It would be worrying if he didn't.

William has a habit of swallowing the ends of his words and trailing off the end of his sentences. He uses words like 'OK' and 'really' a lot and is fond of exaggerated superlatives such as terrific, marvellous, amazing and brilliant. If he doesn't like something it is 'absolutely hideous' or 'foul' – 1950s expressions that sound out of synch with his modern, laidback dress sense.

When it comes to clothes it is Harry who takes more after their mother and shows the greater flair. He gels his hair and whether he's wearing hip hop fashion, polo gear or country tweeds he always adds an individual touch: cowboy boots, maybe a bandana, an Inca hat with a T-shirt and chinos. And he is always careful that the faded Highgrove club polo shirt he is convinced brings him good luck is worn hanging out of his trousers.

The cool image comes with an often wicked sense of humour. His remarks are loaded with sarcasm, especially about members of the opposite sex, who he treats with the feigned indifference of youth. Hiding behind the mask of arrogance and pretending to be confident, he sat next to the supermodel Claudia Schiffer at a Highgrove party in 2001. Having failed to get much of a spark out of the blonde beauty, he later claimed that he found her surprisingly dull.

'Harry is a spirit unto himself,' said his ski organiser Clair Southwell. 'He's very open and affectionate.' He takes exception to being portrayed as a royal tear-away.

But what he also doesn't like is being told what to do. The only person who seemed able to exert any day-to-day authority was his unofficial nanny Tiggy Legge-Bourke. He attended her wedding to divorcé Charles Pettifer in 1999 and is godfather to their first child, Fred, born in August 2001 (William is godfather to their second child, Tom, born in September 2002).

Still he continues to heed her advice. Everyone else, including his father, is likely to be ignored, especially if the opinion has not been asked for. Celebrity sometimes does that to people. As Jodi Kidd, the supermodel sister of Harry's polo playing companion Jack, observed, 'It does change you. You suddenly think you're important. No one says no to you, so you think you can get away with anything,'

His father is hoping that this is a phase his youngest son will grow out of. He is grateful that his eldest never grew into it.

William's humour is more straightforward. He is enough of an Etonian to delight in using non-U words like 'lounge' and 'toilet'. And he is an excellent mimic, not only of television's Ali G but also of his father, whose mannerisms he has turned into a comedy act – a liberty no previous generation of princes would ever have been allowed.

Diana's healer, Simone Simmons, who Diana was close to in the last years of her life, recalled, 'One day he rang me pretending to be his father and I had no idea. Eventually he had to tell me, "It's me Simone. It's me, William." '

William teases his father in other ways, too. When he returned from his gap year he threatened to make Charles eat a bowl of the burnt porridge he had had in Chile. 'I'm going to feed it to my father until he is sick so he can see what we went through,' he said.

Harry's approach and difference in character is reflected in the princes' attitude towards the institution in which they will soon be playing an ever more central part. When William, momentarily overwhelmed by the thought of the responsibilities he was born to shoulder, declared that he did not want to be king, Harry piped up, 'If you don't want to be king, I will be!'

Diana laughed at the memory. 'He loves castles and soldiers,' she said.

There is more to the modern business of royalty than ancient pageantry and a collection of castellated homes, however. Trying to find a direction in which to move, the Royal Family has already caused conflict between the Queen's staff and those who advise the Prince of Wales, and these inter-Palace disagreements have yet to be resolved. It may fall to Prince William to sort out the muddle.

Charles said, 'I'm not unresponsive to change.' He has already set the course for a more open and responsive monarchy, closer to the kind that Diana envisaged than the one the Queen presides over. In that he enjoys the support of William. But Charles remains a traditionalist at heart. William is more his mother's son, keen to push the changes along at a faster pace and, as his father observed, will doubtless do things his own way when his time comes, as is his regal prerogative. One of his best friends said, 'He's got a quiet self-confidence. He knows himself. He's fun, but he knows when to stop.'

He has already established his own style. It is a lot more casual than anything his forebears or even his father would have dared to adopt. He wears jeans, not kilts. He has also been allowed to choose his own friends and girlfriends without first having them vetted by the Palace, and is a lot more confident than his father was at the same age. Charles once told me how gauche he was in his early twenties, and recalled the embarrassing occasion when he took a girl to a restaurant. They were the only people there and had all the waiters hovering around them. To cover his embarrassment he ordered a particularly expensive bottle of wine – and then promptly knocked it over.

William is also a lot more sophisticated. In the summer of 2002 he joined a mixed group of friends on a river trip where everyone, William included, ended up naked in the water. Harry is equally laid back when it comes to his royal image and thinks nothing of cavorting in a carefree and open way with the young women he meets at polo and in the pubs of Gloucestershire.

Diana, the naive kindergarten teacher who married the heir to the British throne, anticipated how her sons would have girls flocking around them. So possessive in other ways, she insisted that she would not be a clinging mother and left them her jewellery in her will to give to their future wives. William already has the gold Cartier watch given to Diana by Charles, and Harry has her sapphire and diamond engagement ring.

They are just the tip of their inheritance. Diana left the bulk of her £17 million divorce settlement in trust for her sons and there will be more monies forthcoming from the royal estates. As heir in line, William will inevitably collect the greater share. He will one day be the outright owner of Balmoral and Sandringham and he, not Harry, will be the custodian of Buckingham Palace and Windsor Castle. That discrepancy in their prospects has sometimes caused difficulties between them, and there have been occasions when Harry has appeared to be jealous of his brother.

'Diana called him her little baby. He always preferred being alone with her. He didn't want to share his mummy and used to sit on her lap and snuggle his head into her shoulder,' Simone remembered. 'I told Harry,

"When William is here, Mummy divides her time, but you need more of her." He always found the excuse of illness to come home so he could be with her.'

'I'm not the important one,' Harry often said. A view that was enforced when he saw his great-grandmother, who only ever focussed her attention on William. That does not mean that he can disappear into anonymity, as his encounter with drugs rammed home to him. After William returned from his gap year, Harry said, 'I get on much better with him now. He's changed a lot.'

The new openness the Royal Family is striving for has brought every aspect of their lives into sharp focus. But that, as they know, goes with the job they were born to. Prince Philip was once asked if he missed not being able to walk unnoticed in a public park. He replied, 'It's like saying, don't you miss going to the moon. I mean, I just haven't the opportunity of going to the moon. You can't go through life desperately wanting to be somebody else, wanting to do something else all the time.'

Being who they are has given William and Harry a lot to contend with. Their childhood was a maelstrom of conflicting emotions that included argument, separation, divorce and death, which turned their lives into an international soap opera. The stability so vital to children's development was denied them, and that would produce problems which even in adulthood they are still trying to resolve.

Yet remarkably they have managed to make it through without cracking up or breaking down. How they did so is the story of this book.

ONE

In the Beginning

To suggest, as some critics have done, that the Prince of Wales regarded Lady Diana Spencer as a convenient brood mare and married her only to ensure the continuation of the Windsor bloodline wilfully discounts the empathy that drew them together.

Diana herself told me, 'It is very hurtful to our children when people say we didn't love each other. We did – very much so.' And a few weeks before she died Diana told me, 'I know he loved me when we got married. If one day anyone sees our letters they will know that we did love each other.'

Charles had been immediately smitten by the gamine, coltish nineteen-year-old who caught his romantic eye at a barbeque at a country house near Petworth in Sussex in July 1980. They sat on a hay bale under the summer stars and talked about the recent funeral of his great-uncle, Earl Mountbatten of Burma. She told him, 'It's wrong you're lonely,' and he made to kiss her.

It was the fateful first move in a relationship that was destined to run a gauntlet of emotions from enchantment to farce and finally to tragedy. Along the way they produced two healthy sons – living testimony to the ardour that was certainly there between them in the beginning.

Children do not necessarily make for a happy marriage, however. They can provide the glue that binds a union together. But they can also expose the divisions and divergences in a relationship and, without ever knowing how or why, William and Harry were fated to feature prominently in their parents' discord.

That was not what Charles had intended. He had gone into his marriage with clear ideas of where his wife's responsibilities would lie. He explained, 'One of the most important roles any woman can ever perform is to be a mother. How children grow up, what attitudes they have, is absolutely vital, both from the social point of view and for the future, and all this stems so much from the role the mother performs.'

Diana was that mother, and this made her the custodian of the Royal Family – of its past, its traditions and its expectations. She had it within her power to shape the monarchy through her sons, as the Queen Mother had done when the opportunity had fallen her way on the abdication of her brother-in-law, Edward VIII. All she had to do was play within the rules.

It was a singular honour and, as the daughter of one of Britain's grandest aristocratic houses, Diana well knew what was expected of her. She knew that dynastic marriages inevitably involved children and there is no more important dynasty in Britain's social hierarchy than the royal one, and she was looking forward to becoming the mother of a future monarch. The fact that she was besotted by Charles was the added bonus.

What she had not taken into account (and what she would refuse to accept) was that her husband might not be quite the Prince Charming who had glowed so glamorously in her teenage imagination. He was twelve years older, old-fashioned and set in his ways. He was also pampered to the point of absurdity. At the age of two he had been given his own valet, called Ian Williams, and one of the first things Diana noticed was that when they travelled he had twenty-two pieces of luggage, while she made do with four or five.

Charles was also labouring under a misconception. He thought he had found someone young enough to be moulded to fit the position of royal wife and mother. His cousin and Gordonstoun school friend, Lord Romsey, was not convinced. He told Charles that Diana had fallen in love with an image rather than an individual. He could have added that the girl the prince described as 'jolly and bouncy' might very well grow up to develop a mind and a will of her own.

Charles had angrily dismissed Romsey's warning out of hand, and at first it looked as though his intuition was right. Diana made every effort to fit into the royal routine, relishing her invitations to Balmoral and making great play of how much she adored the Scottish countryside. Prince Edward's footman Mark Simpson, who would later work with Diana, recalled, 'She would go around telling everybody how much she loved Balmoral and that it was such a magical place and how she loved it beyond imagination.'

It was the autumn of 1980 and Charles was at Balmoral for the grouse shooting. Simpson said, 'Most of the ladies did not get up until after the guns had gone out, but Diana was always up at the crack of dawn. If you looked out of your window at a quarter to eight you could see her walking in the garden. She made a great point of being there to see them off.'

The prince has a deep spiritual attachment to Balmoral which he is thrilled to share with anyone who shares his interest. 'Diana knew full well what she was doing by saying she thought it was such a magical place,' a member of the Household said.

Charles was now thirty years old and at the age when he had said it was time to settle down and get married. By making that remark, he had imposed a time scale on himself and the pressure was mounting on him to find a suitable bride.

The Queen had been keen for him to marry the Duke of Wellington's daughter, Lady Jane Wellesley, but she baulked at joining what she perceived as the royal circus. 'Do you honestly believe I want to be Queen?' she dismissively asked one reporter. 'I don't want another title. I've got one already, thank you.'

Romsey's sister Amanda Knatchbull was another candidate who had met with the Queen's approval. Prince Philip observed that, as the granddaughter of Earl Mountbatten of Burma, she was 'family' and therefore knew how the Royal Family worked. But without the forceful encouragement of Mountbatten, who was assassinated by the IRA in 1979, that romance had lost its impetus.

That left a vacancy in Charles's life which Diana neatly filled. 'You should be with someone to look after you,' she told him during that encounter on the hay bale.

The often indecisive Charles was at first reluctant to commit himself and, according to popular legend, the Queen Mother and her lady-in-waiting, Lady Fermoy, played a large part in helping him to make up his mind. Ruth Fermoy denied that. She was Diana's grandmother, but, well aware of her shortcomings, would later insist that she was against the marriage. She explained that she did not know Charles particularly well and said, 'If I'd said to him, "You're making a great mistake," he probably wouldn't have paid the slightest attention.'

Diana herself discounted the two old ladies' involvement. She told me, 'The Queen Mother and Lady Fermoy were not instrumental in arranging my marriage. It's a myth it was the Queen Mother. She didn't do anything. It was Charles and I.'

The one person who did have a hand was Prince Philip. He warned his son against further procrastination and told him to either ask for Diana's hand or else terminate their relationship before she became 'damaged goods' with a stain on her good name.

Charles decided on the first course of action. He made his proposal at Windsor Castle in the large nursery sitting room where a photograph in a leather frame of the Queen and Philip stood on the mantelpiece, and pictures of Queen Victoria's grandchildren hung from the walls. The footman served them cold poached salmon followed by fresh fruit salad. There was no celebratory champagne. Instead Diana and Charles drank lemon refresher, a favourite royal concoction of Malvern water with lemon squash mixed with Epsom salts now marketed by the Duchy of Cornwall.

In Diana's account, Charles said, 'Will you marry me?' She replied, 'Yeah, OK,' and laughed. He told her, 'You do realise that one day you will be Queen?' She said, 'Yes, I love you so much.' He said, 'Whatever love means' – a phrase he would repeat, to his eternal regret, during the official engagement interview.

Diana slept the night alone in the bottom room of the Queen's Tower. She left the following morning before breakfast and drove herself home to London in her Mini Metro. It was hardly the most romantic of beginnings, but Charles was insisting on doing everything by an out-of-date book.

The engagement was made public at the end of February. The night before the announcement, Diana's father, Lord Spencer, and her stepmother, Raine, went to Buckingham Palace for drinks with Diana and Charles. Raine swept into Charles's apartment, larger than life with her big hair and wearing a large fur coat. Again there was no champagne and after only half an hour Charles rang the staff bell to call a footman to usher them out. Raine was reluctant to leave but Charles quickly rose to help her on with her coat. When he complimented her on the fur she said, 'Oh yes, a little present from me to me,' to which Charles replied, 'How very generous you are!'

The next morning, surrounded by his staff, Charles and Diana stood beside the radio in his office to listen to the official announcement. 'It wasn't very natural,' footman Mark Simpson recalled. 'All those girls in their blue skirts were bobbing away and saying, "Oh, sir, congratulations." From that moment on Diana didn't seem to be as thrilled as she had been.'

The public, however, were captivated. The Royal Family is a symbol of continuity, and in the fresh face of Diana they saw the promise of a new beginning.

It was certainly that for Diana. Before the announcement Diana had gone to Clarence House to spend a couple of nights with the Queen Mother. It was not a happy experience for the ingénue who now carried the hopes for the future on her young shoulders. Diana later told me, 'The Queen Mother was meant to help me, to teach me, but she didn't do anything at all. She's not as nice as she appears – she's tough.'

The public knew nothing of this. Nor were they aware of the strain Diana was under. As Romsey had predicted, she found the reality of royal life very different from what she had imagined when she moved into the second-floor suite at Buckingham Palace, which had once been occupied by Charles's old nanny, Mabel Anderson.

She arrived with just a few bags and a couple of suitcases. Simpson, who was tall, good-looking and gentle and only a couple of years older than Diana, was assigned to look after her. 'She was horribly nervous,' he recalled. 'We started to have great long chats and that was when she told me about the engagement photos and how hideous she thought she looked. She said she was so fat and she had to lose weight.

'She would never eat a proper lunch. Instead she would make me sit with her in the nursery kitchen. She sat on the spin dryer and I sat on the kitchen sink and she used to gorge herself with these huge glass bowls filled with Frosties covered with Windsor cream, which is like double double cream, and topped with lots of sugar and chopped bananas and strawberries.

'Then she would go to the bathroom and I could hear the door being bolted and locked. I didn't know then what bulimia was but I knew she was being sick.'

Her days soon settled down into a stultifying routine that left her confused and fractious. They began at 8.30 a.m. with a cup of coffee and a bath scented with Floris's Rose Geranium bath oil. If anyone asked her why she wasn't eating breakfast she replied that she was on a crash diet for her wedding.

Her mornings were spent either bouncing around in the Palace's music room with a dance teacher, trying to lose weight, or out shopping with her mother, Frances Shand Kydd, who had taken charge of the arrangements for the wedding dress which was being made for her by Elizabeth and David Emanuel.

Diana frequently went swimming in the Palace pool. 'She would go down past all the offices wearing just a towelling robe and all the office staff had their eyes popping out,' said Simpson.

She had been informed that she could invite at least six people to lunch and dinner every night, and the royal chefs were looking forward to showing off for the young lady they confidently believed would one day be mistress of the Palace. But she rarely entertained, and it was only on the urging of the staff that she eventually agreed to invite to lunch Carolyn Pride (later

Bartholomew), Ann Bolton and Virginia Pitman, the girls she had lived with at her flat in Earl's Court.

'I was given another footman to help me because they thought I had too much to do, which obviously I didn't,' Simpson recalled. 'I told her she had to do more entertaining because if she didn't, I would lose my extra help, so she said, "OK, I'll think of some people to ask."'

The luncheon was a success. After they had finished eating the girls all practised curtseying to the princess-to-be. 'Lower, lower, lower,' Diana commanded. Pitman, larger than others, overbalanced and almost fell flat on her face, much to the amusement of everyone else.

After that, her flatmates would be invited at the rate of one of them a week. The Duchess of Westminster was another occasional guest, as was the future Duchess of York. Most of the time, though, Diana continued to lunch by herself, with only her footmen for company. And instead of availing herself of the cordon bleu dishes on offer from the royal kitchens, her diet usually consisted of Kellogg's Frosties eaten out of bowls engraved with the EIIR cipher. Simpson ended up requisitioning so many packets of the cereal that the Royal Pantry store keepers became suspicious and accused him of selling them out of the back door of the Palace. Diana had to go downstairs to vouch that they really were all for her.

It was clearly a trying period for Diana, who became increasingly morose. She talked warmly of her younger brother, Charles Spencer, and her father, who she said was much more intelligent than people imagined. It was the people she disliked that came to preoccupy her, however, and the list was a long one. According to Simpson, it included her prospective sister-in-law, Princess Anne, and her stepmother, Raine Spencer, who she called 'conniving'; the Queen's lady-in-waiting Lady Susan Hussey, whose well-intentioned advice she resented; and her sister, Lady Sarah McCorquodale, because she had gone out with Charles first 'and he had found her very attractive'.

Despite all the help Mrs Shand Kydd was giving her, Diana unkindly called her mother a 'self-promoter'. She also complained that her future mother-in-law was not paying her enough attention, ignoring the fact that, as Sovereign, the Queen had the daily chore of reading and signing her State papers, as well as a full schedule of engagements and receptions to attend, most of which had been fixed months in advance. In private, Diana jokily referred to the Queen as 'Brenda', Prince Philip as 'Keith', and Princess Margaret as 'Yvonne', the nicknames given them by the satirical magazine *Private Eye*.

'I had night after night talking to her,' Simpson said. 'I would go up at 11 p.m. to my room exhausted from listening to her. It was *terribly* mentally draining – I was not the right person to deal with it as I was a product of the Palace. I knew that the Royal Family have huge schedules, which makes ordinary family life almost impossible unless they are at Balmoral. It is how it always worked. I found this quite normal.'

But Diana wasn't listening to the explanations Simpson or anyone else had to offer. The young woman who had captured a prince was losing her mental equilibrium. Up until then she had seemed a perfectly normal young woman – vivacious, outgoing and full of laughter. Within a few short weeks she had become depressed, insecure and lonely.

Carolyn Bartholomew blamed the change in her friend on the transition from a cosy flat in Earl's Court to the impersonal vastness of Buckingham Palace. 'Then the tears started,' she said. 'I was worried about her. She wasn't happy. She was suddenly plunged into all this pressure and it was a nightmare for her.' Diana would later admit, 'I missed my girls so much. I wanted to go back there and sit and giggle like we used to and borrow clothes and chat about silly things, just being in my safe shell again.'

Simpson, who saw her every day, blamed Diana. He said, 'Her misery of being so lonely was brought on by herself. She cut herself off.'

Diana blamed the Royal Family. 'As time went on it was all about how unfeeling the Royal Family were, how they had no emotion,' said Simpson.

And the person she blamed most of all was Prince Charles. She complained bitterly, 'He isn't paying me enough attention.'

Like his mother, the prince was committed to a schedule of meetings and engagements that took him away from the Palace, sometimes for days at a time. He failed to appreciate that the one person who was in greatest need of his presence was the young woman he was about to make a princess.

An engagement is a time when couples are supposed to get to know each other properly, and Diana was in urgent need of physical reassurance and affection. It was not an unreasonable desire. She was barely out of her teens, naive and without any practical sexual experience but, as later events would verify, she was a passionate woman who enjoyed the attentions of men.

With an age advantage of twelve years, Charles should have been qualified to deal with his fiancée in a compassionate and caring way. He had had a number of girlfriends, including the fiery-tempered Anna Wallace, and Sabrina Guinness who had once worked as a nanny for actor Ryan O'Neal and whose friends included Mick Jagger and Jack Nicholson. His experiences had not included actually living with a woman, however. And despite his reputation, he was never the lothario of legend. As he admitted, 'I don't know how the idea got about that I'm amazingly successful with women – my constant battle is to escape.'

There had been occasions when he had been infatuated, but logic had always taken precedence. He explained, 'If I am deciding on whom I want to live with for fifty years, well, that's the last decision on which I would want my head to be ruled by my heart.'

It is a remark that might have been penned by the novelist Jane Austen in the early 1800s. By the emotional standards of the late twentieth century it sounded calculating and a mite prissy. A little more ardour would not have gone amiss, but that seemed to be beyond the prince's emotional range. Brought up in a matriarchal culture where he had to bow to both his mother and his grandmother, he had an idealised and rather naive view of how members of the opposite sex expected or, in Diana's case, wished to be regarded. His was very much a hands-off approach and, to her dismay, Diana discovered that by accepting his proposal of marriage she had inadvertently made herself inviolate.

She tried to force the issue. In the early hours of 2 June 1981, London was hit by a severe thunderstorm. Woken by a crack of lightning, Diana ran out of her bedroom overlooking Constitution Hill and down the long passage to Charles's apartment which looked out over the Mall. She climbed into bed with him. Charles was wearing old-fashioned pyjamas tied with a white cord. It was the first night the couple had spent together. She left his room at 6 a.m., when she was spotted by a housemaid, which sent an inevitable ripple of gossip coursing through the staff corridors.

All was not as the maid had deduced, however. Diana told her staff that the prince had done nothing more than cuddle her and give her a chaste kiss before rolling over and going to back to sleep again. She spoke with regret. It was clearly less than she had been hoping for.

Diana was always astonishingly frank with her dressers and footmen and treated them more like intimate friends than members of staff. One night Simpson had accompanied the prince to the opera in order to serve him drinks and supper during the interval. Diana had been invited but had chosen not to go. When Simpson returned to the Palace, Diana summoned him to her bedroom and questioned him about the evening.

'She was ready for bed and in her nightie,' Simpson recalled. 'She complained that Charles never came to say goodnight to her.'

This was the one night, however, that he did. When he walked in he found the footman sitting on his fiancée's bed, innocently looking at some paintings that had arrived as wedding presents. 'I was horrified,' Simpson said. 'I went bright red and ran.'

The next morning Diana mischievously told Simpson that Charles 'had been very surprised to see you in my bedroom'. She added, 'But it's good for him.'

Simpson suspected that Diana had made Charles promise to look in on her before he retired to his own room – and that she had therefore deliberately created a situation for her own ends. If that was indeed the case, it did not produce the desired result. In the court of Prince Charles, it seemed, courtly love involved no courtship at all.

Charles saw nothing wrong with this. But by behaving in what he considered to be an honourable fashion, he had created a terrible doubt in Diana's mind.

Shortly after their engagement Charles told Diana about his relationship with Camilla Parker Bowles. He insisted that now he was to be married there was no other and never would be another woman in his life. A more worldly man would have known that the past is best kept secret. By admitting that until very recently someone else had been such a central feature of his life, he had only succeeded in planting suspicion.

Diana's thinking was simple. She believed that if Charles was not enjoying her favours, he must be enjoying someone else's.

Her distrust was inflamed when, two weeks before the wedding, she opened a parcel that was sitting on the desk of Michael Colborne, secretary of the prince's office. It contained a gold chain bracelet with a blue enamel disc with the letters G and F stamped on it. The initials stood either for Girl Friday, which is what Charles called Mrs Parker Bowles, or Gladys and Fred, the nicknames Diana facetiously ascribed to them.

It was as nothing compared to the superb pendant of diamonds and emeralds in the shape of the Prince of Wales feathers he had given Diana when she first came to the Palace but, as far as she was concerned, that was beside the point. She was outraged that Charles should give Camilla anything. She believed the bangle provided incontrovertible proof that he was still seeing his mistress. She bearded her fiancé that night and cross-examined him about his relationship with the rival she later called the Rottweiler. When the prince insisted that he was going to personally present the bracelet to Camilla as a 'thank you' for all she had done for him over the years, she burst into tears. Diana later told her sisters about the incident and stated that she was not going to go through with the wedding.

This was the second time in just a few weeks that she had threatened to walk out on her engagement. A few days after the night of the thunderstorm Diana had attended the lavish ball the Queen had given to mark Prince Andrew's twenty-first birthday. More than a thousand guests had congregated at Windsor Castle. Elton John had provided the entertainment and Diana had danced until dawn, when she had suddenly left and driven north to Althorp to tell her father that she intended to cancel her betrothal. Lord Spencer had talked her round. 'Darling Daddy, he always knew what to do for the best,' Diana told me.

Now it was her sisters' turn to calm her down. They made light of the bracelet incident and told her that she couldn't walk out on Charles with just a few days to go before the ceremony at St Paul's Cathedral. 'The tea towels have already been printed,' they teased her.

Diana was easily persuaded. She may have been unhappy, but she was not going to surrender the greatest catch any young woman could aspire to. Not at this stage, anyway.

Two days before the ceremony she attended the pre-wedding ball at Buckingham Palace. The following morning she went to see the Queen, who presented her with Queen Mary's love knot tiara and an emerald necklace. When she returned to her rooms she showed them to Simpson and told him how 'sweet' the Queen had been. Then, Simpson recalled, she gleefully chanted, 'I've got Brenda's rocks!'

The next day the wedding duly went ahead amid all the pomp the British Crown can muster on such occasions. And the world applauded.

The honeymoon, however, turned out to be no more successful than the engagement had been. The couple spent their first two nights together at Broadlands, Lord Mountbatten's old home at Broadlands in Hampshire. Diana recorded, 'It was just grim. I had tremendous hope in me which was slashed by day two. Went to Broadlands. Second night out come the van der Post novels he hadn't read.' She admitted to one of her staff that the first time she slept with Charles, 'I giggled.'

On that second night Diana went upstairs to her room and wrote to Simpson. In her letter she said, 'I just wanted to thank for all your kindness and patience you've shown towards me since I moved into BP. My stay was made so much easier by your company, as it got terribly lonely and we had so many laughs and for that I can't thank you enough. Do hope you were able to enjoy Wednesday and that you noticed my dress?

'Am off to *Britannia* tomorrow. The bad news is that I haven't eaten *any* cereal – sob. How am I going to cope without my bowls of cereal . . .'

Charles seemed astonishingly unaware of his wife's problems. Aboard the Royal Yacht he sat 'hermit-like', as he himself put it, on the veranda deck, writing thank you letters or 'sunk with pure joy into one of Laurens van der Post's books'.

Diana was a normal, healthy woman who had expected a great deal more from her honeymoon. She wanted her husband to pay her more attention than he did his books. She felt physically rejected. She said, 'I was so tired – for all the wrong reasons totally.'

That only served to aggravate her other emotional problems. She would later recall, 'The bulimia was appalling. I remember crying my eyes out.'

Matters did not improve when the couple moved to Balmoral for the next leg of what was supposed to be their nuptial celebrations.

Simpson was at the castle when they arrived and watched them get out of their car at the castle gates. They were then transported up the long drive lined with two hundred cheering staff and estate workers and their families in an old pony trap garlanded with honeysuckle and heather and pulled by four gillies. 'This was her first real royal moment within the family when she found that people were dropping to the floor and saying, "Good morning, Your Royal Highness," etc., and curtseying and bowing and I think she found it all a bit much.'

The trouble was that the staff were curtseying and bowing to a lot of other people, too. It was August and the Royal Family was there in force; instead of being on an intimate honeymoon, Diana found that she was on a family holiday. As well as the Queen and Prince Philip, the Queen Mother was there, as were Princess Margaret and Princess Anne and her children, Peter and Zara Phillips. Rather than being the centre of attention, Diana discovered that she was just one royal among many – and a newcomer at that. She was bitterly disappointed and became ever more depressed.

'She started to miss out on the traditional picnics and evening barbeques, which were held in a log cabin with fires and candlelight,' Simpson recalled. 'She said she wasn't feeling well as an excuse.'

When the rest of the family headed off into the hills at 7 p.m. she would stay behind in the nursery dining room to pick at the sausages and beans she had ordered from the kitchens. This did not make her popular with chefs, as one of the reasons for the barbeques, which the Royal Family cooked themselves, was to give the staff a night off. She did not seem to appreciate that even a plate of nursery food still required a chef to prepare it and a footman to serve it and then clear it away afterwards.

Princess Margaret was sympathetic to her plight and counselled the Queen to 'let her do what she likes'. The Queen, ever anxious to avoid any kind of showdown, gratefully accepted her sister's advice. Charles was not prepared to be so sanguine. Too many nights ended with her tearful accusation that he was still in touch with Camilla. Mountbatten's daughter, Patricia, who succeeded her father to the title, observed, 'Diana had got it into her head that Camilla was still important in his life and absolutely nothing he could say or do would disabuse her of the idea that somewhere she was lurking in the background, which was an absolute tragedy because it was totally untrue.'

The days were equally fraught. Shortly after the couple arrived at Balmoral, a photocall was arranged. It was to be held on the banks of the River Dee. On the morning in question Diana threw a tantrum and said she was not going to take part. Charles pleaded with her but she remained adamant. Charles, always prone to sudden rages, was on the verge of losing his temper when Diana changed her mind. When they arrived at the river to face the photographers she was beaming and relaxed, while her husband, still smarting over the heated exchanged, looked tense and uncomfortable.

Caught in a situation beyond his experience, Charles summoned Laurens van der Post in whose wisdom he trusted, and asked his old friend to have a word with Diana. When that failed to achieve anything (van der Post simply could not fathom her) a doctor was summoned. 'He's my psychiatrist,' Diana declared.

The doctor was picked up from his hotel in nearby Ballater and driven to the castle shortly before 11 o'clock each day. He would be taken up from the Tower Door to the Waleses' large, tartan-decorated sitting room that was almost unchanged since the days of Queen Victoria. Here he would spend half an hour talking to the couple together, followed by another half an hour alone with Diana.

Afterwards Diana would drive the silver Ford Escort that had been put at her disposal to the local shop where she would buy bags of sweets. With Simpson at her side, she would then drive up to the waterfalls at Garowort, to sit on a rock, cast stones into the cascading water, eat her sweets and talk the morning away.

She told Simpson how she longed to start a family of her own and how she hoped her first child would be a boy. Drawing no doubt on the memory of the problems that had ensued in her own family when her mother failed to produce a boy, she said, 'I know how important sons are to men.'

Later, after she had been taken to visit specialists in London, she would complain about having been prescribed Valium and an assortment of other drugs intended to control her depression and mood swings.

'The shrink told her that she needed some young female company,' Simpson recalled. 'A few days later her flatmate Carolyn Pride [later Bartholomew] arrived.'

Her mood lightened. She went stalking and shot a stag and went for long walks through the grounds of Balmoral with Charles at her side. She hadn't a clue what her husband was talking about when he started going on about Jung and the collective subconscious (he was a university graduate, she was a high school drop-out), but at least she listened. For a while she became again the sociable and appealing young woman she had been before she had allowed herself to be drawn into the royal vortex.

It was not to last. When the sun shines on the backdrop of mountains and glens Balmoral presents a glorious sight. On her first visit there Diana had called it 'magical'. But Scotland in autumn is not the best place to be searching for the sunny side of love: when it is shrouded in mist and rain it appears formidable and forbidding, and when the weather took a turn for the worse Diana's spirits mirrored the change. She began to find the formality stifling. The bowing and scraping which had once so amused her started to grate. She complained that she was never alone with her husband. She was irritated at having to change her clothing as many as five times a day, and the endless meals she could not eat became a trial. When coffee was served after dinner one evening, she grumbled, 'Why can't we ever have it on the terrace?'

The answer was that this was her mother-in-law's house and this was the way things were done. It is a problem many new wives have to come to terms with. Diana did not. She was overawed and frightened. She complained, 'They thought I could adapt to being Princess of Wales overnight.'

At the end of their third week at Balmoral the newlyweds moved out of the castle and into Craigowan, a granite lodge set in its own garden about a mile from the castle. Built for Queen Victoria's private secretaries, it has become a honeymoon house for successive generations of the Royal Family. The Duke and Duchess of Kent spent part of their honeymoon there, as did Princess Anne and her second husband, Tim Laurence, and later Prince Edward and Sophie. Double-fronted, it has six bedrooms and staff quarters at the back. The decor is tartan carpets and pine furniture. But if that was not entirely to Diana's taste, she was nonetheless delighted to be out from under her mother-in-law's roof.

'She was happier at Craigowan as she was out of the royal system and could run the house,' observed Charles's valet Stephen Barry, who attended the couple. They were there for four weeks and just before they left in October Charles and Diana treated their half-dozen staff to a special barbeque. The food and equipment were transported in a trailer specially designed by Prince Philip and driven to a log cabin ten miles up the glen. Charles did the cooking and Diana dispensed lethal cocktails.

This was one barbeque she was happy to attend, for she had just found out that she was pregnant with William. The honeymoon had finally lived up to its reputation.

She told Mark Simpson, 'At last I've done something useful.'

TWO

An Heir is Born

Diana was delighted to learn that she was expecting a baby. 'Isn't it lovely,' she happily declared, adding, 'I want *lots* of babies.'

Charles was more circumspect. He wanted children, too. He said he was 'delighted, overwhelmed, over the moon'. But he also admitted, 'I found it rather a shock to my system.'

What he had not anticipated was that paternity would come so soon after their marriage. He felt that it would be a lot wiser if Diana first became accustomed to her royal role before taking on the extra responsibility of motherhood.

There was a practical consideration behind his thinking. Charles was planning a tour of Australia and New Zealand for the spring of 1982. The arrangements were at an advanced stage. These now had to be cancelled. There was no alternative. There was no way that Diana was going to be strong enough to go on a prolonged trip around the Antipodes.

This was a new experience for the prince. For the first time in his adult life he had to put someone else's interest ahead of his own. Even duty, that standing directive in royal life that dominated everything they did, had been outflanked by Diana's pregnancy.

As it turned out, delay might indeed have been the better option. In less than a year Diana had gone from being an anonymous nursery school assistant to a princess whose face adorned the front covers of newspapers and magazines around the world. She was overwhelmed. She was now an international star. However, beneath the glossy veneer of the Hollywood-style make-up and designer clothes chosen for her by *Vogue* magazine's Anna Harvey she was still the same inexperienced ingénue only just out of her teens. The thought of being royal 'terrified' her – a word she used several times.

The transition had been the cause, in part at least, for the bulimia which was making her marriage so difficult. To that was added the problem of severe morning sickness.

Diana was highly embarrassed by her situation. She kept having to leave the table in the middle of dinners to run to the lavatory, and her official functions were often curtailed because of her illness.

Her royal relations advised her to cut down on her engagements and go to bed. She refused. She had been a princess for only a few months but already she had been infused by what she called 'my royal duty'. She said, 'I didn't know which way to turn.'

Yet despite being so unwell, she still felt a great sense of personal achievement. Only two months into her pregnancy and long before the baby had started to show, she proudly started wearing maternity clothes. She took delight in choosing the decorations for the nurseries at Highgrove and Kensington Palace. And she talked enthusiastically about how she was going to bring up her child and how she was determined that he (she intuitively guessed it was going to be a boy) would have as normal a life as possible.

But all that lay in the future. In the meantime she somehow had to find her feet and establish her own position, and that was proving a daunting task. She found Charles's attitude ever more irritating and barely six weeks into her pregnancy wrote to a friend, 'I don't like complaining, but it's not great at the moment. Hubby is going around on a cloud saying how marvellous & clever he is – spend a lot of time reminding him that I'm the one carrying it! – but it doesn't seem to make any difference – sigh!'

She was clearly finding it difficult to adjust, both to her condition and, more pertinently, to her royal situation. Anyone who marries into the Royal

Family has to discard their own traditions and even their own family and fall into the royal way of doing things. That is especially true at Christmas when everyone gathers at the Queen's command. The Yuletide of 1981 was spent at Windsor Castle. It was Diana's first experience of those forced festivities and she would dread them ever afterwards.

It started badly, with a row with Princess Anne, who was ousted to make way for Charles and Diana from the top floor of the Queen's Tower which had been her rooms since she was a child.

Then there was the matter of the presents. In keeping with royal tradition they were exchanged on Christmas Eve. Diana had taken great care in her choice. Too ill to go shopping, she had selected her gifts from glossy catalogues and had spared no expense. Charles would later complain about his wife's 'extravagance', but in those early days he was still prepared to indulge her. He did warn her, though, that no one was expecting anything too elaborate. Diana followed her own taste and bought cashmere sweaters, Floris soap, pretty clothes for younger royal children and a barbeque set for Prince Philip, only to discover that in this household less was more.

In a bizarre game of one-upmanship, the royal women tried to outdo each other in the parsimony of their gifts. Anne, for instance, was fond of handing out woolly socks bought at horse trials and country fairs. Princess Alexandra tied her parcels with old pieces of wool. Diana had wanted to be generous. She ended feeling foolish.

Worse was to come. At 9 o'clock on Christmas morning after communion in the Castle chapel the whole family, which in those days added up to over thirty people, gathered in the State dining room for a sumptuous breakfast of kidneys, eggs, bacon, black pudding, sausages and kedgeree. Even the Queen Mother and Princess Margaret, who rarely rose much before eleven and then only for a slice of toast and a cup of weak tea, turned up for this mammoth morning feast.

After church came an equally elaborate Christmas lunch of turkey served off a sideboard groaning with cold meats, glazed hams and a boar's head. For a woman who by this stage could barely hold down a bowl of cereal, these meals were a ghastly ordeal.

On Boxing Day Charles wrote to a friend, 'We've had such a lovely Christmas – the two of us. It has been extraordinarily happy and cosy being able to share it together.'

The truth was that Diana couldn't wait to leave. But there was to be no escape. After Windsor the caravan of court simply rolled across England to Norfolk, taking Diana with it. And waiting for her there was another succession of breakfasts, lunches, shooting parties, a procession of guests and dinners where everyone was seated where the Queen had put them.

As a little girl, Diana had lived on the Queen's East Anglian estate in Park House. It was only a short walk away from Sandringham House and, as the daughter of one of the Queen's former equerries, she had frequently been invited over. But she had never liked it there. She objected to being made to watch the same film, *Chitty Chitty Bang Bang*, and complained, 'The atmosphere was always very strange.'

Marriage to its future owner had not changed her opinion of a family for whom even something as supposedly straightforward as a cup of afternoon tea came laden with arcane rituals. The cucumber in the sandwiches had to have all its seeds removed and the edges of the bread had to be rounded off because of an ancient belief that anyone who presented them with food with pointed edges was trying to overthrow the throne.

She found these rituals irritating and oppressive and used her pregnancy as an excuse to spend as much time as possible in her room. And the longer she remained there, the more unhappy she became.

With Charles out shooting most days, Diana again sought the company of Mark Simpson, who was on duty at Sandringham. 'She would see me and say, "I've got to talk to you," and push me into a bathroom and lock the door. And I had to listen to her. She wanted attention. I used to agree with what she said so I could get away.'

One day when the rest of the Royal Family were out shooting Diana asked him to go for a walk with her. 'We walked over to Park House and she said it was so wonderful and she wished she still lived there.

'She was not looking very well. I asked her if everything was going all right and she said in a voice full of sarcasm, "Oh lovely, it's never been better."

'I didn't realise it but half the staff at Sandringham were watching us out of the window.'

Royal servants can be more particular than their employers, and Princess Anne's Yorkshire-born nanny, Pat Moss, was one who objected to what she saw as Simpson's over-familiarity. Simpson recalled, 'When I got back in, one of the footmen said to me, "Pat thinks it's wrong that somebody like you should be out walking with the princess." She said it's not right for somebody like you to be mixing with someone like her – it's only going to lead to trouble.'

And so it did. Princess Anne told the nanny not to worry. Mark Phillips got involved and said there were two sides to every story, which only succeeded in drawing his wife's anger his way. Simpson then made a tactical withdrawal. 'After that I tried to keep out of Diana's way,' he said.

The unfortunate consequence of this was that Diana now felt she had no one she could confide in. She was too young to have built up a dependable circle of female friends she could turn to for advice and understanding. The girls she did know were all the same age as her and, apart from her sister Jane, none of them had yet had children. That left her marooned in a strange world in which she felt desperately uncomfortable with only the royal women for company. And they were proving to be less than accommodating.

The Queen, always very matter of fact and down to earth, found Diana's ill-health difficult to understand. With aristocratic understatement, Lady (Prudence) Penn, wife and sister of two of the Queen's senior courtiers and godmother to Princess Margaret's daughter, Lady Sarah, observed that 'it probably tried her patience a little'. Princess Margaret was still sympathetic, but too involved in her own affairs to offer much support. Princess Anne, whose low opinion of her sister-in-law never improved, was obviously a non-starter. The Queen Mother was too old and far too grand for a twenty-year-old to turn to.

Wrapped up in her misery, the stricken child-woman withdrew into herself. She would sit crouched on a chair, her head on her knees, weeping silent tears, ignoring her husband's entreaties.

When she spoke, it was only to blame the Royal Family for her predicament. 'This family has never had anybody who's had morning sickness before, so I was a problem,' she said.

The ambience at Sandringham certainly didn't help. 'The prospect of almost five weeks there was doing her in,' Simpson said.

The start of the New Year saw a further decline in Diana's mental well-being. Charles didn't know how to deal with the endless tears and complaints. He had read the appropriate books on ante-natal care, including *The Expectant Father*, given to him by its author, the former nurse and midwife Betty Parsons, who had helped the Queen through her pregnancies with Prince Andrew and Prince Edward. Parsons had warned him that few women go through a pregnancy without encountering days when they feel depressed about the whole prospect of having a baby. The depression, she said, 'is a bit more than just feeling low. It tends to be a reaction to the woman's feelings of anxiety about what is happening to her in the whole process of reproduction.' She counselled that 'as her husband and the father of the child she is expecting, you are able to give your wife comfort and confidence better than all the doctors, midwives and medical specialists in the world'.

That was not true in this case. Charles had tried his best but it was not enough. Diana needed psychological support, girlfriends to talk to and constant attention. She found none of these in the Royal Family's Norfolk redoubt. Shortly after New Year she decided she could not stand it any longer and threw herself down the North End staircase, which leads from the Queen Mother's rooms to the main hallway.

She was three months pregnant. Diana later told her friend, Elsa Bowker, that she 'did not think it worth living – or having a baby'.

It was obviously a cry for help, although some members of the royal Household unkindly interpreted it as a cry for attention. Either way, it proved to be no more than a momentary aberration which thankfully did no harm to the child she was carrying. Diana said, 'I knew I wasn't going to lose the baby.'

A local doctor was summoned. He said, 'No hint of trouble. She's a strong, healthy young woman.'

Just to make sure, her gynaecologist, George Pinker, was brought to Sandringham and he duly confirmed that both mother and baby remained in perfect physical health.

The visual confirmation of that reassuring prognosis came in February on the island of Eleuthra in the Bahamas, where Charles had taken her in his effort to cheer her up. Diana was photographed on the beach wearing a bikini. The Royal Family, for whom pregnancy is traditionally a very private matter, were appalled by what the Queen called an 'unprecedented breach of privacy'. Diana was not concerned, however. In the heat of the Caribbean she had regained her enthusiasm for life, both her own and the one belonging to the baby she was carrying. Charles wrote to Lady Mountbatten describing the ten days as 'a second honeymoon'.

Diana didn't go quite that far. To her it was very like the first one, when all Charles had done was sunbathe, read and paint. But at least she was finally away from Sandringham, its low Norfolk skies and the claustrophobic atmosphere of the Court. And there were moments, as one eyewitness recounted, when Charles broke off from whatever he was doing to join his wife in the sea, where they splashed each other playfully and kissed affectionately.

She brought her good humour back to Highgrove with her, and the next four months passed off without any major incident.

The Queen had assumed that the heir to her throne would be born at Buckingham Palace. Diana had responded to that suggestion with an emphatic No. She could not bear the idea of giving birth in the Belgian Suite of the Palace, where Prince Charles had been delivered. Her doctor agreed and, at 5 a.m. on Monday, 21 June, she entered through a side door of St Mary's Hospital in London's Paddington, and took the lift to the private Lindo Wing. She was checked into a room at the end of the corridor.

Charles and Diana had decided to have the baby induced. It was a difficult birth and Pinker, with Betty Parsons in attendance, had wanted to perform a Caesarean section. 'I was as sick as a parrot the whole way through,' Diana recalled.

In the end Diana made it on her own and at 9.03 p.m., after sixteen painful hours, she was finally delivered of a son. He weighed 7 pounds 1½ ounces. Her husband was with her throughout. Charles said the baby had 'a wisp of fair hair, sort of blondish, and blue eyes'.

From Kensington Palace he wrote to his friends, Hugh and Emilie van Cutsem, 'I got back here just before midnight, utterly elated but quite shattered. I can't tell you how excited and proud I am.

'He really does look surprisingly appetising and has sausage fingers just like mine.'

The following day church bells were rung and a forty-one-gun salute was fired. The Queen came to see her grandson and dryly observed, 'Thank goodness he hasn't got ears like his father.'

THREE

William's Early Life

Like first-time mothers everywhere, Diana had clear ideas as to how her son was going to be brought up. Many of her ideas were at variance with royal tradition.

She did not want her child consigned to the care of nannies, rarely to be seen, and declared that William would not be 'hidden upstairs with the governess'. Her own experience with them had left her with nothing but unhappy memories and she said, 'A mother's arms are so much more comforting than anyone else's.'

There were to be no dummies, no use of 'pacifiers' as the Americans call them. If he cried it was his mother's finger that would calm him and she intended, she said, 'always to be there to provide it'.

She agreed to William and later, Harry, being circumcised in keeping with royal tradition but turned her nose up at Charles's suggestion that the boy should be called by the ancient name of Arthur. 'Too old-fashioned,' she said.

Diana also insisted on breastfeeding her newborn baby. That was not quite as radical as it sounded at the time. The Queen had nursed all her four children. The difference was that at the time no one knew. When Charles and Anne and, later, Andrew and Edward were babies, the Royal Family were perceived as occupying an unique branch of the human tree where normal corporeal functions were somehow excused (in the 1940s and 1950s schoolchildren were still innocently wondering whether the

Queen actually ever went to the lavatory). It was part of the reverential attitude towards royalty born out of embarrassment and reserve that the British public had wished on itself for the better part of a century.

Diana was having none of that. She was too much a part of the post-Sixties world that was no longer willing to accept the old status quo or the strictures that went with it. She had raised no protest when she had been photographed while she was expecting, something that had angered the rest of the Royal Family, for whom sex and its consequences was a subject always to be scrupulously avoided. And she was quite determined that, when she decided to breastfeed William, everyone should know what she was doing. Her contemporaries did not retire from view when they were pregnant. They carried on with their lives. Nor did they pretend that babies materialised out of thin air and then somehow fed themselves. Having children was 'normal' and, as she said, 'I want my children to have as normal a life as possible.'

There was nothing 'normal' about a child having his own cook, his own policeman on twenty-four-hour guard duty and two nannies, as William eventually would. But then Diana was really talking as much about herself as she was about her son, and she would repeat that remark over and over again. She was the one who wanted to escape the claustrophobic restraints of royal tradition, who wanted to be 'normal', and it would become her cri de coeur in the years to come.

As it turned out, she was able to nurse William for only three weeks before the physical demands proved too great. Nonetheless, in those early days of motherhood she was able to establish her own maternal pattern and there was a freshness and lightness of touch to the way she set about ordering her homes.

Up until then royal nurseries had been lost in a time warp of threadbare carpets, poor furniture and obsolete electric bar fires. Diana spruced everything up. She converted the old attic at Kensington Palace into a day nursery and a night nursery. The furniture was specially scaled down and child-size loos were installed in the bathroom. The decorations were by the South African interior designer Dudley Poplak.

The remote top floor of their houses was where the Royal Family, along with most of the aristocracy, had traditionally confined their children. With Diana in charge, however, there was a new informality that marked a decisive change from what had gone before. When the Queen's children were born, the Household had been invited upstairs to file past the cradle containing the princely infants. It was a courtly ceremony conducted in a respectful silence that was almost religious in its solemnity. The senior members of staff went first, the housemaids and junior footmen bringing up the rear some hours later. Many of the Household lingered to bow deeply before the crib.

Diana dispensed with that act of ritual homage. She simply held up her son and invited the staff to say how lovely he was – which everyone duly did. Instead of bows, her young staff presented gifts. Diana responded with handwritten notes of thanks on paper bearing the royal coat of arms.

To Mark Simpson, the footman to whom she had confided so much, she wrote on 5 July, 'You are so terribly kind to have given us both such lovely presents. William is enormously touched (he said so!) with his goodies, especially his rabbit which is perched in a V.I.P position. As you well know, I adore my Fenjal and Floris soap, thank you so very much for giving me what I love.

'My birthday [she had celebrated her twenty-first four days earlier with a quiet lunch with her future sister-in-law, Fergie] was most confusing. What with W's arrival, endless telegrams & flowers still pouring in.

'Of course, I remembered last birthday – I drank too much Pimm's & ate a mass of chocolate cake. Who would have believed that a year onwards I'd be a mum!'

The letter's easy familiarity was of the kind that any young woman might have written to someone she regarded as 'my good friend'. However, for a member of the Royal Family, even a new one, to write so intimately to a member of staff was unusual to say the least. It was not written by a lady-in-waiting, as was the convention. And it was signed 'With love'. Such intimacy was bound to raise eyebrows among the stuffy members of the Court. Significantly, though, it was an example that Prince William would follow in his own relations with the Palace staff, thereby heralding a new era in which people in royal service would be treated more as well-regarded employees and less as underpaid servants tied by an almost feudal notion of fealty.

Initially at least, Charles was carried along by his wife's enthusiasm. After all, this was his first child, too, and he was as excited by the prospect of parenthood as she was. Overcome with the wonder of it all, he said, 'Being a father is rather a grown-up thing, bit of a shock to my system.'

He wrote to his godmother, Lady Mountbatten, 'The arrival of our small son has been an astonishing experience and one that has meant more to me than I could ever have imagined . . . I *am* so thankful I was beside Diana's bedside the whole time because by the end of the day I felt as though I'd shared deeply in the process of birth and as a result was rewarded by seeing a small creature which belonged to *us* and even though he seemed to belong to everyone else as well.'

When Diana decided to move from the breast to the bottle, he happily joined in the chore of the midnight feeds. And when he was out attending an official function, he was always anxious to leave as quickly as politeness allowed and return home to his family. 'He couldn't wait to get back and do the bottle,' Diana remarked.

He also did his fair share of nappy changing and that, too, represented a break from tradition – his own father, Prince Philip, had taken only a distant interest in his first-born. 'Papa used to send me little notes,' Charles mournfully recalled. Philip rarely looked into the nursery at Buckingham Palace, and never involved himself in the messy business of looking after a baby.

This was not how Charles wanted to bring up *his* son. Just as Diana was determined to dust away the cobwebs and put her own imprint on what was, after all, her baby and not merely a new component for the royal machine, so the prince wanted to give his son the time and attention that he always felt he had been denied (even in middle age, Charles would still be bemoaning what he saw as the unfulfilled wants and needs of his childhood).

There was a limit to how far the prince was ever likely to go along this paternal route, however. He was the heir to the throne, and while he was determined to be as much of a hands-on father as time would allow, he was not prepared to discard all the old precepts simply on his wife's whim. After the break-up of her parents' marriage, Diana had been the one who had comforted her young brother, Charles, and her spell as a nursery school helper had given her some more first-hand experience of dealing with young children. Indeed, at one juncture she talked enthusiastically of setting up her own nursery school within Kensington Palace and, with Lady Susan Hussey assisting, started making plans for the venture.

Charles was happy to go along with the project, but in the end it came to nothing. Diana was not any ordinary young mother. She was now a member of a family which, as the prince gently pointed out, was not free to experiment with whatever popular ideas took its fancy. Conservative by upbringing and instinct, he was suspicious of many of what he called 'these newfangled ideas' about parenthood.

As he observed, 'There are some experts who were very certain about how you should bring up children. But then, after twenty years, they turned round and said they'd been wrong. Well, think of all the people who followed their suggestions!'

One of the experts he had firmly in mind was Dr Benjamin Spock, the American child psychologist whose handbook, *Baby and Child Care*, has sold over 25 million copies, but who later recanted much of his own lenient and often permissive advice.

The first thing Charles broke with his wife over was the question of a nanny. When she returned to Kensington Palace she had a maternity nurse, Sister Anne Wallace, to assist her. Diana said that was all the help she needed. Charles, however, was firmly of the opinion that they needed someone full time for when Diana resumed her official duties.

In the excitement of new motherhood, Diana had given very little thought to the role her marriage had forced on her. Being the Princess of Wales, as she was discovering, meant more than fine clothes and dazzling jewellery and a husband who would devote himself to her every need. It came with a price, just as being the mother of a future king carried with it responsibilities that, in her youthful immaturity, she had never really taken into account. Faced with the logic of her husband's argument, she had had little choice but to agree to his suggestion.

What she was not prepared to compromise on, though, was the type of nanny who should be employed. Charles, forever seeking refuge in the comfort of the past, wanted to hire Mabel Anderson, who had looked after him when he was little. Diana dismissed that out of hand. The Scottish-born Anderson was a nanny of the old school – prim, proper, warm-hearted certainly, but also old-fashioned and quite strict. There was also the matter of her age. She was in her late fifties when Charles suggested re-employing her – far too old for Diana's taste. She wanted someone younger, someone more amenable to her ideas.

The job duly went to Barbara Barnes, the forty-two-year-old daughter of a retired forestry worker on the Earl of Leicester's Norfolk estate, a pheasant's drive from Sandringham. She was told not to wear a uniform. Nor was she to regard the nursery as her private domain. Echoing her mistress's thoughts, Barbara said, 'I'm here to help the princess, not take over.'

That was not how it would work out but, in the beginning, the two got on well enough. Barbara had worked for fourteen years for the Earl of Leicester's daughter, Princess Margaret's lady-in-waiting Lady Glenconner. She had a down-to-earth view of her job. 'I'm not a graduate of any sort of nannies' college. I've accumulated my knowledge from many years of experience.'

In what turned out to be her first and last public utterance on the subject, she added, 'I do not see any different problems in bringing up a royal baby. I treat all children as individuals.'

She also had to put in a lot of caring on Diana's behalf. The princess, already in the throes of bulimia, had started slashing herself, and it was Barbara who frequently had to apply the sticking plaster to the princess's bloodied wrists and arms.

On an altogether healthier note, it was Barbara who reassured Diana that her son was sound and well. As a first-time mother, Diana was forever peering into William's crib, listening to make sure he was breathing properly and asking, 'Is he all right?'

Barbara told her that there were no grounds for fear on that score. William was a healthy, noisy baby who cried a great deal and made his presence felt very early on. As Charles observed, 'He gets noisier and angrier by the day.' Diana later told me, 'He was a bit of handful.'

Charles soon had cause to think the same about his wife. To all outward appearances the Waleses seemed to have the makings of an ideal marriage. Her old flatmate certainly seemed to think so. 'She was thrilled with both herself and her baby – there was contentment about her,' Carolyn Bartholomew observed after visiting her three days after William's birth.

That was not how Diana saw it, however. She was stricken with postnatal depression. She explained, 'It wasn't so much the baby that had produced it; it was the baby that triggered off all else that was going on in my mind.'

While Diana was wrapped in her own misery, 1982 was a momentous year for the Royal Family. Three weeks after William's birth, the intruder Michael Fagan broke into the Queen's bedroom. A week later the Queen went into hospital, ostensibly to have a wisdom tooth removed, but conveniently at the same time as her long-serving police officer, Commander Trestrail, who she was very fond of, had to resign after it was disclosed that he was consorting with male prostitutes. On 20 July an IRA bomb exploded in Hyde Park, murdering eleven soldiers of the Household Cavalry, injuring seven others and killing seven horses, reducing the Queen to tears.

And all the while Britain was at war with Argentina over possession of the Falkland Islands. Diana's brother-in-law, Prince Andrew, who she had known all her life and who she had once been romantically interested in, was serving with the British Task Force in the South Atlantic in the dangerous role of a helicopter pilot.

None of these events appear to have made any impression on Diana. According to Charles's authorised biographer, Jonathan Dimbleby, 'She seemed to resent the interest being shown in the Falklands, rather than her.'

Looking back, Diana blamed her preoccupation – which many in the Household chose to call self-absorption – on her depression. For a woman who insisted that she loved children so much, this should have been a memorable time in her life. It wasn't. She later claimed that the 'pain' was so great that she blotted everything out.

Even the christening on 4 August failed to lighten her spirits. It was on her suggestion that her gynaecologist Mr (later Sir) George Pinker and the nurses who had attended William's birth were invited. Much to Diana's silent irritation, however, the godparents were very much Charles's choice. The only one near Diana's age was the Duke of Westminster's wife, 'Tally'. The others – Princess Alexandra, Lady Susan Hussey, ex-King Constantine of Greece, Earl Mountbatten of Burma's grandson, Lord Romsey, and Sir Laurens van der Post – were much older people with whom Diana found it extremely difficult to communicate.

The ceremony was held in the Music Room at Buckingham Palace at 11 a.m. The baby was named William Arthur Philip Louis (Charles had managed to slip the Arthur in). He was baptised by the Archbishop of Canterbury, Dr Robert Runcie, with water drawn from the River Jordan in the Holy Land, a custom dating back to the Crusades. He was dressed in a robe of Honiton lace over satin, made in 1841, worn by all Queen Victoria's children, grandchildren and after them by George VI, his brothers, sisters, nephews, nieces and by his own two daughters, the Queen and Princess Margaret. Charles, too, had worn it when he was christened.

William was unimpressed by the ancient rites and cried loudly. True to her promise, Diana tried to quieten him by putting her finger in his mouth. It didn't work. But then nothing was working for Diana that day. The whole occasion infuriated her. She complained that William, the Queen, her husband and the Queen Mother whose eighty-second birthday it was got all the attention, and that 11 o'clock, the traditional hour for such services, interfered with her one-month-old son's 'morning sleep'.

'I was excluded totally that day,' she complained bitterly. 'I wasn't very well and I just blubbed my eyes out.'

The person she held most responsible for her tears was her husband of barely a year. Like most newlyweds, little niggles had crept into their relationship as they set about trying to adjust to each other. To Diana's annoyance, for instance, Charles had insisted on painting over the murals in William's bedroom because he thought the characters she had chosen would terrify little children. But such disagreements were almost bound to occur. Most couples, especially those labouring under a twelve-year age gap, suffer their share of disagreements as they go about the business of making the compromises necessary for a successful marriage, and Charles and Diana were no exception – after all, she was young and totally inexperienced in dealing with men, while he was a pampered prince set in his bachelor ways. What gave their problems a particularly wounding edge was the incompatibility caused by sexual distrust.

Charles would maintain, on his honour, that he was not unfaithful to his wife until their marriage had 'irretrievably broken down'. Diana was convinced that his long-standing relationship with Camilla Parker Bowles remained intimate and ongoing. It became her obsession and that, regardless of what the facts may have been, only succeeded in allowing Camilla into her husband's life to stake her claim on his affections.

As Princess of Wales, Diana initially held most of the cards in this contest for the affections of the prince. As Princess Michael of Kent observed, 'How many Princes of Wales are there?' The answer was only the one – and Diana had married him. Now she had produced him an heir and Charles, whose commitment to duty had always circumscribed his behaviour, was never going to abandon her. He wanted his marriage to work. What Diana's frequently erratic behaviour could do, however, was drive him to seek comfort from a mistress. And there, poised in the wings, waiting to provide him with the solace and reassurance he needed, was Camilla.

It was a desperate situation that would later divide the country, with Diana's account of what went wrong very much to the forefront.

It would have been a sad beginning for any marriage, never mind one conducted under the searching glare of public scrutiny as theirs was. It was also a disruptive background against which to embark on the serious business of bringing up a child, any child, but especially one destined to be king, and it would leave a profound imprint on their son.

It wasn't all black clouds, however. When William was nine months old the Prince and Princess of Wales were preparing to set off on a long-planned tour of Australia. Diana was resigned to leaving her son behind. That was the royal way. Back in the high summer of the British Empire, the future Queen Mother had left her daughter, Elizabeth, for all of six months when she accompanied her husband, the soon-to-be King George VI, on a six-month tour of the Antipodes. That was how things were done in 1927, when steamships were the only means of crossing the globe and it would have been regarded as strange, if not downright disloyal, if the Queen Mother had placed the welfare of her daughter ahead of duty.

The parting had been heartbreaking nonetheless and, as George VI's official biographer, Sir John Wheeler-Bennett, noted, the car that took the royal couple to the station to catch the train to Portsmouth where they embarked on the battle cruiser HMS *Renown* 'had to be driven around until she was composed enough to face the crowds'. When she eventually returned, the baby had grown into a toddler who did not recognise her mother, would not to go to her arms and, despite all the entreaties of her nanny, refused to say 'Mother' or even 'Mama'.

The advent of the aeroplane had brought distant lands within easier reach, but such separations carried through into the next generation. The Queen had left Prince Charles for long periods in his early, formative years. When he was eleven months old his father, Prince Philip, then an officer in the Royal Navy, was posted to Malta and his mother spent more of the next two years with her husband in the Mediterranean than she did with her son in England. Charles was not to see his father again for almost a year and his mother only intermittently. Philip missed his son's first two birthdays, and on his third both parents were away on tour in North America. In 1953, shortly after the coronation, his mother and father went on a six-month tour of the Commonwealth.

Like her own mother before her, the Queen had cried when she was parted from Charles and his young sister, Anne. When they were reunited the Queen poignantly observed, 'I don't think they really knew who we were.'

Diana had settled herself for a similar heart-wrenching separation. 'I accepted that as part of duty, albeit it wasn't going to be easy,' she said. It was Australia's then Prime Minister Malcolm Fraser who stepped in with a solution. He wrote to the princess suggesting that 'being such a young family, would you like to bring your child out?'

Both Charles and Diana jumped at the chance. It was the ideal way of combining royal commitment with personal wishes. It also meant that the Waleses would be able to include New Zealand on their tour. The Queen was never consulted officially on the matter but raised no objection when Charles told her of the new arrangements.

The royal party touched down in Alice Springs on 22 March 1983, with an entourage of twenty staff. Their baggage included the baby paraphernalia of nappies, clothes, special food supplements, fluoride drops and multi-vitamins, all carefully packed by Nanny Barnes with Diana fussing around in attendance, checking to make sure that nothing was forgotten.

Shortly after landing, Barbara took William off in a private plane to a sheep station called Woomargama in the fast Outback of New South Wales. This would be their base throughout their stay in Australia, and where they returned to recharge their physical batteries and revel in their son when their schedule allowed. Charles wrote, 'I still can't get over our luck in finding such an ideal place. We were extremely happy there whenever we were allowed to escape. The great joy was that we were totally alone together.'

This trip was no holiday, though, and Charles and Diana spent four weeks criss-crossing the continent, attending dinners, openings and functions surrounded by vast crowds desperate, as Charles discovered to his chagrin, not for a sight of him, but of his wife. The prince wrote, 'All is chaos, crowds, cameras, politicians, cynicism, sarcasm and intense scrutiny outside.'

He was understandably concerned at the effect this was having on his wife. 'How can anyone, let alone a twenty-one-year-old, be expected to come out of all this obsessed and crazed attention unscathed?'

The answer was that she couldn't. She was overwhelmed by the attention and frequently burst into tears. She was also sick, a result of her eating disorder which was already well developed. At one point she went to her lady-in-waiting, Anne Beckwith-Smith, and said, 'I can't cope with this.'

At the same time, though, she was starting to grasp the power the wielded over people's imagination. Australia saw the birth of the cult of Diana. It was, she said, where she 'learnt to be "royal" '. The inverted commas were hers and Diana used them to underline her new-found position, for hers was royalty of a kind that replaced understated reverence with the frenzy of Hollywood-style celebrity.

William was spared the mass hysteria that now greeted his parents wherever they went. In the seclusion of Woomargama he was able to develop in an ordinary way, without a camera following his every movement. Charles was entranced by the speed William was growing. He expressed his excitement in letters quoted by Jonathan Dimbleby.

To Lady Susan Hussey he wrote, 'I must tell you that your godson could not be in better form. He looks horribly well and is expanding with visible and frightening rapidity. Today he actually crawled for the first time. We laughed and laughed with sheer hysterical pleasure.'

He later informed the van Cutsems how William was crawling at high speed and 'knocking everything off the tables and causing unbelievable destruction. He will be walking before long and it is the greatest possible fun.'

The picture was not quite as idyllic as Charles painted it. Diana's mood swung erratically from euphoria to tearful despair, and while she was 'thrilled' to be with her son she also resented the good time his carers were enjoying at Woomargama. As well as Barbara Barnes, William had a police bodyguard and a chef in attendance. Diana had talked about the pleasure of sharing the 'same sky' with William but because of her official commitments she was able to snatch only a few moments beside the sheep station's inviting swimming pool. The staff was having a better time than she was – and that, she complained, wasn't fair.

What having William with her did do, though, was to give her something to talk about on her seemingly endless round of engagements. She was untrained in the art of making small talk and, in a rare compliment to her husband, wrote admiringly of his ability to engage people he had never met and would never meet again in a friendly and, for them at least, memorable way. William allowed her to follow suit. Wherever she went, she was asked how he was getting along and was he walking and what he was getting up to, and Diana used the questions as a means of establishing a rapport with whomever she happened to be speaking to.

On a radio phone-in she was asked what William's favourite toy was. She replied that it was a plastic whale that spouted water and which he took into the bath with him. It was hardly a revelation of significance but it endeared her to the listeners, and in the years to come she would issue regular William updates. She told how he kept breaking his toys, pressing the panic button in the nursery and trying to flush anything that came to hand, including a pair of his father's handmade shoes, down the lavatory. On a visit to a hospital she informed the beaming patients that William was 'a mini tornado'.

By the time the royal party arrived in New Zealand, the public fascination with the little prince had become an industry. He disembarked from the New Zealand air force jet on the hip of Barbara Barnes and was whisked away by limousine to the specially prepared nursery at Government House. Before he got there he was already the unsuspecting figurehead in a campaign for child road safety. The car had been fitted with a child safety harness and it was promptly claimed that the example set by Charles and Diana would encourage others to strap their babies in properly.

William's other restraint was a baby bouncer that had been fitted at the top of the staircase at Government House. It was a useful diversion, for by this stage William's crawling ability was getting him into all sorts of trouble. 'He keeps crawling away – especially into wastepaper baskets,' his father said.

Like Woomargama, Government House offered the family near complete privacy. Too much so, in fact. Neither Charles nor Diana liked it there. It was shielded by trees and built on the side of a hill named Mount Eden, but it was also surrounded by buildings and guarded by scores of police, and Charles likened it to 'being imprisoned'. But at least Nanny Barnes was able to take William for his afternoon walks, propped up in a grand old-fashioned blue English pram that had previously been used by the governor's children, unmolested by photographers. They were there soon enough, however, for it was in those gardens that William was presented for his first photocall.

It was held at 9 o'clock in the morning, with thirty journalists, forty photographers and several television crews in attendance. His nanny had dressed him in an expensive silk smocked peach-coloured romper suit, and a floral woollen carpet had been spread out on the damp lawn as an invitation for William to perform the crawl his father had been talking about so much. His parents warned that there was no guarantee that he would perform on cue, but no sooner was he down than he was off, heading for the grass or lifting the fringe of the carpet to see what was underneath. 'He performed like a true professional in front of the cameras and did everything that could be expected of him,' Charles proudly observed.

Later that day his father was presented with a miniature polo stick for William's use. Charles declared, 'I suspect the first thing he will do with it is to chew it, the second thing will be to hit me sharply on the nose, but I hope in twenty years' time he will be galloping up this field with me in a bathchair on the sideline.'

Twenty years later William would indeed be playing polo – with his father by his side and nowhere near a bathchair. But the happy family frozen in those photographs was long gone.

FOUR

A Brother for William

William was not terribly pleased by the arrival of his brother. Up until then he had been the cynosure of his parents' affection and the centre of attention for the squad of nannies, policemen, chefs, butlers and housemaids who were always on hand to keep an eye on him. His mother would firmly deny it, but he had been more than a little spoilt.

That was all but inevitable, given who he was. He was still too young to realise just how important he was in the regal scheme of things, but the royal attendants knew exactly where he stood in the hierarchy and treated him accordingly.

So did a public eager for any sighting of the prince. His parents duly obliged. At the age of eighteen months he had toddled before the cameras in the walled garden of Kensington Palace. Six months later he was back there again, to celebrate his second birthday and take his father's hand. He kicked a ball with his left foot and uttered the time-honoured word, 'Daddy'.

Diana noted that William revelled in the notice paid to him. It was what he had grown used to. As a member of the Kensington Palace household recalled, 'He couldn't even fall down without at least a couple of people rushing to pick him up and see if he was all right.'

But the birth of a baby was bound to shift the focus away from the little prince, if only for a while. Diana did all the things a mother is supposed to do to placate her first-born. William had been taken to the hospital to greet his brother and his mother arranged for a little soft toy to be handed to

47

him, a gift ostensibly from the new addition to their family. There were moments when Harry himself appeared to be the toy. 'William spends the entire time pouring an endless supply of hugs and kisses on to Harry and we are hardly allowed near,' Diana said.

Try as they might, however, his parents could not totally stem William's initial jealousy.

Charles took the view that that was only 'to be expected', and added, 'You have to be slightly careful because, you know, a tractor comes winging through the air and things like that.'

Harry was sublimely unaware of his brother's resentment. While William had been a boisterous child almost from the moment of birth, Harry, so his father observed, was 'extraordinarily good, sleeps marvellously and eats well'. He was, or so Charles insisted, 'the one with the gentle nature'.

In the light of the troubles to come, that was a premature judgement. At the time, though, he was a welcome contrast to his more rumbustious brother.

Harry had been conceived 'as if by a miracle', as Diana tellingly put it, during the Royal Family's long winter break at Sandringham, a house she would later profess to detest. Just before the official announcement was made, Diana flew to Norway on her first official solo trip. She returned to a love note written by her husband. It read, 'We were so proud of you', and Charles had signed it, 'Willie Wombat and I'.

Despite the obvious good intentions, the message did little to boost the princess's faltering confidence. The pregnancy was not an easy one. Once again she suffered from morning sickness made worse by what had by then been diagnosed as bulimia. She was tired, overwrought and feeling thoroughly miserable. William was still teething and her nights were often disturbed by his cries.

In March she declared, 'I've not felt well since day one. I don't think I'm made for the production line.'

To friends she complained, 'If men had babies, they would only have one each.' It was a remark that carried with it a sour subtext. She was less than three years into her marriage but already her relationship with Charles was teetering towards the unresolvable crisis that would break up the family. The two were discovering that they had little in common, and not even a son and the promise of another child could fill that yawning emotional gap.

Diana had started questioning Charles's every action. She grew suspicious when his duties took him away from home, convincing herself that he was having clandestine assignations with Camilla. Such was her distrust that she had even taken to steaming open his letters. In one of her school reports a teacher had written, 'She must try to be less emotional in her dealings with others,' but that self-discipline proved to be beyond her. Unable to cope with his wife's behaviour, Charles became increasingly distant, which only exacerbated the problem.

In August her uncle Edmund Fermoy committed suicide, aged forty-five. Diana wrote to friends from Balmoral, 'Depression is a disease like cancer – only in so many ways worse because it is often misunderstood and the battle against it so lonely.' She was quoting from personal experience.

The Queen had been aware for a while that her daughter-in-law was finding it difficult to adapt to the pressures of her royal role, but assumed that she would eventually find her feet. And to outwards appearances at least, that is what Diana seemed to be doing. She carried on performing her royal duties until July, to the admiration of the people she met. They saw only the beautiful princess and mother-to-be and not the troubled young woman who cried herself to sleep most nights. There were even periods when Diana herself bought into the popular illusion.

During the final six weeks of her pregnancy, for instance, she said she was closer to Charles than she had ever been before, and he was with her at 7.30 on the morning on Saturday, 15 September 1984, when she booked into the Lindo Wing with a suitcase containing a cotton nightgown, earplugs, lip salve and water spray.

Charles remained at her side throughout the nine-hour labour. He gave her ice cubes to suck when she was thirsty and when she needed comfort he held her hand. He admitted that he had fallen asleep during the long wait but said it was only a 'little doze'.

The boy weighed in at 6 pounds 14 ounces at 4.20 p.m. Charles came out of the Lindo Wing to tell the crowd outside that the birth had been 'much quicker than last time' and that his son had 'pale blue eyes and hair of an intermediate colour', and how delighted he was. In Diana's memory, Charles's first comment when he saw the baby had been, 'Oh God, it's a boy.'

It was no secret that the prince had been looking forward to having a daughter. Diana had known for several months that she was carrying a son (she had seen it on a scan). Yet despite the 'closeness' she said she felt towards Charles over the previous few weeks, she had chosen to keep that important bit of information from her husband.

In the first flurry of excitement, that did not matter. At 6.35 p.m. he left the hospital and returned to Kensington Palace, declaring, 'I need a drink' (he had a large dry martini when he got home). He returned to the hospital the following morning, bringing Barbara Barnes and William with him. As soon as he emerged from the lift the little prince went scampering down the corridor, calling for his mother. In the ensuing bustle Diana's bodyguard knocked over the screen outside the princess's door, which brought Diana from her bed to see what the commotion was about. Looking out of the door, she saw William running towards her. She picked him up and it was therefore from the comfort of his mother's arms that he saw his brother for the first time, swaddled in a white blanket. William rushed forward and planted a kiss on his forehead. He then sat down on the bed beside his mother and held the newborn gingerly in his arms.

Once again Diana had resolved to leave hospital as quickly as possible, and at 2.30 that afternoon she returned to 'KP', as she called Kensington Palace. As soon as she was home Charles went off to play a game of polo at Windsor. To leave his wife and newborn son so soon struck Diana as odd.

The prince saw nothing untoward in what he was doing. The Royal Family, their lives regulated by never ending schedules of commitments and anniversaries, pay scant regard to the conventions that bind most families. They frequently overlook each other's birthdays, and on this occasion that casual approach extended so far as to include the actual day of birth. The Queen and Prince Philip, for instance, were out shooting when they received the news that they had become grandparents for the fourth time, and did not return from Scotland until a week later. And while the Queen did at least go and see Harry as soon as she got back to Windsor, it would be several weeks more before Prince Philip managed to fit him into his schedule. After flying down to Windsor, he went to a carriage driving event and then flew off to Canada for a state visit with the Queen. Asked what he thought of his grandson, he replied, 'I haven't seen him yet – I've been too busy.'

Although Charles was nothing like his father as a parent, in some matters he could be similarly off-hand. The polo was a long-standing engagement and to his way of thinking he was merely giving his wife time to settle in while he went to take some strenuous exercise, which was always his way of relieving tension. Diana, he explained, was 'very tired – I reckoned it was time she was left alone to recuperate'.

At the game played at Smith's Lawn he was presented with a magnum of champagne by the captain of the opposing team, Johnny Kidd, grandson of the newspaper magnate Lord Beaverbrook and father of the model, Jodie. An impromptu party ensued, with champagne being gulped from a makeshift bar in the back of a Land Rover. In polo there are four players on each side. With the birth of a second son, Charles happily announced, 'We nearly have a full polo team.'

By then the baby's name had already been announced. The Queen's assistant press secretary, the bluff and privately outspoken former Canadian football layer, Vic Chapman, had declared from the steps of the Lindo Wing, 'OK, the name is Prince Henry Charles Albert David. They intend to call him Prince Harry.'

By royal precedent the speed of announcement was unusual. The Royal Family do not like being rushed in these matters. But Diana already knew what the gender of her child was going to be, and while Charles was still mulling over suitable girls' names, she had forced him to decide on appropriate ones 'just in case' it turned out to be a boy. Diana's persistence in this matter should have given her husband a clue that she knew more than she was letting on, but this was not the first and nor would it be the last time when he failed to read her mind.

While Charles was unable to read his wife's mind, Diana was under the impression that she could read his, and what she thought she saw there was a total lack of feeling. The consideration Charles had shown towards her throughout her pregnancy should have calmed her insecurities. It was certainly an opportunity for a new beginning, for whatever else Charles may have been – and he could veer between selfishness and self-pity to a point that drove Diana to tearful irritation – he was deeply committed to his family.

That was partly for reasons of state. Royalty was still a family with a capital F and at that point a separation, never mind divorce, was far beyond the boundary of contemplation for the future head of an institution for whose members the usual matrimonial escape routes are fraught with political dangers. There was more than expediency at work here, for Charles truly wanted his marriage to work. Like his grandfather, King George VI, who had referred to himself, his wife and their two daughters as 'the four of us', he craved the security and stability of a family unit. He told his friends so. And while it was impossible to deny that Diana could be what he called 'a bit tricky', he still harboured the belief, just as his mother did, that given time she would calm down and settle in.

But that prognosis was entirely dependent on Diana's willingness to abide by the rules as laid down by her in-laws – and that was something she was loath to do. Instead of bringing her closer to Charles, the birth of Harry only succeeded in driving them further apart. She put on a winning smile for the cameras as she left the Lindo Wing, her baby cradled in her arms. Her unhappiness, however, negated whatever joy she might be feeling. It was Diana herself who said, 'Suddenly, as Harry was born, it just went bang, our marriage, the whole thing went down the drain.'

She would blame that partly on what she maintained was her husband continuing his relationship with Camilla, but also, more mundanely, on his wish for a daughter. She said he told her mother, 'I'm so disappointed – I thought it would be a girl,' and that Frances Shand Kydd had snapped back, 'You should be thankful that you had a child that was normal.'

According to Mrs Shand Kydd's account of the incident, she said to the prince, 'Just be grateful he's healthy.' It was a remark drawn from cruel personal experience. A year before Diana was born, she had given birth to a son, named John, who was immediately taken away from her by worried doctors; he died eleven hours later before she even had the opportunity to hold him in her arms.

In Diana's fragile state of mental health, however, the prince's attitude was enough to add another dark shadow to a 'fairytale' that now looked as if it had been penned by the Brothers Grimm in one of their more gruesome moods.

In their early years William and Harry were unaware of the problems that were besetting their parents. Both Charles and Diana were careful to leave their disagreements behind when they stepped into the nursery.

When he entered his sons' domain Charles discarded the artifice of his public persona – and his clothes with it. The Queen, on the few occasions she joined her children at bath time, had sat majestically out of the way of any splashes on a crimson upholstered chair carried in by a footman. 'I don't recall the Queen ever actually bathing the children herself,' said Eileen, wife of Prince Philip's private secretary and roustabout companion Michael Parker. Charles took an altogether more relaxed approach to this intimate aspect of parenthood, getting into the bath himself and then lifting one boy or the other in with him for a good half-hour of laughter and play with the rubber toys hidden among the bubbles. A fleet of plastic battleships were sunk during these evening romps.

Diana was equally informal. When she returned home from the hospital she took Harry to the servant quarters at KP so that the cooks, Mervyn Wycherley and Graham Newbold, dressers Evelyn Dagley and Valerie Gibbs, Frances the housekeeper and the new butler Harold Brown could get their glimpse of the little prince. William enlivened the proceedings by smothering his brother in kisses. When he tried to grab Harry, however, Barbara

Barnes pulled him away – but not before he had attempted to headbutt the infant.

He was just as boisterous at the christening at St George's Chapel, Windsor, four days before Christmas. This time Diana had insisted on having the final say in the choice of godparents. They were Princess Margaret's daughter, Lady Sarah Armstrong-Jones, her old flatmate Carolyn Bartholomew, Old Etonian farmer Gerald Ward, the artist Bryan Organ who had painted Diana in 1981, and meat baron Lord Vestey's second wife, Cece.

Prince Philip had hinted none too subtly that Princess Anne should be one of the godmothers. Diana refused. The two women had never hit it off and Anne, who keeps pit bull terriers for pets, still made no attempt to conceal her disdain for her highly strung sister-in-law. In a gesture of contempt, she went rabbit shooting on the day of the christening.

It was William who dominated the proceedings, however.

As a little girl the Queen had been taught to control her bladder in return for the reward of a biscuit, and had had the pockets in her dress sewn up. 'Teach that child not to fidget,' her grandmother, the formidable Queen Mary, was forever commanding her nanny, Clara Knight. She had also learnt at a very early age how to pose for photographers. William had received no such instruction. He kept grabbing for the ancient Honiton lace robe which would doubtless have disintegrated if he had managed to get hold of it, and protested loudly when he was not allowed to hold the baby.

The Earl of Snowdon, who was taking Harry's official photographs, eventually managed to divert his attention by giving him an antique bird cage to play with. It silenced him long enough for Snowdon to take his pictures, but his assistant was surprised at the way he had been allowed to run amok, noting, 'Every time he did something naughty they roared with laughter. No one admonished him and he was a thorough pest.'

The christening was shown in the Queen's televised Christmas broadcast. It showed him chasing his cousin, Zara Phillips, round the legs of the Archbishop of Canterbury. In another sequence Diana was seen trying to

Prince Charles and six-month-old Prince William at Kensington Palace (*Alpha*)

At the wedding of Prince Andrew and Sarah Ferguson in 1986, William fiddles and jiggles in his itchy pageboy's outfit while his bridesmaid cousin Laura Fellowes looks on (*Rex Features*)

William takes a pretend pot shot at the crowds watched by the Duke of Gloucester's daughter, Lady Rose Windsor, in June 1988 (*UK Press*)

(Above) Four-year-old Prince Harry gets a ride on his father's horse in the Quadrangle of Buckingham Palace after Trooping the Colour (*Alpha*); (below) Diana and William in the Royal Box for the men's finals at Wimbledon in 1991 (*Alpha*)

William guides the Queen Mother through the Dean's gate after the traditional Easter service at St George's Chapel, Windsor, in 1992. William later said that this was one of his favourite pictures taken with his great-grandmother (*John Selley*)

Duty calls: (above) William sitting between his mother and great-grandmother at Trooping the Colour (*Alpha*); (below) William and Harry smartly dressed in matching blazers, shirts and ties for their ride in an open carriage (*Alpha*)

William, hat askew, at a local gymkhana near Highgrove (*Alpha*)

Eight-year-old William and six-year-old Harry on the steps of Wetherby, their prep school in Notting Hill Gate, in 1990 (*Rex Features*)

explain to William how many generations of royalty had worn the robe he had tried to tear to pieces. 'Great-granny was christened in it,' she said. Charles quickly interjected, 'And I was christened in it.' He was trying to cover up his wife's mistake, for the 'great-granny' in question was the Queen Mother who, like Diana, was an earl's daughter and therefore had most definitely not worn the regal robe.

But then, Diana never did get a firm gasp on the Royal Family's history or its traditions. She was more concerned with the present than she was with 'stuffy' customs handed down like threadbare christening robes. And it was through her sons that she sought to give expression to her ideas.

She would talk for ages with her sister, Lady Jane Fellowes, about the best way to ensure that William and Harry had the kind of rounded education that would prepare them for lives which, for all their privileges, were certain to be very different to anything the previous generations of the Royal Family had experienced. Charles wanted to entrust his sons' early education to the care of governesses, but Diana had made it clear the moment William was born that this was a non-starter. Jane agreed with her. She had given birth to a daughter, named Laura, in 1980, and a son, Alexander, three years later. Her children were therefore almost exact contemporaries of their royal cousins and the two young mothers, neighbours at KP where Jane and her husband Robert, then the Queen's assistant private secretary, enjoyed a 'grace and favour' apartment, would meet to discuss the educational future of their offspring.

Despite their occasional disagreements – Diana had a habit of blowing hot and cold towards her sister, sometimes refusing to speak to her for days on end – they concluded that it was vital that William and Harry should be allowed to mix with 'ordinary' children. What Diana didn't want, as she had made clear right from the start, was for her children to be confined to a schoolroom at the top of the house with only a few carefully selected playmates. That had been Charles's lot and in Diana's opinion it had left him socially unsure, emotionally withdrawn and incapable of dealing with anyone who contradicted him (after his confrontation with her mother over the gender of Prince Harry, Diana said 'the shutters have come down and that's what he does when he gets somebody answering back at him').

Just how far William was already removed from the hustle of ordinary childhood was brought home to her when she took him on a visit to the Young England kindergarten where she had worked as a helper. William, always active and outgoing, had joined in enthusiastically. What he couldn't play, however, was Galloping Horses, that simple child's game that involves putting one foot in front of the other and charging round the room pretending to be a horse. He didn't know how. His only contact with other children up until then had been with his cousins and the children of her very few friends.

Diana was upset by the incident. She felt that William had been made to feel an outsider, a horrible thought for any mother. She discussed it with her husband and impressed on him how essential it was that William be taken out of royalty's traditional ivory tower and be allowed to mix in with children of his own age. And that, she said, meant sending him to an 'ordinary' school.

By 'ordinary' she did not mean the local state school; she was too much the aristocrat to make that social concession. What she had in mind was one of the private nursery schools that proliferate in the wealthy enclaves of central London to care for the children of the upper middle classes. These, as she said, would be the very people William would be mixing with in the years ahead. Charles saw the sense in her argument and the couple set about choosing an appropriate establishment.

For reasons of familiarity Diana was keen on Young England. But everyone she spoke to impressed on her the importance of accessibility, and Young England was in Pimlico, a fraught drive from KP during the morning rush-hour traffic. They cast around for something nearer to home and eventually decided on the £200-a-term school run by Mrs Jane Mynors, a few minutes' walk away in Chepstow Villas, a quiet, tree-lined street in Notting Hill. Several members of the royal circle already had their children there, including Sir John Riddell, Charles's newly appointed private secretary.

At 9.30 on the warm morning of Tuesday, 24 September 1985, aged three years and three months, William arrived for his first day carrying a flask decorated with a picture of Postman Pat, a cartoon character popular at the time. He was wearing a striped jumper, red checked shirt and red shorts – clothes, Diana revealed, he had chosen himself. 'It's best to let him do that if you want him to smile,' Diana explained.

All the other pupils had gone in – he was half an hour late. That was not anything to do with tardiness on Diana's part. It was to give the 150 waiting photographers and reporters a clear look at the young prince. To make sure that William's schooldays did not turn into a media bunfight, Charles and Diana had sent a letter signed by them both to the editors of all the Fleet Street newspapers, politely requesting that after that one photocall he be left alone.

The daughter of a bishop, Jane Mynors had reinforced that appeal for privacy. Her husband, Robert, worked in the City and the school was in the basement of their family home. She had visited all the neighbours to inform them that William would be attending her classes and that, although he was a prince and this was the first time that an heir to the throne had attended a school at such a young age, would they kindly contain their interest and treat him as they would any of her other pupils. She was more forthright with the parents, warning them that under no circumstances must they speak to the press. The consequences of any breach in that rule were implicit.

After shaking hands with Mrs Mynors and giving a wave and smiling to the cameramen as his mother had promised he would, William disappeared down the steps. Diana confessed that she was nervous. Her son wasn't. He couldn't wait to get into the classroom and meet his fellows.

There were thirty-six children, who were divided into three classes of twelve, depending on their age, called Big Swans, Little Swans and, for the youngest like Prince William, Cygnets. As befitting the daughter of a bishop, Mrs Mynors started the day with a short morning prayer. That was followed by painting, cutting out, modelling and singing and movement lessons around the piano. Lessons ended at noon. 'His classmates hardly know who he is,' Mrs Mynors said.

That was not quite true. Life in the royal redoubts of KP and Highgrove had already left its mark on the youngster and, if his fellow pupils were not quite sure who he was, he was in no doubt. 'My daddy's a real prince – and my daddy can beat up your daddy,' he would declare.

The royal detective who sat quietly at the back of the classroom would try to moderate his young charge's behaviour, gently pointing out, 'That's not a very nice thing to say, is it, William?' William rarely took any notice. He was high-spirited boy who spent most of his art lessons splashing paint on his own and his friends' faces rather than on the paper the teachers had provided. He preferred to run rather than walk. And he was more than willing to fight his corner – a trait he inherited from his mother rather than his father who, as a child, had been sat upon, quite literally, by his ferocious younger sister, Anne, and was bullied throughout most of his schooldays. It was not long before William was called 'Basher Wills', which translated into the press as 'Billy the Basher'.

Diana, whose own temper was never anything other than mercurial, nevertheless took a grim view of her son's behaviour. She had insisted that there be no shouting in the nursery and that discipline should be imposed only after the rights and wrongs of the situation had been carefully explained. 'I'll listen to both sides of an argument, then make a decision,' she said.

Practice did not always match Dr Spock-style theory, however. That sometimes led to no punishment at all being imposed, as happened when William once went missing at Highgrove. After a frantic search of the house and gardens, with Diana in a state of near panic, he was discovered in a larder clutching a bottle of cherry pop, most of which he succeeded in spilling over himself. Diana was so relieved that she broke out laughing.

Yet on other occasions she was not averse to resorting to more old-fashioned methods of child control. She smacked his bottom in public on several occasions. When he climbed into a policeman's car at Highgrove to fiddle with the radio she spanked him and made him apologise. And when he became bored and obstreperous at polo at Smith's Lawn one afternoon, demanding, 'Where's Papa? Can I have a drink? I want a drink,' she had bundled him unceremoniously into the car, taken him back to Windsor and confined him to his room.

William became adept at playing up to his mother as he learnt how to turn her anger to indulgent good humour in a way his father never managed, but he was not always successful. Because of Diana's policy of discussing his misdemeanours before taking any action, he sometimes ended up being punished for something he had forgotten having done. And when she was in one of her darker moods he was in risk of a sudden whack across his legs or backside.

On at least one occasion the two modes blended in one. Once, when William was in the Royal Mews at the back of Buckingham Palace and was about to get into one of the carriages, he delivered a sharp kick to the leg of the footman helping him in. Diana immediately slapped her son on his bottom. William started crying loudly – and then cuddled up to his mother. Feeling guilty about the tears she had provoked, Diana picked him up and hugged him, thereby negating the punishment she had just administered.

This inconsistency in Diana's approach was not what any child psychologist would recommend. It also subjected her to public criticism of a kind she had not encountered before.

As a boy, Charles had preferred a swift smack to the alternative of being sent to his room for the afternoon, but physical chastisement was no longer a popular option and would be banned in British schools in 1985. When five years later Diana was again pictured angrily hitting her son, on this occasion for refusing to end the game of tag he was playing with some friends and accompany her home, it aroused predictable controversy.

Child psychologist Penelope Leach, who had written a no-smacking guide for a children's charity, observed, 'Good discipline and smacking don't go together. A smack can't prevent bad behaviour that has already happened or prevent it in the future. It just makes children feel so angry and humiliated that they can't even remember what they were smacked for.' Parents often smacked in public, she added, because they are 'embarrassed or afraid that onlookers will think they don't discipline their children properly'.

Diana was badly shaken by the reaction. She prided herself on her abilities as a mother and enjoyed the kudos that brought her. 'My children are the most important things in my life,' she plaintively told me. She certainly did not think that she was maltreating them in any way. 'I love them to death,' she said. It was a chance comment but it did hint at affection of an overpowering variety. However, with two boys making their conflicting demands on her attention and a hectic schedule of official engagements to fulfil, there was a limit to how much smothering she could do.

She also had Nanny Barnes to contend with. The forestry worker's daughter had turned out to be a lot more independent-minded and strong-willed than Diana had anticipated, and the two were soon at silent loggerheads.

'Barbara guarded the nursery floor like the Vatican,' one member of the Kensington Palace staff recalled. 'Trays would be grabbed and doors would be shut. It was her kingdom. But she was very good with the children. She treated them as people and never talked down to them. If there were tears she diverted their attention to something else. And if the boys refused to put on the clothes she had chosen for them, she would divert their attention again and gently lead them round to her way of thinking. She never went into head-on confrontation, but she somehow always managed to get them to do what she wanted.'

She achieved the remarkable feat of having both William and Harry sitting up straight before their first birthdays. They were made to say 'Please' and 'Thank you' almost as soon as they could talk. She would not allow them comfort blankets and refused to put their little feet into shoes until they had learnt to walk properly. And when they did get their first pairs of footwear, she insisted on classic Start-rites with buttoned straps that were shaped to the boys' feet. Trainers were banned.

Diana bowed to Barbara's greater experience in these matters. She was nonetheless 'very hands-on', always playing with them, in the nurseries, in the walled garden opposite her front door at Kensington Palace or in her sitting room at Highgrove. And it had been on her suggestion that the official photographs released to mark Harry's first birthday were casual and relaxed.

They were taken by his uncle, Prince Andrew, while the Royal Family were cruising the Western Isles of Scotland aboard the Royal Yacht *Britannia*, and they showed the prince clutching a bucket and smiling happily. They were not 'classic shots', as Buckingham Palace was forced to concede. Tim Hughes, assistant editor of the *British Journal of Photography*, marked them a poor 'three out of ten'. Andrew defended his pictures. 'They were actually taken as family snaps. I was just sitting on the deck, snapping away. If there was one that the princess liked and one that the prince liked, then it would be used as a birthday photograph. They weren't looking for a formal portrait. I don't think it's fair on a small one-year-old baby to have a formal portrait taken.'

The formality Diana had set her face against was already starting to reassert itself, however. Aboard the Royal Yacht, the Queen insisted that each child had his own sailor to make sure that he did not get into trouble. There was to be no repeat of the incident when Princess Anne's young son, Peter Phillips, had looked out of one of *Britannia*'s portholes at the crowds gathered on the quay to wave to the Royal Family and loudly proclaimed, 'Look at the poor people.' His nanny, Pat Moss, had pulled him away and furiously told him, 'Those poor people you're referring to keep you where you are, young man, so show some respect.'

That respect was what William and Harry were also expected to exhibit, and the lessons started at home. They were not allowed the free run of Kensington Palace, which was Charles and Diana's office as well as their home, and were brought downstairs only at certain times of the day. 'It was a very organised way of life,' a member of staff recalled. 'It was certainly a lot more formal than a normal household.'

When the Royal Family moved to Sandringham or Balmoral, William and Harry went with it and, as it was at Kensington Palace, their lives revolved around the nursery.

Prince Philip never went near the children's floors as far as anyone who was there can remember. 'The boys were wary of him and he did not have much time for them,' a member of the nursery staff recalled. That did not prevent the Queen they called 'Granny' taking a close interest in their welfare, though. Before they arrived she would fuss around their rooms, moving chairs and arranging toys, and when they were in residence she would often stop by to enquire how they were and what they had been doing, and sometimes to linger and do a jigsaw puzzle with them.

The Queen Mother, too, paid them a suitable amount of attention when the fancy took her. She would tell them stories and sometimes hide their stuffed animals behind her back, asking playfully, 'Where's Teddy gone?' as they squealed with delight.

This was still a court, however, bound by rules and conventions that had changed little since Victoria was on the throne, and in the presence of the woman who was their Sovereign as well as their grandmother they were expected to be on their Sunday best behaviour. One of the first things Nanny Barnes had been required to teach them was to bow to the Queen and the Queen Mother. This mark of royal respect to two anointed queens was rigorously enforced. One of the longest-serving members of the royal staff observed, 'When they came to visit the boys would wait by the door. When they entered the boys bowed – and then kissed them on the cheek and gave them a hug. It sounds a bit strange but it was not uncomfortable; it was so natural the boys didn't think anything of it.'

Despite those protocols, William would sometimes evade his minders and make it to the front door where he would stand and salute people as they came and went. Diana encouraged him. 'I want him to meet as many people as possible,' she told me, explaining that it was better to learn how to 'mix in' while he was still young, rather than having to do so when he was older.

Those meetings were not always an unqualified success. William was a naturally unruly boy with an easy-going father and a mother often distracted by her own problems, and like Peter Phillips before him there were moments when his exuberance was allowed to get the better of his manners. Brought up in an enclosed environment, he had little experience of the unconventional and reacted accordingly when he encountered it. When Bob Geldof, the pop singer who had galvanised the world with Live Aid, called on Charles at Kensington Palace to discuss the famine sweeping the Horn of Africa, he was greeted by William and Charles. The little boy took one look at the dishevelled Irishman and loudly asked his father, 'Why do you talk to that man?'

'Because we have work to do,' Charles replied.

William was not to be deflected. 'He's all dirty. He's got scruffy hair and wet shoes,' he declared.

Geldof, never one to stand on ceremony even in the presence of two princes, shot back, 'Shut up, you horrible little boy. Your hair's scruffy, too.'

William was nonplussed. 'No, it's not – my mother brushed it,' he protested.

It was not the kind of exchange that met with his nanny's approval. She was determined that William and Harry should display the good manners expected of princes. To Diana's way of thinking, however, they were just two 'ordinary' little boys who should be allowed what she called their 'right' to express their personalities.

FIVE

Life at Highgrove

Highgrove stands in the quiet Cotswold countryside just off the main road that wends from the picturesque township of Tetbury down to the M4 motorway.

It is not a grand house, not by royal standards. Nor does it boast of any great architectural merit. Built in the late eighteenth century, it is ungainly and, when Charles first saw it on a day when the sky was low and the rain was driving across the flat fields, rather forbidding. Diana told me she 'hated the place'.

As far as William and Harry were concerned, however, this was home. It still is. It is where they spent the happiest days of their childhood. It is where they return to whenever they can. It is the house that William will inherit when their father becomes king.

'Life there was about as normal for them as they were ever going to get,' observed Wendy Berry, Highgrove's former housekeeper.

It was where they could behave, Berry said, 'like ordinary boys'.

They had the run of the estate that Charles was painstakingly transforming from a plain, workaday farm into a rich tableau of kitchen gardens and formal flower beds, topiarised yew, and meadows sprinkled with wild cowslips, poppies, cornflowers and ox-eye daisies. There were cows and black Hebridean sheep and horses in the fields, chickens in the barn, dogs, guineas pigs and a pet rabbit to look after. And in this vast wonderland there was no end of hidden nooks and secret crannies waiting to be discovered by two boys in short trousers enthused by a sense of mischievous adventure. It was somewhere to escape the formality of London, with its petty rules and endless restrictions. It was also the place where, until they were old enough to know better, they could enjoy the family idyll that was popularly presumed to be their royal birthright.

No wonder, then, that they rushed shouting with excitement to clamber into the estate car that drove them down to Highgrove on Friday afternoons. Or that, once there, they would tumble out of the back seat and run to the back door calling out, 'Where's Papa? Where are you hiding?'

Charles was usually to be found in the garden, surveying the landscape, planning another improvement or simply communing with nature in a way that sometimes exposed him to ridicule but which to his sons seemed perfectly normal. He always broke off from whatever he was doing to greet them as they came tearing across the lawns.

'You could see how much he loved them,' said Berry. 'And they him – they wouldn't be so close to him now if they hadn't. You don't suddenly pose with your arm around your father, as William does, if you haven't always been close.'

Diana rarely ventured outdoors except for an occasional sulky walk through the fields, the sound of the countryside cut out by the headphones of her Walkman, or to go to the swimming pool tucked away to the side of the house near the stables. The daughter of a rustic earl, she had spent her own childhood in the country, first in Norfolk then in Northamptonshire, but rural life no longer held any appeal for her. 'It's always raining, there are too many flies and it's damp,' she complained to me.

Her sons did not share her dour opinion. They loved it there. William had a small arsenal of plastic weaponry including machine-guns, pistols, rifles and swords. When he was two years old he was given a replica of a Jaguar XJS cabriolet with leather seats and walnut fascia, powered by an electric motor capable of propelling him around the Highgrove grounds at speeds up to 15 miles an hour. Two years later he crashed into a garage wall at which point his mother said it was 'too dangerous, I won't ever allow him to use it again', and took it away.

That did not leave him and his brother bereft of amusements, however. They had their pet guinea pig and rabbit to care for, a tree house for a camp, and they liked nothing better than playing in the bales of hay in the barns looking for the eggs the hens had laid. When they found them they would burst into the kitchen, brandishing them aloft in triumph. In his haste William stumbled one day and sent two freshly laid eggs crashing on to the tiled floor where they broke into a slippery mess.

Mervyn Wycherley and Graham Newbolt were the full-time chefs, later to be joined by Chris Barber. They treated the boys with the amused tolerance that the staffs in aristocratic establishments usually employ in their relations with the sons of the house. Which was just as well, considering the amount of time William and Harry spent in the farmhouse kitchen with its large industrial-sized oven, scrubbed tables and, in the corner, their tank of exotic fish.

Diana never cooked. The most she ever did in all the time she was at Highgrove, according to one member of the kitchen staff, 'was make herself a cup of Horlicks'.

Her sons, on the other hand, delighted in the culinary process. Charles had given them their own little vegetable patch where they grew the lettuces and radishes they proudly presented to the chefs. Charles was forever telling his sons, 'Plants have feelings, too,' but that did not prevent them setting about what they had grown and anything else they could get their hands on with fiendish relish.

Harry became adept at chopping up vegetables, standing at the wooden chopping table attacking the carrots and potatoes with a sharp knife. William's forte was baking cakes. Harry somehow managed to avoid cutting himself. William was not so fortunate. On one occasion he burnt his hand on the oven door and scalded it badly.

'He let out a hell of yell,' a member of staff recalled. Ice was applied to bring down the swelling, but not quickly enough to escape the notice of Charles, who brought the cooks into his study to warn them, 'We won't let this happen again, will we?'

It would take more than a princely decree to keep his boys out of trouble. Running around the kitchen one day, Harry collided with the edge of the table and ended up needing several stitches above his nose. Mother and father were distraught, as they were when Harry was sick in his bed on one of the rare nights when there was no nanny in attendance. Diana ran to fetch clean linen out of the airing cupboard, and she and Charles then changed the sheets and sat with their son until he settled down again.

But these were no more than the common ailments and mishaps that all children are subjected to, and they certainly did not dampen down the boys' boisterousness. Indeed, there were times when visitors formed the impression that Highgrove had been converted into a giant playground.

Two soda siphons were kept to hand to mop up after Charles's Jack Russell terriers, Tigger and Roo, which were never fully housetrained. They were an irresistible temptation to the boys, who on more than one occasion squirted the entire contents over the floor. They terrorised the gardeners with catapults loaded with little water bombs made out of plastic bags. Harry also liked dropping ice cubes down the backs of the household staff. And when he was old enough he became a royal highwayman like his brother.

As a youngster, William was very keen on playing at being a soldier and, with Harry as his accomplice, he graduated to ambushing guests, demanding money with menaces before allowing them to pass. They never collected very much and 20p was usually enough to secure a safe passage past their water pistols. But for two boys who never received any pocket money (they were learning at an early age that royalty does not carry money) it seemed like a princely booty and it enabled them to buy themselves an extra helping of ice-cream when their detectives or their mother took them shopping in nearby Cirencester.

Less engaging was the way they treated the visitors who came to view Prince Charles's ever more exotic gardens. Charles had expanded them considerably since he bought the house for £750,000 in 1981 against the advice of the accountants acting for the Duchy of Cornwall who were concerned at the cost of turning a high-yield investment into a low-yield agricultural property. He kept buying up the surrounding land to add to his property and every season saw the addition of some new and often eccentric feature: a herb garden, an avenue of lime trees, a Spanish garden, a black and white garden, a bog garden, Tuscan vistas, lavenders specially selected for their oils, a stumpery of old driftwood.

Diana took a rather disparaging view of her husband's obsession ('He'd rather talk to his plants than to me,' was one comment) and sourly noted that not all his experiments were resounding successes. The butterflies he imported from Jersey churlishly flew away, and his attempt to found a colony of hooting owls came to an end when the mother ate her chicks the moment they were born. But he persisted and, in the opinion of Sir Roy Strong, the former director of the Victoria and Albert Museum, 'It is the most important garden to be made in the decade of the Eighties.'

When Charles invited me to Highgrove, he admitted that in the beginning he 'knew nothing about horticulture'. He was nonetheless always immensely proud of his creations and was more than happy to show them off to fellow gardening enthusiasts. There were times, though, when he wished he had kept his gates firmly bolted. As Diana told me, 'There was the day when he was working in his study, he looked and saw a group of gardening ladies peering in. He was so embarrassed that he ducked behind the window ledge so that they couldn't see him.'

His sons were a lot less retiring. Whenever they encountered one of the tours, they made a point of running up and sticking their tongues out. It was rudeness of a kind that would soon get them into serious trouble with the Queen. In those early days when they were young, they were still allowed to behave very much as they pleased and there were inevitably times when they took their sights off the visitors and set about each other.

Initially William had bossed his little brother around. He would order, 'Don't do that, Harry,' or, more imperiously 'Come here, Harry – now.' If Harry had a new toy, William was bound to want it. Charles's observation that Harry was the one 'with the more gentle nature' appeared to be holding true. A member of the household said, 'William was the leader. He was big, strong, very adult and Harry was like an irritating, ineffectual little brother who was very much in William's shadow.'

As Harry started to find his feet, however, he learnt to give as good as he got, as younger brothers usually do. He was no longer willing to hand over his possessions on demand. No member of staff can recall a supposedly enraged William ever hanging Harry out of a window, as was widely reported at the time, but they certainly had their share of squabbles, with William, as the elder, usually the instigator.

Wendy Berry thought he was 'just like any other boy'. Other members of the staff took a more trenchant view of his behaviour. Diana's dresser Evelyn Dagley, for one, called him 'naughty' – especially when their cousin, Zara Phillips, who was just a year older than William, came to stay. One of their favourite tricks was to blow through straws and send their jellies sploshing over the nursery table. 'They were a terror,' one member of staff recalled. So on occasion was Harry, but it was William who earned most of the black marks in those early years.

If he was made to wear clothes he didn't like he was quite likely to go into a rage – typical childhood tantrums. One weekend when Diana, bored at Highgrove, insisted on taking him back to London early, William shouted at her, 'I hate you, Mummy,' and ran off and hid. Diana eventually had to drag him to the car.

Charles tried to be the stricter of his two parents (it was Charles who told him off when he squirted his detectives with his water pistol, while Diana was inclined to laugh). He was rarely able to sustain his irritation for very long, however, which meant that William often ended up getting his own way.

The one instance when Charles did put his foot down and kept it there was over the matter of breakfast. When the prince he called Wombat and Diana referred to as 'William Wales' was four, his father decided it would be a good idea if he joined him for breakfast. The meal ended in shambolic disaster, with William spilling his food over the table and on to the floor. Afterwards Charles declared, 'We'll all get to ten o'clock a lot happier if we don't repeat this experiment.' William was duly banished back upstairs to the nursery.

Bedtimes could be equally trying. Like all small children, William objected to being packed off to bed. His cries of protest were liable to set his brother off as well.

The late Spike Milligan recalled visiting Highgrove and being asked by Charles to give a rendition of 'Ying Tong Iddle I Po'. Milligan recounted, 'For the first time I started to feel embarrassed and he noticed and said, "Look, don't tell me you've forgotten it." And I had to say, "If you must know, I have." And he said, "We'll do it." '

Charles went on to his knees to bring himself down to his sons' height and sang the old song from Milligan's *Goon Show*, followed by his own scat version. 'It left me helpless with laughter,' Milligan said. 'He finished on a double-forte high note, which must have put a great strain on his nethers.'

Diana was not overly impressed. 'She turned to me and said, "I don't know what's come over him," and I said, "Well, whatever it is, it's lasting quite a while." '

His performance at an end, Charles turned to William and Harry and said, 'That's it, off you go to bed.' Milligan observed, 'The boys didn't seem to want to go and he said, "You little rascals, you must go to bed, your mother and I have guests." I thought the boys must think guests was some awful disease because one of the boys said, "I hope you get better soon, Daddy." '

Charles eventually persuaded them upstairs and Milligan heard him say, 'Don't forget your prayers.' William and Harry replied, 'Do we have to?'

As the future Supreme Governor of the Church of England, Charles might have been expected to take a vigorous approach to his sons' religious education. But in this matter, too, he tended to be easygoing. The family never attended church when they were at Highgrove, a fact reflected in William and Harry's off-hand approach to the rituals of faith. They were far more interested in bringing their father to his knees than getting down on their own, and when Charles made it downstairs again he was panting and his hair was tousled. 'I had to wrestle with those little buggers before they would go to bed,' he explained.

Such bedtime scenes were typical, with William and Harry drawing them out for as long as possible. In the effort to settle them down Charles would read them stories (Rudyard Kipling's *Jungle Book* was a great favourite). All too often, however, he got drawn into a rough and tumble pillow fight or a noisy game of Big Bad Wolf that, instead of calming them down, left them even more agitated than they had been when he went upstairs. Diana observed, 'He really is good with children – but I don't think the children are good with him.'

Charles didn't seem to mind. He liked the easy familiarity and he was prepared to permit them liberties beyond anything any princes belonging to the House of Windsor had ever enjoyed.

As befitting their royal position, the boys' bedroom slippers were embroidered with the Prince of Wales feathers. And when they went to visit the home of their aunt, Princess Anne, at Gatcombe Park, their mother always insisted on dressing them neatly in shiny shoes and neatly pressed shorts – much to the amusement of their cousins, Zara and Peter, who were usually dressed in old jeans and Wellington boots. But they were allowed to have friends to stay, and to spend the night in some of the grander houses in the area with families that had children their own age. Of greater social significance, their detectives took them to the travelling fairs when they came into the neighbourhood, and to the public playgrounds where they mixed with the local children and shared the cakes and sandwiches their chefs had prepared for them.

On Saturdays Diana would drive them into Cirencester. Diana would complain that there was usually a photographer lying in wait for them on those regular visits to the local market town. Her detectives pointed out that as she always parked in exactly the same place, the paparazzi knew exactly where to be and at approximately what time and that if she changed her routine she would probably avoid them. Diana deliberately ignored their advice. It was the beginning of that strange (and ultimately tragic) relationship, wherein Diana telegraphed her movements to the photographers and then moaned afterwards when they seized her bait.

Fortunately, William and Harry were too young to notice or care about the portentous drama developing around them. All they were interested in was buying one of their favourite Magnum ice-creams or the latest video featuring Mr Bean, the Chaplinesque character created by Rowan Atkinson that had them howling with laughter. They also delighted in going to the butcher's and helping to choose the different-flavoured sausages that were a feature of the barbecues which enlivened the summer evenings at Highgrove.

Charles did not attend those casual al fresco feasts where the princes cavorted with Nick and Alex, the children of the butler Paul Burrell and his wife Maria, who acted as Diana's maid until the princess dismissed her. He excused himself by claiming pressure of work. Every day his papers would arrive by car in blue bags and he would retire to his study to read and, where appropriate, to sign them. 'I never have time to relax,' he said. The staff suspected that the real reason for his absence was that he was uncomfortable mixing with them when they were off-duty.

He did not object to his sons joining in the revelries, however. Prompted by Diana, it was exactly the kind of upbringing he wanted for his children. He had seen the benefits it had given his nephew and niece, Peter and Zara Phillips, and agreed that in an age with the old divisions between court and country no longer held fast, it was important that William and Harry should learn to mingle with people from beyond the confines of the royal enclave. And if that led to occasional lapses of behaviour, so be it. He was determined that they should not be isolated in the way he believed he had been when he was little. He accepted the sibling rivalry and the 'terrible twos' and even the odd tantrum as a natural part of his sons' development. He was forever talking about their latest escapades. He even took an interest in their potty training, and when William called down that he had been successful, Charles would shout back, 'Good, very good, Wombat.'

Diana was amused by her husband's easy-going approach to fatherhood. What she could not stomach was the fastidious way he handled just about everything else at Highgrove. He was obsessed by details, no matter how trivial, and that only served to exacerbate their fraying relationship. Charles's authorised biographer, Jonathan Dimbleby, formed the opinion that she wanted to 'possess' Charles. Diana saw it differently. She believed that she was the one who was being hemmed in and restricted by a man who insisted on having his own way – and was prone to fits of sudden rage if he didn't get it. She told me, 'All the Windsor men have appalling tempers.' By her account it didn't take much to set Charles off.

By his own admission he demands perfection and expects it. But while concentrating on the minutiae of life he often leaves making decisions about more important issues to the last minute.

On one occasion he called his unfortunate valet away from his supper to ask why he had not unbuttoned the shirt he was about to wear and on another broke a pane of glass with the heel of his shoe when he was unable to open the window. He was adamant that the clocks in the house should all keep precise time. If he noticed that one had stopped he would shake his hands and proclaim, 'My clocks, my clocks, what am I to do?' and then threaten the staff, 'There'll be hell to pay.'

If one of the lights above the collection of fine pictures from the Royal Collection that adorned the walls happened to fail, a memo would be dispatched to the staff, again warning against a repeat of such a 'calamity'.

His gardens were full of flowers for every season, but he refused to allow anyone to pick them, which meant that the floral arrangements for the house had to be bought at a shop in Tetbury.

In late summer the house was full of flies. 'The ceilings were often black with them,' Wendy Berry recalled. They so disturbed the actress Emma Thompson when she stayed that she started pressing frantically on the panic button in her bedroom to summon the staff to her aid. When they got there she asked them to bring some fly spray – only to be told that the prince did not hold with fly spray because it was not ozone-friendly.

If little pieces of gravel were inadvertently brought into the house from the driveway, Charles would reprimand the housekeeper and warn that it must never happen again, regardless of the possibility that he might very well have been the person responsible.

He often slept in the bed in his first-floor dressing room with only his faded yellow teddy for company. The bear had to be tucked up every night 'to stop him getting cold'. Whenever teddy needed patching he was sent by chauffeur-driven car to his old nanny Mabel Anderson at her retirement cottage in Windsor Great Park.

It was the valet's job to double guess where the prince would be spending the night and make sure that the one and only pillow he would sleep on was there waiting for him. Once he made the mistake of not putting the pillow slip on, leaving Charles to struggle with that simple domestic chore (the lessons learnt during his six years at Gordonstoun, when he had to make his own bed complete with hospital corners, were seemingly long forgotten).

The monogrammed towels in the cloakroom had to be changed and the washbasin cleaned each time he used them. In a rage, he once ripped a washbasin from the wall and smashed it to the ground.

While he was in the bath his valet would pick up the clothes he had so insouciantly left lying on the floor. And when he stepped out of the bath there was always a fluffy towel waiting for him on a chair. It was folded on two sides that met in the middle so he could wrap it around him without having to exert himself.

At Sandringham one year, he changed his mind about which cuff-links to wear and sent his valet on a 300-mile round trip to Highgrove to collect the right pair. He often dispatched a chauffeur to pick up vegetables. And when he forgot the box of chocolates he was going to give to the Queen on her sixtieth birthday, he insisted that one of his staff drive all the way from Highgrove to Windsor to deliver them on time.

He hated wooden tables and insisted that they be covered with freshly laundered linen – except, contrarily, for dinner parties when they had to be polished to a glass-like finish.

Diana was askance at the way the staff pampered him. She said, 'It was as if he was married to them, not to me, and they were so patronising it drove me mad.'

Such idiosyncrasies aroused little comment in the Royal Family, however, although the Queen has felt moved to remark more than once that she thought her first-born was getting 'a little grand'.

What did upset the Queen was the behaviour of her two grandsons, and William in particular. She had noticed how unruly they were becoming when they stayed with her at Balmoral, Sandringham, Windsor and aboard the Royal Yacht *Britannia*. She had not been prepared to tolerate it in her own children and would certainly not put up with it from this little boy who would one day be king.

Notwithstanding the fact that he was required to bow to her whenever they met, William had enjoyed an affectionate and informal relationship with the Queen. As far as his young mind was concerned she was simply his grandmother and his detective recalled how, when his teacher was discussing her in class one day, he had innocently asked, 'Are you talking about my Granny?'

In her role as sovereign, however, 'Granny' could be stern and demanding. Diana had long been aware of her mother-in-law's mounting disapproval at the way he was being brought up and admitted that she was very worried about taking him to the Service of Thanksgiving at St George's Chapel, Windsor, to mark the Queen's sixtieth birthday 'in case he misbehaved'. He was still not four and it was only at the last minute that she agreed to chance it and allow William to attend – and then only after he had been given the strictest of instructions from Barbara Barnes as to how he should conduct himself.

As it turned out, William thoroughly enjoyed himself. He was still young enough to relish the excitement of such occasions without concerning himself with the procedures or the attention which soon would later start to so upset him.

He was fussed over by Diana's hairdresser, Richard Dalton, who cut his hair on the morning. During the ceremony he bobbed up and down in his pew, full of wide-eyed wonder as he looked to see who else was there (there were forty-four members of the Royal Family on parade that day).

It was the horses, however, who provided the high point of his day. On the way back from the chapel he had ridden with his mother and father in a state coach with an escort of outriders. When he got back to Highgrove the staff asked him what he had most enjoyed. He replied, 'The horses. They went plop.' Warming to his theme, he galloped off as he had been taught at Mrs Mynors', shouting, 'Plop, plop, plop.' He was a little boy delighting in using what he thought was a naughty word and everyone laughed.

Three months later, however, William's exuberance would get him into the most serious trouble of his young life when his antics at the wedding of his uncle, Prince Andrew, to Sarah Ferguson infuriated his grandmother.

William had been chosen to be one of the four page boys at the ceremony in Westminster Abbey. Diana was nervous from the start. 'I'm going to put down a line of Smarties in the aisle of Westminster Abbey so that William will know where to stand – and he's got to stay there,' she said. 'He's terribly excited, I only hope he behaves in the Abbey. He will rise to the occasion – at least I hope he will . . .'

Her doubts turned out to be well founded. William was required to wear the uniform of a sailor in the Royal Navy of 1846, specially made by the Savile Row tailoring firm of Gieves and Hawkes. Diana had insisted on extra fittings 'so that William will at least be comfortable'. For his efforts William received one groat dated 1846, worth in today's money less than 2p but a great deal more to a collector.

Fergie's five-year-old nephew, Seamus Makin, was another of the pages. He would later recall that they were under firm instructions to keep their hands out of their pockets and their fingers out of their noses. He said, 'Our little suits had scabbards down the side with decorative knives on the inside. At the rehearsal William and I kept pulling them out and sparring with each other, so my mum and Sarah glued and sewed them closed.'

That proved to be a less than adequate restriction. The trouble started as soon as the wedding ceremony began. The four pages were required to walk hand-in-hand up the aisle behind the bride and her father, the late Major Ronald Ferguson. The progress was a little slow for William, who quickened his step, dragging his cousin, six-year-old Laura Fellowes, with him. A modicum of peace was restored when they took their places beside the sanctuary steps. Half-way through the ceremony, boredom got the better of William and he began to fiddle with his hat cord, scratch his head and finger the knife that had fortunately been glued fast. He rolled his order of service into a trumpet, put his fingers into his mouth and then covered his face with his hands. When Laura Fellowes refused to join in his game he poked his tongue out at her. By the time he left the Abbey his hat was perched on the back of his head.

He was no better during the official photographic session in the Throne Room at Buckingham Palace. The Scottish-born, New York-based photographer Albert Watson remarked, 'Prince William was supercharged and his nanny kept coming up to tell me that he was sticking his tongue out in every shot.'

Diana tried to bluff it out. On a visit to the Shetland Isles on the day after the wedding she disingenuously enquired, 'Did you see William? I'm glad he behaved himself because he can be a bit of a prankster. It was terribly hot in the Abbey but he did very well considering he is only four.'

Unfortunately for Diana, the cameras had recorded William's misbehaviour. The Queen was not amused. He may have been only four but, as far as she was concerned, that was no excuse. As a child aged three she had already learnt how to sit upright and still when called upon to do so. Yet there was her grandson behaving as if he was in a playground.

Up until then the Queen had avoided making any direct criticism of the way her grandsons were being brought up. She had no compunction about telling her daughter's children to watch themselves when they stepped out of line and, indeed, had once shook Zara forcefully when she was running riot aboard *Britannia*. 'She was always chastising her and Peter,' a rating aboard the Royal Yacht recalled. When it came to William and Harry, however, she was more circumspect.

Diana's own mother had made it clear from the beginning that she had no intention of interfering in her daughter's way of bringing up her children. 'I think mothers-in-law should be seen and not heard,' Mrs Shand Kydd declared. 'When daughters marry, they set up a new home and they don't want mothers-in-law hanging around. They should be free to make their own decisions and, maybe, to make their own mistakes.'

The Queen would have liked to adopt the same attitude. William and Harry were her son's children and she did not want to undermine the authority of their mother, who she rightly deduced needed careful handling. She therefore confined herself to dropping opportune hints when the Waleses came to stay at any one of her homes for those immutable family gatherings centred on Easter, Christmas, and the sporting seasons for stag, salmon, grouse and pheasant of autumn and winter.

Sandringham, Balmoral and Windsor were nowhere near as carefree as Highgrove. When they were with the Queen, they were treated as princes. The staff called them by their Christian names but they could not fail to sense the deference accorded them. They had their own nursery footman to clean there shoes, press their clothes and do their fetching and carrying, and it started to dawn on William and Harry that they were different to the children they met in the playgrounds of Gloucestershire or even their cousins, Zara and Peter. But if this was privilege, it came with the price of good manners and self-control.

It may have been an old-fashioned view but, as the Queen observed, William was not as other boys and his behaviour therefore mattered more than it might in other children. Charles had insisted, 'It's so important to have an adequate amount of discipline at an early age, which is the only way, it seems to me, to enable you to be a self-disciplined person.' But for all his good intentions, Charles proved to be a rather easy-going parent. One member of staff observed at the time, 'What William wants he usually gets.'

During her four decades on the throne the Queen had built for herself a wide-ranging intelligence network that kept her abreast of what was going on in politics – and within her own family. She was a good listener – when she telephoned Highgrove, for instance, she would often spend a long time chatting to the butler Paul Burrell before asking to be put through to the Prince of Wales – and had become adept at picking up on rumours and gossip. She rarely acted on the information she received. In the case of

William and Harry, however, there was a limit to how far she was prepared to let the situation drift. She knew they were running wild. She had seen it with her own eyes.

During a fire drill at Sandringham, William started clambering over the engines and when one fireman asked him if he would like to wear his helmet, William replied, 'Yes please' – and then refused to take it back. Diana pleaded, 'Be a good boy and give it back.' William stamped his foot, declared, 'I want it,' and ran off. Diana giggled. The Queen did not.

This was not a case of a meddlesome mother-in-law interfering in the private workings of Diana's family. That was the last thing the Queen wanted to do (or, indeed, was psychologically capable of doing). When it came to safeguarding the reputation of her dynasty, however, she felt compelled to take a firm line. The wedding of the Duke and Duchess of York had merely been the final straw. It was clear evidence for what she had suspect for some while, which was that Charles and Diana were over-indulgent parents who were not facing up to their royal responsibilities.

The Queen expresses her displeasure succinctly. There is no loss of temper, no histrionics, just a few clipped words accompanied by a withering look. A lifetime of royal training has given her a formidable authority that can quash even the most bombastic politician. There is no mistaking her meaning.

Diana's sister, Lady Sarah McCorquodale, tried to defend the manner of William's upbringing. She said, 'It's bound to be different to Prince Charles's experience. After all, that was thirty years ago.'

And so it was. But while there was clearly going to be no repeat of the Victorian style of childhood Charles has endured, the same criteria – of politeness and restraint – still applied.

The Queen had pointed this out to Barbara Barnes. As a member of the nursery staff said, 'If William or Harry were badly behaved she would tell the nanny.'

The trouble was that Barnes's authority over the boys was waning badly as her relationship with Diana deteriorated.

Barnes had proved herself to be competent and caring. 'She had a real bond with the boys, especially William,' Wendy Berry recalled.

The nursery floor at Highgrove was a self-contained unit. It had a light and airy communal sitting room with a fireplace, large bookcases with cupboards underneath for their toys and a television and video in one corner. There were two sofas and some large, squashy cushions on the floor, with windows overlooking the front drive. The small kitchen was off to one side, the boys' bathroom to another. William's bedroom with its brass bed and his stuffed wombat toy was next to the kitchen above his father's dressing room. Harry's room was next to the bathroom. The detective who was in constant attendance had his own quarters through a door on the backstairs. The nanny had her own suite comprising a bedroom, a separate sitting room and her own bathroom. A member of staff described it as being like 'a semi-detached house', and in a way it was. It was there that the boys' days began and ended, only a staircase away but effectively cut off from the main body of the house.

They woke shortly after seven. Eyes full of sleep, William would make a beeline for Barnes's bedroom and climb into bed with her for his morning cuddle, dragging his toy Australian marsupial in with him. Harry would sometimes toddle in later.

Breakfast, prepared by Nanny from a tray taken up the night before, was eaten in the communal sitting room, with the boys wearing their dressing gowns over their pyjamas. They were then taken downstairs to see their mother. William often went ahead to climb into bed with Diana for a second cuddle of the morning. They were then dressed and then went out for their morning ride, which in Harry's case when he was young amounted to no more than sitting for a few minutes on the backs of the Shetland ponies, Smokey and Trigger.

Later in the morning they would drive into Cirencester with Diana or accompany their father around the farm. William liked to put on jeans and Wellingtons and follow Charles around as he chatted to the gardeners and estate workers.

They would return to the nursery for lunch. It was brought up to them on a tray from the main kitchen. Sometimes there were as many as three fully trained chefs cooking their sausage and chips, pasta and fish fingers for them.

On Saturdays, it was Charles who spent the afternoon walking around the estate with their sons, while Diana, disliking the country and increasingly uncomfortable in her husband's company, remained in the chintz-decorated sitting room on the ground floor, reading magazines, listening to pop music or making telephone calls to friends. If Charles was away she would have the boys in the room with her, snuggled up on the sofa to spend the afternoon watching television. There were plenty of other things that the boys might have doing, but Diana wanted to have them with her.

In the early evening they would be handed back to nanny and taken upstairs for supper, again brought up to them on a tray, via the backstairs, from the main kitchen. Then came bathtime, a frolic Diana liked to share – unless Charles had got there first.

Afterwards the Waleses would take their own baths. They rarely had guests to stay and, with the boys finally asleep, on the evenings they weren't going out Charles and Diana would then dine casually off a card table in front of the fire in the sitting room, dressed in towelling robes.

It was a simple enough routine that would be familiar to many families. In their case, though, it required a large staff of chefs, butlers, maids, detectives, valet, dresser and Gurkha soldiers to keep it running smoothly. There was no such thing as a night off for them in a household where the mistress never cooked and never once washed up. Housekeeper Wendy Berry recalled, 'It was very theatrical, like working on the stage. We would set up the props and then get out of the way.'

Essential to this performance was Nanny Barnes. She was the dresser, prompter and director of the two boys who were now starring in the Royal Family's latest domestic production. It was Diana who commanded centre stage, however, and she was growing increasingly unhappy with Barbara's role.

The first sign that all was not well between them arose over the question of the clothes William and Harry should wear. Diana had allowed Barnes to decide when they should first wear shoes, but as the boys grew older she insisted that she had the final say in what they wore. The nanny dug her heels in. She believed that, as the one who had the day-to-day responsibility for them, she knew best what they required. Diana did not agree. She wanted to choose what they should wear but all too often, by the time she had made up her mind, Barbara already had them dressed. The situation degenerated into a running feud, with Diana objecting to almost everything Barbara put them in.

The way the boys were to be controlled was another area of conflict. Diana ruled that on no account was Barnes to raise her voice to William and Harry. She was also forbidden to spank them, no matter how trying the circumstances and despite the fact that Diana herself was not averse to delivering the odd slap. When a dispute arose between the nanny and her young charges, Diana would insist on being the judge. She often sided with her sons, which only served to undermine the nanny's authority. After the Queen's intervention this disciplinary problem became a major source of contention.

At the heart of their disagreements, however, lay something much more basic. It came down to jealousy.

It was Barnes who was always there for them, always waiting to pick them up when they fell down, clean them up when they got dirty, comfort them at night should they wake up crying. It was Barnes who took them away on holiday to the Scilly Isles and up to Scotland – Diana sometimes only managed to join them in time for the photocall. Barnes was the guard at the nursery door who shielded the boys from the disharmony seeping into their parents' marriage. No hint of discord was allowed to enter into her domain. The boys, as one observer said, 'sailed from house to house under Nanny's calm captaincy'.

It was inevitable, given her fondness for them, that Harry and more especially William grew extremely attached to the woman he called Baba. There was nothing unusual in this. Children often develop close ties to their nannies. It does not override or negate their feelings for their parents. Diana, however, did not see it that way. The consensus among the staff was that Diana felt that Barbara was supplanting her in William and Harry's affections.

There was only ever going to be one winner in this situation and that was Diana. In the five years since her marriage, she had either fired or forced into resignation some forty members of staff. Barbara Barnes was about to become the latest name on her casualty list.

Just before Christmas 1986, Barnes attended the birthday party of her former employer, Lord Glenconner, on the Caribbean island of Mustique, which he owned. She was photographed with such luminaries as Princess Margaret, Jerry Hall and Raquel Welch. That angered Diana, who felt that it was out of order for the nanny to be cavorting with celebrities in the West Indies while she was part of the Wales's household and employed to look after the heir to the throne.

When Barnes returned with her suntan to Britain she discovered that Diana's coolness towards her had turned stone cold. The princess hardly spoke a word to her until after the winter break at Sandringham, when Diana told her that it would 'better', as she put it, if Barbara left her employment.

'One weekend she just wasn't there any more,' Wendy Berry said. 'Her bags had been packed by the part-time housekeeper Joan Bodmin and no one saw her again.' She left without a job to go to and before a replacement had been found.

The announcement was made on 15 January 1987, William's first day at his new school.

'I thought no one would notice,' Diana said, 'but I was wrong, wasn't I?'

She was indeed. The story of Barbara Barnes's departure made the front page of most of the newspapers.

The one person who really noticed that Nanny had gone was, of course, Prince William.

SIX

School Days

It was a bitterly cold January morning when William alighted from the chauffeured car outside Wetherby School at 11 Pembridge Square in London's Notting Hill. Nervous and shy, he was clutching his mother's legs.

Diana pushed him forward to shake the hand of his new headmistress, Frederika Blair Turner. He was not yet tall enough to negotiate the steps with any ease and stumbled as he made his way up to the front door. He looked self-conscious in his new grey and red uniform (available only from Harrods) as he faced the battery of waiting photographers.

Charles, always more pragmatic when it came to dealing with the attention that is the price the Royal Family must pay for their position, might have brought a calming influence to the situation. But he was snowbound in Sandringham, and slipping out of the domestic frame as his marital problems mounted. It was Diana who was in charge of this royal performance.

As she led William up the steps she lent down and whispered to him, 'Don't smile at the cameras.'

It was an extraordinary instruction to give a four-and-a-half-year-old destined to be photographed for the rest of his life. He had been told by his father always to be polite to the media. The fact that his mother had a broad grin on her own face only made matters worse. Diana later told friends that she had 'wanted to die laughing' when she saw Miss Blair

85

Turner, 6 foot 2 inches tall, dressed entirely in blue, her hair in plaits 'and looking more like a Viking figurehead' than a schoolmistress.

To add to his confusion, his mother then ordered him to wave to the cameras she had just told him to ignore.

On the second day there were few journalists waiting to greet him. 'Where have all the photographers gone?' he asked.

The princess, whose relationship with the press was always ambiguous, was herself somewhat nonplussed by their absence. She replied irritably, 'Don't be so grand.'

William's detectives were not impressed by the princess's behaviour. As Ken Wharfe, who had recently started in his job as Royal Protection Officer, later observed, 'When she told William not to smile he didn't know what his mother was talking about. It wasn't the kind of thing she should have said to the prince. It's not surprising that he is so reticent now.'

Diana was unaware that she might be establishing a pattern in her son's life that would persist into adulthood. Always capricious, she was oblivious to the possibility that an impressionable youngster might remember her words long after she had forgotten ever uttering them. As far she was concerned, they were merely throwaway remarks uttered on the spur of the moment, and later that morning, when she arrived at an old folks' home in Islington, she was talking cheerfully about how well adjusted William was, how smart he looked in his new uniform, and what a perfect little gentleman he was becoming.

'He's already opening doors for ladies,' she said, 'and he's calling men "sir".'

Diana, aware of the Queen's watchful disapproval, was anxious to give the impression that William's manners were on the mend. To ensure they were, Diana had done the rounds of all the local schools before finally settling on Wetherby's, which was near Kensington Palace and offered good security and a curriculum that matched the royal needs.

Charles had done some checking of his own. He had consulted Camilla, whose husband's nephews, Luke and Sam, were pupils there. She spoke highly of the establishment. A pre-preparatory school for boys aged between four and a half and nine, Wetherby's placed great emphasis on 'courtesy and reasonable discipline'. Another aim was 'to instil confidence and a sense of responsibility'. That fitted in with Charles's evolving views as to how his son and heir should be brought up. It was the natural step after Mrs Mynors', an experiment that Charles now judged to have been a success.

There had been a few ups and downs, of course. William had burst into tears on his acting debut when he was called upon to play a wolf. But he did manage to progress to a speaking part playing an innkeeper in his final Christmas nativity play. He had displayed a delight in signing his name and his classroom papers were covered with 'William's, scratched left-handedly in crayon. His last report read, 'Prince William was very popular with the other children, and was known for his kindness, sense of fun and quality of thoughtfulness.'

School reports on royalty are inclined to highlight the positive while overlooking any shortcomings, but that glowing reference was enough to convince Charles that his wife had been right to insist that William be educated at school – and not, as he had initially wanted, by governesses in the lonely privacy of a palace. Signalling his change of attitude, Charles said, 'We're open-minded about William and his education. I would like to try and bring our children up to be well mannered, to think of other people, to put themselves in other people's position. That way, even if they turn out to be not very bright or well-qualified, at least if they have reasonable manners they will get so much further in life than if they did not have any at all.'

William would go on to prove himself bright enough to earn himself a university place on merit. It was the good conduct that was always going to be the tricky part. Good manners do not come naturally to little boys and especially not to someone as high-spirited as William. Despite Diana's insistence to the contrary, there were times when his behaviour fell a long way short of what his grandmother expected.

At one children's tea party he threw his food on the floor, shouting that he hated sandwiches and jelly and ice-cream. That did not endear him to his contemporaries. One fellow complained to his mother, 'Who is William anyway – he's really boring. But everyone talks about him all the time.'

The mother explained that one day William would be king, 'so he's obviously interesting to people'. 'Not to me, he's not,' came the sharp reply.

His position was certainly of growing importance to William. Asked to recount what he had done on the weekend, he often wrote about visiting 'my granny's castles'. 'The boasting doesn't go down well,' Diana admitted. Nor did his threat to one boy who had the temerity to challenge him: 'When I'm king I'm going to send my knights around to kill you.'

Harry was drawn along in his brother's riotous wake and the two were forever disappearing into horse boxes and cellars, provoking frantic searches of houses and woods. William got a sharp smack for teasing the gundogs at Sandringham and both parents were particularly upset to hear reports of William bossing the guardsman on duty at Balmoral during the summer holidays of 1987. In a moment of exasperation, Diana remarked that they appeared to have 'grown into a couple of little thugs'.

Charles tried to defend their sons' behaviour. 'They're normal little boys who are unlucky enough to create an abnormal amount of attention,' he said. Charles and Diana nonetheless decided it wise not to risk the Queen's displeasure further by taking them to the Highland Games at Braemar that year.

Part of the problem, as any child psychologist would doubtless have pointed out, had one been consulted, was the disruption in the Waleses' household. By the autumn of 1987 Charles and Diana were barely on speaking terms. She was in London while he spent most of the autumn in gloomy retreat in Scotland, with a hardly a word passing between them. On the rare occasion they were together, the tension was palpable. He disliked being in the same room as her and when they were she took a malicious delight in putting him down. One evening, when he was extolling the charms of Rudyard Kipling's *Just So* stories he was reading to William and Harry, she rounded on her husband and declared, 'Just so what, Charles.'

Despite that unpleasant emotional undertow, life in the nursery remained pleasant enough for William and his little brother. At this juncture both

Diana and Charles tried to avoid embroiling their sons in their own disaster and, when the family was together, did their best to act as if that nothing was amiss. But it was. And the worst thing, as far as William and Harry were concerned, was the sudden removal of their nanny, Barbara Barnes.

She had been with them since they were born and they had come to depend on her. It was her bed they climbed into in the morning and she was the last person they saw at night. When they were sick or unhappy she was usually the one who comforted them and while she had never supplanted Diana in their affections, they had forged an intimate bond with her. Professor of Family and Developmental Psychology at Lancaster University Charlie Lewis explained, 'However fraught the parents' relationship might be and however often they are absent from home, a loving nanny can stabilise the situation for the children and fulfil the parents' role quite happily.' That was exactly what Barbara Barnes had done. Now that protective bulwark had been summarily removed.

William was particularly upset by her disappearance. The Highgrove housekeeper Wendy Berry said, 'He was very upset. I don't think anyone else formed such a bond with him.'

He would cry out, 'Where's Baba?' and 'I want my nanny.' He started to blame himself for her abrupt departure. Staff recalled him asking, 'Why did she go? What did I do wrong?' His final plaintive cry was always, 'Is she coming back?'

The answer was no. Diana cut her out of their lives completely. Barbara Barnes would be allowed no further contact with the boys she had nurtured from birth until William's confirmation all of eleven years later.

The princess was convinced that her sons would get over their grief in a few weeks. That was wishful thinking. In his book, *The Rise and Fall of the British Nanny*, Jonathan Gathorne-Hardy stated, 'If this early relationship is suddenly severed, if, in effect, he is punished (for so it seems) for loving, and not rewarded, he will naturally be very wary about how he sets about it in the future. It will be much more difficult for him to commit himself.'

According to the authoritative book *Child Development and Personality* by Mussen, Conger and Kagan, children deprived of contact with someone they have come to love enter a 'phase of detachment' and as a result are 'incapable of experiencing separation, anxiety or grief'. They may well grow up to give the impression of 'unusually vigorous independence'. In a flight of literary fancy rare in such serious textbooks, the authors concluded, 'Analysis shows that the springs of love are frozen and that their independence is hollow.'

There is a large chasm between medical theory and royal practice, and both William and Harry became very friendly with many of the people employed to look after them, and with their police protection officers in particular. However, the staff at Highgrove were quick to note that after Barbara Barnes left William never again allowed himself to become emotionally dependent on anyone.

According to one member of the household, 'William and Harry loved their mother and father but they learnt very early on how to transfer their affections.'

From the age of four onwards William would sit with the staff in their dining rooms. 'He knew the names of everyone in all the houses,' Wendy Berry said. 'He was quite forthcoming and seemed very grown up for his age.'

In the opinion of another staff member, however, the interest was superficial. 'After Barbara, William never appeared to miss people after they were gone.'

Diana had dispensed with Barbara Barnes because she felt her sons were becoming more attached to their nanny than they were to her. It would be a sad irony indeed if, in her attempt to draw them closer to her, she had only succeeded in making them more like their emotionally withdrawn father and Prince Philip, the father-in-law whose self-containment she came to detest. But that, if the staff were accurate in their observations, is exactly what happened.

In an effort to bring some calm to the overwrought prince, Diana enrolled William in 'Fun with Music'. Its founder, Ann Rachlin, explained, 'Music is a wonderful way of getting rid of pent-up emotion.'

Based on the theory that learning should be enjoyable, her pupils were treated to an afternoon of stories woven around a musical theme. 'For them it's tea and stories,' Rachlin explained. 'You can't take them out of school and sit them down to another lesson, so I tell them, "I'm going to do all the work and all you have to do is sit and listen and draw if you feel like it."

'William's drawings were wonderful. The drawing enforces the story I am telling, which is set to the music. I match my voice in pitch, mood and excitement. They absorb the story and at the same time they totally absorb the music. When my voice is removed they remember and identify the music with the story, saying, for instance, "I know that, it's Beethoven – and he was going deaf when he wrote that." '

The Waleses first heard about the classes through Princess Michael of Kent, who had enrolled her son, Freddie, when he was three. They were held in a church hall in St John's Wood. Ann Rachlin sat on a high-backed wicker chair while the children sat in three groups of ten around little tables, tucking into their afternoon tea of jam and Marmite sandwiches. With Princess Michael's daughter, Ella, as his classmate, William attended Fun with Music for four years. It gave him an introduction to the great classical composers and helped develop his interest in music which has remained with him.

It also tapped into that feeling of compassion for others his father was so keen for his son to develop. While listening to a piece of music by Johann Sebastian Bach, whose parents died before he was ten, Rachlin told the prince how distressing it was to lose a loved one. 'I know, because I lost my father, too,' she said.

The prince, who was sitting next to her, snuggled up and said, 'Oh, Ann, how sad.' The next time he came he brought her a box of chocolates. When he later learnt that she had also lost her mother, he brought her a bouquet of flowers.

When Harry was old enough, he joined his brother in the chauffeur-driven car that took William to St John's Wood. 'My aim was to open their ears to music and provide tomorrow's audiences,' Rachlin said.

Harry much preferred performing and loved taking his turn at singing and conducting. Because Ann Rachlin had a hard and fast rule that no parents were ever allowed into the hall, they were performances that Diana was never allowed to witness. The princess could not but help noticing, however, that the little boy was starting to emerge from under his brother's shadow.

School had a lot to do with that. In the nurseries at Highgrove and St James's Palace he had been very much the junior partner in the sibling relationship, little more than an accessory in whatever game William wanted to play. Now, in the company of children of his own age, he was at last able to give rein to his own personality. It was a challenge he responded to with alacrity.

Harry started at Mrs Mynors' in September 1987, the day after his third birthday which had been spent looking at the animals at London Zoo. Charles was at Diana's side as they delivered their youngest son into the care of his teachers. It was a poignant moment for them both. Despite the show of familial unity, they knew that Harry was going to be their last child together. 'I had a lump in my throat when we left Harry,' Charles said. Diana agreed. 'I was upset about leaving Harry,' she admitted.

Harry was equally sorry to see his parents depart. William, keen to show off, had dragged him down the basement steps and into his old classroom. He told him where he used to sit, and what he had done and what fun he used to have. There was no malice aforethought in what he was doing, but Harry was left in no doubt that he was in his brother's territory. He didn't like that. When William pushed him into the room the little boy tried to run away. He wanted to go home and he cried when his parents left.

There were a lot more tears in the days that followed. Where William had been aggressive, Harry was retiring, and the mother of one of his classmates called him a 'shrinking violet'. Norman Myers, who as Smarty Arty the clown had entertained two generations of royal children, pointed out the difference between the two brothers. William, he said, was 'extrovert and a bit cheeky, like Prince Andrew. Harry's more like Prince Edward, more shy and introverted.'

They were not the best of traits to take into the rough and tumble of a classroom, and Harry found himself at the wrong end of the school pecking order. He had been brought up in the cloistered environment of royalty, and mixing with other children did not come easily. He refused to join in the playground games, preferring to hide away behind the playhouse in a corner of the garden. He hardly spoke in class and would not fight back when pushed. 'He just won't stick up for himself,' another mother observed – with the sad result that the other children, sensing a weakness, started picking on him. Like his father before him, he was teased about the size of his ears. Comments were also made about his red hair.

Confused and lonely, he was too embarrassed even to put his hand up to ask to be 'excused' to go to the loo. His teachers had to keep a watchful eye on him and then cart him off to one of the school's two lavatories before an accident happened.

Diana was understandably worried, and made a point of rearranging her official engagements in order to pick him up at lunch time and take him back to Kensington Palace for a homely dish of his favourite fish fingers or spaghetti prepared for him by the duty chef.

There was a lot more to Harry than either his mother or his father had first discerned, however, and it soon became obvious that his supposed shyness was the product not of nature, but of his position as the younger brother to the energetic William. Too small to compete physically, Harry had chosen the only sensible option open to him, which was fall into line with his brother's plans. There was nothing unusual in that. It is a situation all younger children have to deal with.

But once away from William's intimidating influence, Harry found his feet and within a few weeks his own personality started to exert itself. And he made it quite clear during a clay modelling lesson that he was no longer prepared to tolerate being endlessly compared to his brother. When his teacher told him how good William had been at making models, Harry picked up his clay, threw it on the floor and refused to have anything more to do with it for the rest of the day. So wilful did he become that his mother felt moved to threaten him, 'If you don't behave, I'll swap you for a girl.'

To some onlookers, it seemed almost as if the boys' roles were being reversed. Since Nanny Barnes's departure William had become notably more circumspect. Harry, on the other hand, was exhibiting the wild traits that had once been his brother's prerogative. He was a page at the wedding of his uncle Charles Spencer to the model Victoria Lockwood in 1989. William had made a spectacle of himself at Westminster Abbey. Harry did the same in the twelfth-century church at Great Brington, two miles from Althorp. At the rehearsal he was in playful mood. As the rector, Norman Knibbs, observed, 'The prince was, how shall I say, in a fun mood, but it was all healthy naughtiness. What do you expect a little boy to do when things drag on? He stood when he should have sat and sat when he should have walked and jumped about when he should have stayed still and played with hassocks when they were meant to be left alone.'

Behaviour that was unbecoming in an heir was more acceptable in the 'spare', however, and Harry got through the ceremony without incurring the displeasure of his grandmother. Indeed, this show of spirit was regarded as something of a welcome change from the timidity he had exhibited in his infancy. It showed that he was starting to hold his own, a good sign in a younger son.

He was also becoming braver. On Charles's insistence and as part of their training for jobs that would involve many hours sitting on horses, both boys started taking riding lessons. When they were at Highgrove they were taken out every morning by the groom, Marion Cox, on their Shetland ponies. Their ponies went with them to Balmoral where they were expected to carry on their lessons in the castle grounds. William showed no great enthusiasm for this equestrian training programme. Like his mother, he was somewhat fearful and had to be cajoled into the saddle. Not Harry. Before his fourth birthday he was competent enough to control his mount on his own without the necessity of a leading rein.

This new-found courage could lead Harry into extremely hazardous situations. One winter's morning he was making a snowman with Ken Wharfe in the garden at Kensington Palace when a snowball fight broke out. To get a better vantage point from which to pelt his detective he ran into the house to reappear, much to Wharfe's horror, on the roof. The prince took a fiendish glee in the situation and it took a lot of delicate negotiating to get him back inside to safety.

Charles and Diana were not told about the incident. That was probably just as well. Both were extremely protective towards their children and the repercussions would have been drastic – for Wharfe, but also for Harry, who would henceforth have found his liberties severely curtailed. As it was, Harry had learnt his lesson and, after Wharfe gave him a stern telling off, never again attempted anything so reckless.

That did not curtail his sense of adventure, however, and his parents were understandably delighted by what they saw of Harry's growing confidence. It gave them something safe to talk about when they were together, although Charles, forever in search of a theory to explain what Diana took for granted, was inclined to irritate his wife by pontificating endlessly about the psychology behind the transformation.

As part of that process, Harry started to gravitate more towards his father. Diana had always referred to Harry as 'my little Spencer'. But now, instead of curling up on a sofa with his mother and watching a video, he preferred to spend his afternoons going around the Highgrove gardens with Charles, looking at the trees and shrubbery. They went on long walks together. 'Harry loves animals and plants,' Charles said. He tried to pass on his New Age philosophy. 'I tell him all about them and say they have feelings too and mustn't be hurt.'

Diana did not join them. She had no interest whatsoever in listening to Charles expounding on the feelings of plants. She was more interested in her own feelings and they were ones of hurt and anger.

Her sons were only vaguely aware of just how precarious their parents' marriage had become. It would not be long before the crisis would engulf them, but in the mid to late 1980s they were too young to realise how fraught the situation was. They had their own lives to get on with and that meant school, learning to read and count and the exciting business of making new friends.

The difficulties that all children face when they venture out from the comfortable security of home into a wider and often confusing world was made doubly so by the fact that their royal status marked them out as being in some way 'different' – a handicap for any child. Both parents did their best to help. They were insistent that William and Harry should be treated exactly like everyone else and while that was never going to happen (human nature being what it is, both were treated by their teachers with a degree of deference that few other children were afforded), at least they were spared the embarrassments that had disturbed Charles's boyhood.

At school he had been regarded as something akin to a freak and treated with a mixture of envy, awe and distaste that manifested itself in verbal and sometimes physical abuse. He was seldom allowed to invite anyone home and never visited any of his classmates at theirs.

The ballyhoo surrounding his parents' visits served only to accentuate his sense of isolation. When the Queen went to see him at Cheam and, later, at Gordonstoun, her arrival resembled a state visit, with masters lining up to bow and scrape before their sovereign. Her son was mortified. School was difficult enough as it was for that sensitive youngster without having to contend with the extra burden of being singled out in such a way.

If anything, the arrival of his father was even worse. In the 1960s Philip was still in his forties, lean, handsome and with a lithe athleticism that stood in marked contrast to his altogether more pedestrian son. Charles used to cringe when Philip piloted his helicopter down on to the school lawn at Gordonstoun and leapt out like a Douglas Fairbanks stand-in, radiating brusque bonhomie. Charles couldn't wait for his father to leave. But when he did, that brought new problems and on at least one occasion he hid away in his study to escape the taunts of his contemporaries invariably hurled at him the moment Philip flew off.

With such memories very much to the fore, Charles was anxious that his visits to see his sons should be as low key as security and media interest allowed. When he and Diana went to watch Harry play a goblin in his first Christmas play at Mrs Mynors', they mingled informally with the other parents and joined them on the short walk to the little hall across the road – something the Queen had never done. Harry rather spoilt the show by sticking his tongue out at the photographers, provoking a predictable postbag of criticism about his manners. But he did at least acquit himself well on stage. When William appeared in the same play two years earlier he had been dressed as a wolf and had promptly burst into tears the moment he saw his parents sitting in the front row. Harry, wearing a fetching green tunic and red cap, appeared to relish his moment in the limelight.

So did Diana. Despite the warning she had given to William on his first day at Wetherby's, she always gave the cameramen the photogenic smile they were looking for. This was not mere artifice. The princess had come to realise the power of her image and had learnt how to manipulate it to her advantage. But she genuinely enjoyed these visits. They brought her into contact with female contemporaries, and she made friends with several other mothers her own age. They made a welcome change, she said, from the 'stuffy' dignitaries she met on her non-stop round of official engagements. 'They're just like me,' she explained, and if that wasn't quite true, she did feel able to 'let my hair down' in their company.

Her refusal to stand on the ceremony that had hitherto governed royalty's involvement in their children's schooling carried through to sports days. In the June of 1987 she kicked off her high-heel shoes to run barefoot in the mothers' race – and won by a clear distance of three yards. She even persuaded her husband to loosen his tie, remove the jacket of his bespoke Savile Row suit and take part in the fathers' race.

Charles was reluctant to subject himself to the indignity of this kind of competition. Despite the Action Man image foisted on him by the press, he had been a poor athlete at school and he had not improved with age. Only his wife's chivvying and his wish not to let his sons down persuaded him to take part. He duly came last. William followed in his father's less than fleet footsteps and ended up as what the school politely called 'an also-ran' in the 60-metre dash.

In many British state schools competitive sport, with its accent on winners and losers, is regarded as politically unacceptable. In the public school system, however, athletic ability is still highly prized. Diana appeared unconcerned by the failures of her menfolk, however. She was basking in her own success and spent the afternoon happily taking snapshots with her SLR camera of William and Charles running and Harry watching from the stand.

Such was her enthusiasm that the Wetherby sports day, held at the Richmond athletic ground, became a regular fixture on the Waleses' calendar. In 1988 she again won the mothers' race and was rewarded with a potted plant. 'My mummy's won, my mummy's won,' chanted the delighted William, who had improved on his previous performance and earned himself a chocolate bar for coming third in the egg and spoon race.

Harry, however, got trounced in the brothers' race and burst into tears, while the fastest movement Charles managed was a quick sprint to the car waiting to take him to Windsor to play polo, the one game he was proficient at.

He was back competing the following year – and again wished he hadn't bothered. Required to run with a plastic bag around his shoe, he got hopelessly left at the start and never managed to catch up. He was last again in 1990.

In 1991 he wisely refused to take part at all, citing the bad back he had sustained in a polo accident. By then Diana, too, had had enough. In 1989 she came second in her race. She was third the following year and, in her post-race irritation, delivered a resounding smack to William's backside when he started playing up. By 1991, a month short of her thirtieth birthday, she could only manage fourth place. It was time for the barefoot athlete to step back into the high-heeled shoes she called 'my tart's trotters'.

But although Diana's winning days were at an end (and Charles's had never begun), the Waleses had succeeded in what they set out to do, which was to set their sons an example of normality. The Queen, cocooned in her majesty, had never kicked off her shoes or taken part in a race, barefoot or otherwise. According to royal precepts, it would have been unthinkable for her to have done so. When she was a little girl, even such a simple exercise as swimming had been conducted in the decorous seclusion of the private Bath Club in London's Mayfair, well out of public sight.

Diana was too modern to put up with such archaic restrictions. As she repeated time and time again, she wanted William and Harry to have a normal childhood. And that, she concluded, meant involving herself in all the activities other parents engaged in. Charles had his doubts but, as in most matters pertaining to the boys' upbringing, he gave way before his wife's resolve. 'Anything for a quiet life,' as he put it.

Her policy was of some benefit to the boys. As the Wetherby mother rightly observed, they were always going to attract people's interest. But at least they escaped the isolation Charles was forced to endure because of his princely position. It was Diana who broke down those barriers. She wanted her sons to have parents who behaved normally. And she wanted them 'to have the knocks and fights other children face', as one courtier explained.

On her instigation William and Harry were allowed to go to their classmates' parties and have friends round to join them for afternoon teas of cheese on toast, boiled eggs, sausages and mounds of chips served in the Kensington Palace nursery. On her instructions the chefs made them baked potatoes with a lightly poached egg on top, drizzled with cheese sauce and sprinkled with Parmesan. 'She was a great fan of this type of food, less so the prince,' said royal chef Graham Newbould.

Charles disapproved of the menu. 'I'm afraid they'd rather eat the things that are bad for them,' he complained. He would ask, 'Why are they having chips again?' He also objected to the amounts of fizzy cola they drank.

His own taste was veering ever more towards healthy and preferably organic eating. He wrote to one of his chefs, 'Just a thought about chickens! I am so appalled at the idea of what they do nowadays to intensively rear chickens, ie hormones, antibiotics, etc, etc, that I *very* much hope that whenever you happen to buy a chicken you buy one that is *properly* free range? Personally I hope we can always eat game – ie pheasant, duck, grouse, etc – from now on as that is the most natural.'

Charles was given little opportunity to impose his dietary fads on his family, however. It was Diana who told the chefs what to prepare for the boys and she ordered what they liked. And it was the princess who arranged for them to be taken to McDonald's, to the spooky London Dungeon, and to Harrods and Selfridges department stores to meet Santa Claus.

She was also behind their visits to a council play scheme in Coram's Fields in London's Holborn where they played with children from the nearby council tower blocks. 'We were taken aback when we noticed who they were,' said the scheme's administrator Chris Nicholls. When one suspicious little boy pointed at William and asked, 'What's his name?' the prince's quick-witted bodyguard replied, 'Roger.' 'No, it's not – it's William,' the boy born to be king shouted angrily.

The play group was sponsored by the Inner London Education Authority which had close links with the left-wing Camden council. It was intended for the children of working parents. A council spokesman sniffily remarked, 'By working parents, we did not have in mind the heir to the throne.'

This modern-day enactment of the princes and the paupers did not go down well with the Queen. She felt that Diana was playing to the crowd. She also had another, deeper concern.

The Queen had been taught that mystery was essential to the monarchy's survival. In the effort to safeguard its prestige, her father, George VI, and grandfather, George V, had discouraged their children from mixing with anyone from outside the royal circle. They did not want their offspring contaminated by the bad example of people George V dismissed as 'cads', a term which to his way of thinking embraced just about everyone not of royal blood.

The advance of democracy and the development of cameras, microphones and television had made such remoteness impossible to maintain. The Royal Family was forced to adapt. It had even tried to use the new technologies to its advantage, most notably in the fly-on-the-wall television documentary broadcast in 1969. But as the Queen's uncle David, who had reigned for ten months as Edward VIII, had warned, 'These new means of communication whetted the public appetite for what was termed "human interest" and the more "human interest" people got, the more they wanted.'

There was only so far along this path the Queen wished to go. It was her strongly held belief that the monarchy was there to do a job of constitutional importance. She did not wish to see it turned into a branch of the entertainment industry.

That, of course, was precisely what was happening. In their determination to be 'ordinary', the Waleses began to discard the protective mantle of regal mystique. And the more the public learnt of their faults and foibles, the more the Royal Family came to be judged by the standards that applied to everyone else – an unwelcome prospect indeed for the Windsors.

When the Queen was in her youth there was no unfavourable analysis of her behaviour or her abilities. Quite the contrary. In a book published in 1930 when she was six years old and entitled *The Story of Princess Elizabeth and Princess Margaret*, readers were informed that when the future Queen, then aged six, had to go to bed, 'there were no poutings or protests, just a few joyous skips and impromptu dance steps, a few last minute laughs at Mummy's delicious bedtime jokes'.

Now every misdemeanour committed by her family made news, with the emphasis on the dysfunctional.

In 1988, when Harry entered Great Ormond Street Hospital for an emergency hernia operation, Charles's absence was duly noted. The prince was on a painting trip in Italy. 'I love William and Harry dearly,' he explained, 'but sometimes I just have to get away from home to get some peace.' He saw no reason to cut short his holiday to be at his son's bedside while he underwent what the doctors assured him was a simple and safe operation. The fact that he telephoned every half-hour to be updated on Harry's progress did not prevent him being labelled as uncaring, however.

Despite the change in his disposition since Nanny Barnes's departure, William continued to attract his share of the criticism. In 1989 one headline proclaimed, 'Rascal typed words wee and bottom into school computer'. The rascal in question was Prince William, aged six and three-quarters. Despite what Wetherby's described as his 'flair' for English, he had misspelt 'bottom' as 'botem'. The article went on to record that the prince had failed to make the top academic stream.

Even a visit to a local swimming bath could become the stuff of mild controversy. During the Easter break in 1989 William and Harry were taken to the four-star Craigdarroch Hotel near Balmoral for a splash in the heated indoor pool. Harry got embroiled in a brawl with another boy. Despite his parents' directive that the boys should be left to fight their own corners, his bodyguard felt it advisable to haul him out of the water and take him away. 'It was one of those things that happen when youngsters are playing together in a swimming pool,' a royal aide observed.

The Queen was not pleased by the publicity her grandsons were generating. She said it was bad for the monarchy and bad for the boys. What they needed, she said, was the chance to grow up at their own pace, without the pressure of being constantly on show. In a belated attempt to put a cap on the interest, it was agreed that henceforth William and Harry's public appearances should be limited, especially during the holidays.

There was a limit to what Diana would agree to, however. She was not going to hide her sons away. As she told her husband firmly, there was to be no going back to the old ways. They continued to get out and mix with people with an easy freedom that would have been unthinkable even a generation earlier. And they were regularly pictured with their father at the Sunday polo matches at Windsor.

In some other respects, though, they were very much the children of their background. Royalty has always been keenly involved in hunting and many of Britain's laws pertaining to property and trespass were first introduced in order to allow the reigning monarchs of the day uninterrupted opportunity to pursue they passion. This enthusiasm for what they call 'country pursuits' and its opponents term 'blood sports' continues to the present day, and both William and Harry were introduced to shooting at a young age.

William was just four years old when he accompanied his father on a shoot at Sandringham attended by ex-King Constantine of Greece and Spain's King Juan Carlos who had entertained the Waleses in Majorca that summer. He was armed with nothing more deadly than a toy silver pistol, but animal rights campaigners took predicable exception to his presence there. 'It is horrific for a child of his age to be indoctrinated into slaughter,' local RSPCA committee member Beki Barthelmie complained.

There was much the same reaction two years later when Harry, also aged four and wearing outsized ear muffs to protect his hearing from the bang of the guns, joined Prince Charles on another Sandringham shoot. 'I think the prince has been highly irresponsible,' said League Against Cruel Sports director James Barrington. 'He is brandishing a deadly weapon. It is showing young Harry the glamorous side of guns. He is keen on other sorts of conservation, in architecture and farming, but not wild animals.'

The protests got even more vociferous when William and Harry went to see their father ride out with the Beaufort Hunt in pursuit of fox (it is a peculiarity of royal and aristocratic language that the plural of animals which are hunted are expressed in the singular).

The Prince of Wales took not the slightest bit of notice. He pointed out that the hunting of foxes was necessary vermin control, while the shooting of birds was a vital part of the rural economy. Like his father before him, he had served as president of the Game Conservancy, which he argued, 'was the first organisation to regard game quite rationally as a crop, a valuable by-product of the land, which deserved good husbandry as much as corn and cattle'.

He diplomatically refrained from adding that hunting in its various guises is also exhilarating and entertaining. His sons certainly found it so, and as they grew older they came to like nothing better than tramping across the fields and moors and through streams and glens after game of all kinds – deer, pheasant, partridge, woodcock, pigeon, fox and salmon, all of which, the fox excepted, they started to enjoy eating. It became their passion and in later years it would take precedence over almost everything else.

Diana never raised an objection to this bloody enthusiasm. She called her sons 'my killer Wales'.

Early in her marriage it was widely assumed that she was against hunting and that she had persuaded her husband to give up shooting and give the pair of Purdey shotguns he had inherited from his grandfather, George VI, to his brother Andrew. That, she insisted, simply wasn't true. Charles's decision, she said, was just another of his 'fads'. (And an expensive one: when he took up shooting again a year later, Andrew refused to hand back the Purdeys and Charles had to buy himself another pair – at a cost of some £20,000.)

'I don't know why I'm always being portrayed as an Anti, because I'm not,' she told me. 'After all, I was brought up in the country.'

Shooting lunches had been a highlight of her childhood and she had shot stag on the Balmoral estate and been taught to fish in the River Dee. She had even overcome her fear of horses to ride out in 1987 with the Belvoir, one of the toughest and most gung-ho of fox hunts. This new-found confidence in the saddle was a tribute to her riding instructor, a certain James Hewitt.

Country pursuits did not really appeal to her, however, and she eventually gave them up. 'I'm just not interested any more,' she told me. But she was always quite happy for William and Harry to carry on shooting and never tried to curb their enthusiasm. What she did not want was for them to photographed with guns in their hands. Unlike her husband, who regarded the Antis as ill-informed 'busy-bodies', Diana had an intuitive understanding of public susceptibilities. She was well aware of the anger stirred by the killing of animals and was anxious to protect her sons from the backlash of criticism.

She recounted to me, 'I told them, "Remember, there is always someone in a high rise flat who does not want you to shoot Bambis." '

Their other sporting interests required no such warnings. Like his mother before him, William turned out to be fast and capable swimmer and, aged seven, won Wetherby's Grunfield Cup for the best overall style.

Like most other boys, he also developed a keen interest in football. For reasons that made no geographical sense and which he could not really remember he became a fan of Aston Villa, the Birmingham team that had won the European Cup in 1982 but had been languishing in mediocrity ever since. In the manner of supporters everywhere, he would listen to the football results on Saturday afternoon and then moan with disappointment when Villa failed to achieve his optimistic predictions.

Harry, meanwhile, was developing into a first class rider. No less a judge than his aunt, Princess Anne, who won the European Three-Day Event Championship when she was twenty-one and represented Britain at the Montreal in 1976, said that he had the talent to reach international standard. 'He has got a good seat,' she observed. It was a singular compliment from a woman who gives them rarely.

In the September of 1989 Harry followed William to Wetherby's. He arrived a week late due to a viral infection but, once there, he settled in quickly. There were no tears and no hiding away as had happened when he first started at Mrs Mynors'. He was much better adjusted by then.

Taken all together, the boys were turning out well. Like parents everywhere, Charles and Diana spent a lot of time analysing William and Harry's characteristics and traits and discussing how they were doing at school. They concluded that, while there had been a fair share of problems, the overall result justified their decision to bring their sons up as if they were two ordinary little boys.

But no matter how hard their parents tried (and how hard they tried to pretend otherwise), William and Harry were destined to be marked apart. William, especially, found that trying. The impish grin was replaced by a more sombre demeanour. He was growing older and that brought with it the dawning awareness of who he was.

Dr Elizabeth Newson, joint director of the child research unit at Nottingham University, explained, 'He is obviously an intelligent boy who is realising he is different from the others. It is being brought home to him that he is a prince. And that is a lot to think about.'

The Highgrove housekeeper, Wendy Berry, put it more succinctly when she said, 'He knew he was the one.'

SEVEN

The Royal Protectors

On wet afternoons the Highgrove nursery resembled a miniature battlefield. Tables and chairs had been moved to create make-believe fortresses and redoubts and the floor was covered with the decimated armies of scattered toy soldiers.

When one campaign was over, William would deploy his Action Man dolls and another brutal skirmish would be waged over the Ribena-stained cream carpet.

Harry found himself drawn into the confrontations, to suffer the inevitable rout as William literally threw his plastic troops into action.

Presiding over this mayhem and sometimes taking part were the Personal Protection Officers, the PPOs. They were robust policemen, armed and trained in the martial arts, and they were destined to play a formative role in the lives of the young princes.

William would sometimes tell these officers, 'I want to be a soldier when I grow up.'

It was the PPOs and not the staid and conventional military men who attended their father, however, who set the more vivid example and in the imagination of childhood they acquired a heroic lustre. With guns in their holsters underneath their Savile Row suits (the PPOs were given a special clothing allowance that allowed them to dress appropriately and blend into the royal scene) and their endless stories of derring-do, they appeared to be very much the James Bond-types that little boys look up to. Such was

William's admiration for them that one day he declared, 'I don't want to be king – I want to be a policeman.'

The remark was a measure of the high regard in which they were held, first by William, then by his younger brother. All had been selected for their professional abilities, but it was their ability to relate to two lively boys that ensured their continued employment. Inspector Ken Wharfe, who started looking after the princes in 1987, said, 'In terms of security it was essential to develop a good rapport with the boys and they had to trust completely whoever was looking after them.'

They were not surrogate fathers, as has often been suggested. Charles and Diana had no intention of allowing their position to be usurped by their own bodyguards. As a former member of the Highgrove staff observed, 'The prince and princess knew the policemen became close to the boys, but they did not like to see it rammed down their throats. If the prince, in particular, happened to be around, they made themselves scarce.'

Nonetheless, because of their position they spent more time with the princes than Charles or Diana ever did. A courtier explained, 'The Prince of Wales loved his sons, but he always seemed a little wrapped up in his work.' It was therefore left to the policemen to join in the princes' activities.

When, for instance, Charles declined to take part in the fathers' race at the Wetherby sports day in 1988, Ken Wharfe took his place – and won, much to the boys' delight. And on holiday to the Scilly Isles off the coast of Cornwall, it was the bodyguards who organised William and Harry's games of baseball and their beach picnics. The princes liked having them around, especially when, to their young eyes, their primary duty appeared to consist of amusing them. 'They regarded us as jovial uncles,' Wharfe said.

Ex-Marine Reg Spinney, assigned to look after Harry, was among the first to win their confidence. He was their archetypal idea of a tough guy. Fit and disciplined, he was also adept at answering their persistent childish questions. One of his hobbies was yoga, and he showed William and Harry how to do some of the stretches, explaining how the movements complemented the body. Always the professional, Spinney never allowed himself to become overawed by his position.

Sergeant Dave Sharpe, nicknamed 'Razor', was out of the same mould. Married and with two children of his own, he was considered ideal for the job. On a royal holiday in Majorca in 1988, while Charles and Diana were sunning themselves on board King Juan Carlos's yacht, he was photographed on a public beach with William and Harry building sandcastles, romping in the sea and taking them out on a pedalo. And when Harry was seen in tears on his fourth birthday it was assumed that it was because Charles had banned Dave from attending the party. 'It wasn't true, but Dave was teased about that,' a member of staff recalled.

Some of the PPOs enjoyed the celebrity of their positions but, like Spinney, Sharpe was one of those who simply got on with his job. It was to his considerable embarrassment, therefore, that he started being referred to as William and Harry's 'deputy dad'.

It wasn't the only nickname the PPOs had to put up with. In the small community that made up the Waleses' household, many of the officers soon acquired nicknames, often bestowed by Wharfe.

As well as Razor, there was Tony Blackman, who filled in for Diana. As a former employee of British Airways, he knew a lot about aeroplanes, which made him a favourite of the boys. He was an expert barbecue chef who entertained the boys at Highgrove with his stories and impressions. He was known at Sooty.

Chris Tarr, who stayed on to look after Harry at Eton, was always called Jack. He was assisted by Trevor Bettles who, Wharfe decided, looked like one of the characters in *'Allo, 'Allo*, the hit television comedy set in France during the Nazi occupation, and as a consequence was always called 'Heindrick'.

The most bizarre name went to Chief Inspector Graham Smith, Diana's senior police protection officer, who headed up her security until he fell ill with the cancer that finally killed him in 1993. The boys, too young to pronounce Graham, called him 'Gay Gay'. Much to his discomfort, the moniker stuck.

Graham was held in high regard by the Waleses and in the final stages of his illness accompanied the family as a guest to Necker, Virgin boss Richard

Branson's private island in the Caribbean, and aboard the Greek ship owner John Latsis's yacht.

Another officer who commanded their particular affection was Sergeant Graham Cracker, who everyone called 'Crackers'. Tall and thin but with a personality that one of his colleagues compared to an 'overgrown school-boy's', he made it his business to keep the boys amused by cracking a succession of juvenile jokes. His wife was drowned in a lake in 1991 but he somehow managed to recover his cheerfulness. His hobby was framing pictures, and he mounted many of the photographs of the princes that subsequently disappeared.

The nannies who replaced Barbara Barnes were happy to share their responsibilities with this retinue of policemen. Which was just as well, because they had little choice. After Barnes, Diana ensured that no nanny was again allowed to occupy such a central position in her sons' affection.

Ruth Wallace, who took over from Barnes, stayed three years but, with the boys away at school, her influence was more muted. She had previously worked for Princess Michael of Kent, who was not best pleased to lose the services of someone whose help she had come to value.

Wallace was very different from her predecessor. A nurse by profession (she had trained at St Bartholomew's hospital), she had once worked as a disc jockey at Raffles, a fashionable nightclub in London's King's Road. She was also a cordon bleu cook and had run her own catering business called 'Britain at Your Service' from her home in an old railway cottage in North London. With interests beyond the self-contained world of the nursery floor, she preferred to eat with the rest of the household in the staff dining room rather than upstairs with William and Harry, enjoyed a drink with the detectives and was a keen participant in the games of Trivial Pursuit that occupied the staff's winter evenings.

Diana liked Ruth's relaxed approach to her job. The nanny, however, found the mounting furore surrounding the Waleses' marriage difficult to deal with and in 1990 handed in her notice and left to take a long trip up the Amazon.

'Working for the royals was an exceptional highlight in my life,' she said. But she had done her stint and it was time to move on. 'I would like to try everything at least once in my life, as long as it's legal,' she said. When she returned from Brazil she took a job working in guest relations at the Sheraton Belgravia hotel.

Ruth Wallace was followed by Jessie Webb. She had formerly worked for Nina Campbell, the interior designer responsible for the decor at Annabel's, the night club in Berkeley Square, Mayfair, which Diana and Fergie had visited disguised as policewomen on the evening of Prince Andrew's stag night in 1986.

Wendy Berry described Webb as a 'battleship in full sail', adding, 'She was great fun and very outspoken. She brought a welcome air of Cockney normality into the boys' lives.'

Jessie had firm ideas about how the boys should be treated. That did not always correspond with what they were used to. Having decided that Harry was too thin, she insisted on feeding him up, much to the chagrin of the little boy and to the chefs who objected to the way she filled the nursery fridge with sausages, buns and doughnuts she had bought herself.

She also had no compunction about criticising the way the princes were being brought up. After one particularly fraught Christmas at Sandringham, she complained to the Highgrove staff about the way Diana had spent most of the time in tears, leaving William and Harry to be 'thoroughly spoilt' by the Queen's staff. 'There they are treated like princes – here they are treated like ordinary little boys,' she said.

When Diana insisted on taking William and Harry back to London instead of allowing them to stay at Highgrove and attend the large party in a marquee their father had organised, Webb said to the staff, 'It's ridiculous going back to London. The boys would have just loved to have gone to the party.'

By 1992 relations between the princess and her nanny had sunk to the point where Diana had ceased talking to her. It was agreed that Webb would leave when both boys were at boarding school. Webb later went to work for Charles's cousin, Viscount Linley, and his wife, Serena.

That left William and Harry in the care of their relief nanny, Olga Powell, who had been with the Waleses since William was six months old. Quiet, unassuming and long widowed, her job had been to fold their clothes and pack their trunks and stand in when the head nannies were on holiday or on one of their occasional days off. Like Nanny Webb, she did not hesitate to give her charges a stern ticking-off when they misbehaved. But she had no interest in the in-house politics or the gossip that animated the staff quarters, which was why she managed to outlast the others.

'She was very just and firm and when she was on duty she always took her supper in the nursery,' a member of staff recalled. The princes were both fond of her, but she was too old to keep up with two lively boys and it was the men whose companionship they wanted.

In Scotland they always sought out Willie Potts, a gillie who had given long service to the Balmoral estate. His dark hair had turned white after a heart attack. Because of his medical condition he was no longer able to spend whole days in exhausting pursuit of stags up 3,000-foot-high mountains, which the Scots, as thrifty with their language as they are reputed to be with their money, insist on calling 'the hills'. But he did take William and Harry shooting for rabbits and taught them how to cast a line for salmon with elegant assurance. He would greet the princes in his broad Highland brogue with a cheerful, 'Hello, boys,' followed by a strange harrumphing sound – a voice affliction sustained after his heart problems, which everyone, including the boys, found extremely funny.

This easy relationship between the princes and those who served them was no new phenomenon. Young men from aristocratic families had traditionally enjoyed the company of the gamekeepers, gillies and farm hands whose labours supported their great estates. There was no inverted snobbery to this. In the countryside – and the Queen's family consider themselves country men and women at heart – this affinity between the classes was regarded as the mark of a happy and well-run estate.

Predictably, there were some households where the relationship had extended beyond the bounds of moral propriety to include the young women of the estate. Diana's family was one, and in times past a standing joke in the upper reaches of society was the way so many of their workers were said to look like Spencers.

In William and Harry's case, the pleasure was in the adventures these men introduced them to. Holidays at Balmoral and Sandringham were like their own private Scout camps, with each day offering a new activity, and long before they had reached their teens both had become proficient with gun and rod. They had learnt how to track, kill, gut and skin an animal, how to make fires, and how to smoke a fish, which they would eat beside the river where they had caught it.

According to Highgrove staff, however, it was Inspector Ken Wharfe, the floppy-haired policeman from Canterbury in Kent, who was 'the greatest influence of all' on the princes. 'Get a grip' was one of his favourite expressions and he was forever bursting into song. Possessed of a fine baritone voice (he is a member of the English Chamber Choir), he showed them how to open their mouths wide and enunciate the words properly to achieve the maximum effect, and then led the boys in singing along to their favourite show, *The Phantom of the Opera*, as it played on the car stereo on their weekly drives to and from Highgrove.

On trips to the Caribbean he took them snorkelling and led them on expeditions into the interior of whichever island they were staying on to re-enact their own version of Robinson Crusoe. Getting lost, which he did on at least one occasion, added to the fun.

When Wharfe was on duty in London his bedroom was next to the nursery, and William would often tap on the door to demand that he come and play with them. This usually consisted of rough and tumble fights with Wharfe in the middle. Once, when he was being used as a punch bag by the royal brothers and had taken off his shirt to stop it being torn to shreds, Charles appeared at the doorway.

'I felt very awkward,' the policeman recalled. 'William said, "Oh, Daddy, please take off your shirt and come and fight with us too." '

The Prince of Wales was appalled by the suggestion. He told his son, 'No, I can't do that,' and beat a hasty retreat.

Like all the other policemen seconded to royal service, Wharfe had to be careful not to overstep the mark. It was a delicate tightrope the PPOs were required to walk. Diana was a possessive mother, who was quite likely to become irritated if she felt her position was being usurped, as had happened with Barbara Barnes.

'I don't envy your job,' the princess told Wharfe when they first met. The princes, she said, 'can be a bit of a handful'. She then added, 'But remember I am always around if you need me.'

It was a reminder of where Wharfe and the other members of the household staff stood in the pecking order of the princes' affection.

Charles could be equally sharp. At Highgrove, Wharfe started teasing William about his pronunciation. Before he developed his distinctive Eton slur, a strange combination of working-class English mixed with American vowels, the prince sounded very much like his father. Words like 'out' were pronounced as 'ite', and house was made to rhyme with mice. Ken said this was wrong. William insisted he was correct because 'Papa speaks like that.'

William ran out into the garden and told his father what the detective had just told him. Charles went over to Wharfe, the son of a welder, and said, 'I hear you have been giving William elocution lessons.' There was an edge in his voice, which Wharfe took as a clear reprimand.

'It was a tough job,' Wharfe said. But despite his memoirs of royal life published in 2002, which led to him being branded as a 'traitor', no one denied that Wharfe was good with William and Harry.

'They idolised him,' a member of staff recalled. 'He would sing to them and play with them. He would also do great impersonations of their mother to make them laugh. But never of their father, the Prince of Wales. He was too canny to do that.'

Like the other PPOs, Wharfe learnt what the parameters were. They were certainly much wider when Charles was away. Then Diana would join 'my boys', as she called them, at the staff barbecues and parties. These sometimes involved the kind of high jinks that would never have been permitted if Charles had been in residence.

A fellow member of staff remembered, 'Ken and I were chasing Diana around the garden to throw her into the swimming pool. There was much screaming and laughter. Ken finally rugby tackled her and we both grabbed hold of a leg each, carried her screaming to the pool and threw her in.'

Several of the Household were uncomfortable with this casual behaviour. Diana had dusted away many of the cobwebs of royal decorum, but royal staff can be even more concerned with position and protocols than their employers and the sight of the princess and her sons frolicking with such abandon was an informality too far. Said one, 'I thought, "Hold on a moment, what are we doing?" It was all very informal, but there were serious undertones. After all, she was the Princess of Wales – and William and Harry are the Queen's grandchildren.'

William, on the other hand, was unconcerned by his mother's behaviour. He liked to see her laughing, an increasingly rare occurrence as her marriage edged towards its final collapse. Wharfe appeared to make her happy and that was enough to convince him that Diana had taken a fancy to the jovial policeman.

In the summer of 1989 the family (minus Charles who had become an ever more peripheral figure in their lives) spent a week's holiday at the home of Diana's mother, Frances Shand Kydd, on the isle of Seil off the West Coast of Scotland.

Wharfe later recounted to me, 'One night I was using the washing machine to wash my shirts and the princess asked me what I was doing. I replied, "Washing my shirts, ma'am.' She said, "I will do them." I replied, "No, ma'am, you can't," and thought no more about it.'

The next morning Wharfe came downstairs to find the princess had taken the clean shirts out of the machine and put them in the drier, and was standing at the ironing board with her hair in a towel and only a towel wrapped around her body, energetically pressing his shirts.

Wharfe said, 'Ma'am, this is the last time you do this, you really can't.' Diana giggled and replied. 'I enjoy it.'

At that moment William walked into the room and asked his mother what she was doing. 'I am ironing Ken's shirts,' the princess replied.

'You're going to marry Ken, aren't you, Mummy?' the seven-year-old William asked.

'Don't be silly,' the princess replied.

William walked across the room and cheekily pulled off her towel. She had nothing on underneath. For a moment the mother of the future King of England stood before her bodyguard, naked except for the iron in her hand. Diana laughed.

Indulging the Royal Family in a string of risqué frolics is not the primary task of the PPOs, of course. The 185 police officers who provide security for the Royal Family are not members of the royal household. They belong to the Royalty and Diplomatic Protection Department of the Metropolitan Police and it is their job to act as human shields, with all the dangers that entails and regardless of the risk to their own lives.

In 1974, Inspector Jim Beaton was shot three times when he threw himself in front of a gunman attempting to kidnap Princess Anne. The last bullet missed his spine by only a fraction of an inch. Beaton was awarded the George Cross, the civilian equivalent of the Victoria Cross.

After Michael Fagan broke into the Queen's bedroom at Buckingham Palace a few days after William was born, a major review of royal security was undertaken. Bodyguards were no longer viewed as an extra pair of hands to keep over-enthusiastic members of the press at bay, but an essential part of modern royal life.

The Royalty Protection Department is divided into two units. The first comprises those who wear uniform, who man the gates at the royal residences and patrol the grounds with guard dogs. The second is the plain-clothes branch, which provides the royal police protection officers. They all belong to the uniform branch of 'A' Division and work under the supervision of a deputy assistant commissioner at New Scotland Yard. The hours are long and unsociable and there is no extra pay, but there is no shortage of candidates and there are twenty applicants for each vacancy.

Throughout the 1980s the greatest threat they faced was posed by the IRA. In 1979 Irish republican terrorists had killed Prince Charles's great uncle, Earl Mountbatten, and several members of his family. The intelligence services uncovered plans to perpetrate similar outrages. The gang who blew up the hotel in Brighton in 1984 in their attempt to murder Prime Minister Margaret Thatcher had put the Royal Family at the top of their death list, and Special Branch chiefs warned that it had drawn up detailed plans for an attack on Balmoral.

To counter the danger, new high-tech surveillance equipment was installed and all the royal residences were linked to the police station at Buckingham Palace, which is manned twenty-four hours a day. If William or Harry broke so much as a window at Highgrove, an alarm would ring at the Palace.

As a further protection, the security chiefs decided in 1988 that it was too risky to have just one bodyguard guarding both William and Harry. Henceforth the princes each had up to three armed police protection officers working on a rota system divided into one week on, one week off and one week doing reconnaissance work.

This put inevitable restrictions of the Royal Family's freedom of movement. There was no spontaneity. Everything the princes did had to be carefully choreographed in advance. If the boys wanted to go to an amusement park with their mother, one PPO would recce the site, liaise with the local police and check all the entrances and exits, while two others accompanied the royal brothers.

It was even more of a performance when Charles took the boys out. During half term in February 1989 he took William and Harry to Windsor Safari Park. They went to see Winnie the killer whale before spending the remainder of their short visit swooshing down the 30-foot-high water slide and yelling to their father below, 'Watch me, Papa. Papa, watch me.'

It was an innocuous family outing, yet it was deemed necessary to have no fewer than four policemen to trail around the park after the future king and his 'heir and spare'.

Diana resented having her movements so closely monitored, especially when she started forging a life for herself beyond the confines of the marital home. She started to complain about being constantly watched, which she was – though not, as she came to believe, in order to acquire evidence against her, but for her own safety.

William and Harry were not averse to offering their mother a little protection of their own. On a second vacation to Richard Branson's private Caribbean island Necker in 1990, the royal party included their grand-mother, Frances Shand Kydd, uncle Charles Spencer and his new wife, Victoria, aunts Lady Sarah McCorquodale and Lady Jane Fellowes and five cousins. With the Waleses' marriage now in free fall, they were besieged by photographers. To distract them, Wharfe organised 'war games' with catapults and balloons full of water, which the children used to fire at each other in mini battles.

These gave William the idea to catapult the press photographers with water-filled balloons when they returned in their flotilla of boats. After enthusing Harry and his cousins with his plan, he told Wharfe, who in turn informed Diana. The Princess gave it the go-ahead.

'As the boats carrying the paparazzi approached, I gave the children the order to unleash their stack of coloured water bombs,' Wharfe later wrote. 'The unfortunate photographers did not know what had hit them, and after twenty minutes and several direct hits they retired hurt and did not return.' William was delighted with his 'victory'. So was Diana.

There were occasions, however, when these confrontations took on an altogether darker hue. On a skiing trip to Lech one year, Diana and her sons were suddenly besieged by a crowd of foreign photo-graphers. When one particularly persistent Italian refused to be moved on, insisting he wanted an interview with William, the detective lost his patience.

The good life as a member of the royal circus had left its impression on Wharfe's waistline. 'But even if I can't run as fast as I used,' the onetime winner of the Wetherby's fathers' race coolly observed, 'I can shoot straight.' He could also punch hard. As Diana started to fluster, he unleashed a jab that sent the photographer crashing into the snow.

William and Harry were delighted. 'Do it again,' they chorused.

For all their urging, a street brawl was not on the policeman's agenda, however. Instead, he quickly shepherded his wards into the safety of their hotel.

Diana said afterwards, 'I wasn't worried for myself, only for the boys. People forget they were only eight and ten years old.'

Wharfe interpreted the situation differently. 'I was very angry,' he told me later. 'It was a nasty situation. The princess's panic was frightening the boys, which was why I did what I did.'

The PPOs had certainly left their impression on the youngsters. They had joined the princes in their escapades and encouraged them to get out and do things that might otherwise have been forbidden to them. That had helped develop their independence and gave them insight and experience of the world beyond the enclave of their background. That was what Diana wanted.

They were not going to affect the fundamentals of their lives, however. As Wharfe observed, 'Even aged five and three years, they knew they were special, different from others.' In other words, they were royal, and no welder's son from Kent or forestry worker's daughter from Norfolk, no matter how capable or well-intentioned, were going to change that immutable fact.

Like all little boys, William and Harry were entitled to their boyhood dreams of growing up to be soldiers. But Prince William was never going to be a policeman. He was going to be king.

EIGHT

Life at Ludgrove

Children have more resilience than adults give them credit for. They can adapt to the strange and the new without mourning too deeply for a past which quickly fades from their memories. Intuition rather than experience guides their judgement, and instinct informs them to keep their heads down and deal with life as it is, not as it should be.

Unfortunately, that does not grant them immunity from confusion, anger, anguish and fear – far from it – and William and Harry needed all their inborn survival mechanisms as they grew towards adolescence.

They had much with which to contend, and William especially. Sensitive by nature, he found it difficult to deal with the fact that he was not like other children. In their determination to give him a rounded childhood, his parents insisted that he should be treated like any other boy of his age. But that was always going to be an impossibility. He was 'special', as his bodyguard Ken Wharfe had noted. His brother recognised that, too. He was different.

He had begun to realise that at Mrs Mynors' kindergarten and at Wetherby's. It was confirmed at Ludgrove, his prep school near Wokingham in Berkshire where he booked in on 11 September 1990.

The other new boys were taken straight to their dormitories. Not William. As befitting his status, he was made to shake hands with the headmaster, Gerald Barber, and Barber's wife, Janet. He was then taken on a conducted tour of the school which, in readiness for his arrival, had been protected by new fencing, reinforced glass and video cameras.

'We shall treat Prince William exactly the same as other pupils,' Barber insisted. No other little boy at a school whose past pupils included the dukes of Kent and Wellington and the former British Prime Minister Lord Home had been referred to by their titles. That singled him out from day one.

'He was very nervous,' a member of the Household recalled.

So were his parents. Ludgrove is a boarding school and William was leaving home for the first time. Diana had burst into tears when she said goodbye to her eight-year-old son. 'Dived into the Kleenex box,' she wrote to her friend, the Duchess of York's stepmother Sue Ferguson. 'It's quite something, putting one's eldest into school.'

There was another reason for the princess's discomfort, and that was the presence of her husband.

Diana had driven William down from London. Charles was chauffeured from Highgrove. They only met up fifty yards from the school gates where they all climbed into Charles's Bentley in order to arrive together.

They spent twenty minutes accompanying William as he was shown his classrooms and the dormitory he would share with four other boys. While Charles gave their son a reassuring pep talk, Diana placed William's duvet on his little pine bed, folded a blanket at the foot and propped his stuffed wombat up on the pillow. They helped him store his trunk of clothes which had been packed by his under-nanny, Olga Powell, then assisted him as he arranged the family photographs he brought with him on the chair beside his bed.

It was a show of family unity which belied the sad truth that Charles and Diana had reached a point where they struggled to exchange a civil word. As soon as they had kissed their son goodbye, they went their separate ways – Diana to London, Charles back to Highgrove and then on to France with his physiotherapist Sarah Keay, who was attending to the arm he had broken playing polo three months before. It would be several weeks before they met again, and then only because William was having his first outing from school.

Ludgrove, like most British preparatory schools, has a strict disciplinary code which new boys like William at first found confusing and sometimes intimidating. But the rules did bring some order to a prince whose home life was spinning out of control.

His day began at 7.15 a.m. when he clambered out of bed and into the uniform of blue or grey corduroy trousers, checked shirt and blue, green or purple sweater that can only be bought at Harrods. A tweed jacket was worn instead of the traditional blazer. Once dressed, the boys were summoned to breakfast on the long trestle tables in the dining room of the mock Tudor house by 'Mr Gerald', as they were required to call the headmaster, marching up and down the corridor ringing a large bell.

After breakfast the boys were allowed out of doors for free time, during which they were encouraged to take part in walking and running exercises. Lessons began at 9 a.m. and continued through the day, with breaks for lunch and sport, until 5.20 p.m. Supper was a simple meal, often pasta, sausages and the ubiquitous chips. There were prayers before supper, grace was said before eating and the boys all attended chapel on Sundays. In the evenings there was prep. At 8 p.m. the cry went up, 'Lights out in the dorm.'

Any boy who misbehaved was punished by being sent to bed early or, worse, being denied his twice-weekly helping of sweets, called 'grub' at Ludgrove. 'That was a fate worse than death,' William said.

It took him a while to settle into this alien regime, where there were no footmen or nannies to attend him. He had to make his own bed, something he had never done before.

A PPO, usually Graham 'Crackers' Cracker, was always on duty and close by. But it was not his job to interfere when William became involved in pillow fights in the dorm, even though his own bedroom was next door. He was under firm instruction to remain in the background. William had a buzzer beside his bed and another on his wrist which he carried with him at all times, but they were only for emergencies. If he was going to make a go of it away from the protective embrace of his royal background, he was going to have to do so on his own.

It was four weeks before he saw both his parents again and then only for a weekend. Worried about appearing soppy in front of the other boys, he refused to greet Diana with a kiss. Only when he was in the safety of the car did he give his mother a quick peck on the cheek. When anyone told the princess that she had no reason to worry, that he would soon settle in, it only seemed to draw her back to her own unhappy childhood. 'He's so young,' she would say. 'I can't imagine having to go through that stage of my life all over again.'

Once back at school, William was not allowed food parcels. Nor was he allowed to telephone home. He wrote letters instead and his mother wrote to him every day on cards decorated with little animals that she had carefully chosen.

He kept these notes hidden in his tuck box, which he was careful to fasten with the lock he had asked his mother to send him. Janet Barber, the headmaster's wife, said, 'It does not mean a problem with security. They are just normal little boys who like to have their own keys.' William guarded his box diligently. At the end of term he took it home, sorted out which notes he wished to keep and, with the help of Olga Powell, carefully destroyed the rest. As he told one of his contemporaries, 'I don't want them to fall into enemy hands.' Clair Southwell, a part-time member of the Prince's staff, told the court during the trial of butler Paul Burrell, 'Prince William was always very conscientious about where he left his letters. He was aware of what would happen if they fell into the wrong hands.'

He did not give them to anyone for 'safe keeping', Burrell included. By the age of eight he was already royal enough to appreciate the need for discretion.

There was a plaintive tone to Diana's missives. After one brief meeting, she wrote, 'My Darling Wombat . . . It was lovely to catch a kiss and a hug off you this morning even though I would love to have run away with you.'

There was no escape, not for William at least. Running away was not an option for the closely guarded little prince. He was stuck where he was, homesick, lonely and in awe of the older boys who called him 'squit'. One fellow pupil remembered how William spent the first few days wandering through the school grounds on his own, aimlessly kicking up the gravel.

At night he often felt tearful, but he was not the only one. The first few weeks at boarding school can be a frightening experience, especially for those whose backgrounds were already troubled. Many of the boys at Ludgrove came from broken homes. That is a common enough situation in an age where nearly half of all marriages end in divorce, but one which according to the American psychiatrist M. Scott Peck can have a disruptive effect. Peck maintains that 'Those who grow up in warm, nurturing, loving homes usually have relatively little difficulty in leaving those homes, while children who grow up in homes filled with back-biting, hostility, coldness and viciousness often have a great deal of trouble leaving.'

Peck's book, *The Road Less Travelled*, has sold over five million copies and continues to sell 500,000 a year, making him one of the best-selling authors in history. He continued, 'Those who grow up in nurturing homes tend to see the world as a warm, loving place and say, "Hey, let me at it." Children who grow up in a home filled with hostility and viciousness tend to see the world as a cold, hostile and dangerous place.'

It is to William's credit that he was able to adjust as well as he did. Once he learnt to find his way around, he discovered that the school was not quite as forbidding as he first thought. He started enjoying sport and in his first term was in the team that won the under-nine football competition.

His studies improved and he worked his way into the top stream. The pupils had tests every few weeks and his results were pinned up on the notice board like everyone else's. 'He was usually in the top four,' another student recalled.

He started making friends. Among them were Edward Corry-Reid, the son of a London businessman; Andrew Charlton, whose father had once been a proficient racing driver; and Viscount Galway's grandson, Simon, whose mother, Charlotte Morrison, owns much of London's Holland Park and is, appropriately enough, the richest woman in Britain after the Queen and one of the few people other than the sovereign who is allowed to own her own swans.

William became wrapped in the fads that swept the school. At one point it was coloured key rings on a curly plastic cord. At other times it was Swatch watches and BB guns that fired plastic bullets.

And in Janet Barber he found someone who was both receptive and perceptive when it came to dealing with little boys and their problems. She helped them pin up their posters (Mutant Turtles were the craze when William arrived), and comforted him when he had a cold. 'She even knew when a tooth came loose,' one parent observed, and William was at a stage when his were still falling out.

To shield him from the outside world, the Barbers also banned newspapers and radios. There was only so much the school could do, however. At the Christmas play that first year William played a shepherd. Diana and Charles sat in the front next to the Barbers. When another father tried to take a photograph of his own son who was also in the play, the PPO rushed forward and told him to put his camera away. The father refused and a heated discussion ensued. Gerald Barber left his seat and said, 'Oh dear, we have a problem here.'

The row was resolved in favour of the father. The incident nonetheless served to highlight the attention William was bound to attract. The Waleses were the focus of everyone's interest and, if boys didn't gossip, their parents certainly did. As Prince Michael of Kent told me, 'Bad news has a way of filtering through. You discover that they have been got at or teased about something and that upsets them.'

William had every reason to be upset. When he went home for half term and then for his Christmas holidays, he found himself a central part of a story that was making headline news, most of it as bad as a young boy could imagine.

During his first term at Ludgrove his father, then aged forty-two, had come perilously close to a nervous breakdown. He became morose, uncommunicative and racked with self-doubt. His friends – including his cousin, Norton Knatchbull, and his extra equerry, Sir Winston Churchill's grandson Nicholas Soames – tried to make light of it by saying he was in the throes of a mid-life crisis. It was much more than that, and in private one chum went so far as to say that he was suffering from 'clinical depression'.

Diana was almost as distraught. Her only comfort was her children. At Christmas she took William and Harry, dressed alike in matching blazers and grey flannels, to the International Horse Show at Olympia. She also took William to a Christmas concert at London's Barbican where he signed his visitors' book, confirming that he was left-handed.

The rest of her holiday was spent under a cloud of emotional gloom. The traditional sojourn to Sandringham was a particularly unhappy occasion. The big house, filled with her prattling royal relations, made Diana feel claustrophobic and she kept disappearing for long walks along Norfolk's deserted wind-swept beaches.

This bitter atmosphere accompanied the fragmenting family back to Gloucestershire.

In February William came home on his first 'long weekend' (Friday afternoon to Sunday evening) out of school. Diana brought Harry down from London and Charles arrived on the Highgrove lawn at 5 o'clock in a red helicopter, much to the excitement of his sons.

Charles was very much looking forward to seeing his first-born. 'He really is shooting up,' he said.

That evening they ate supper together off a card table that had been set up in front of the wood fire in Diana's bright and light sitting room decorated in white chintz with yellow flowers, while the dogs Tigger and Roo sat on the window seats. Charles was at his most animated, softening William's complaints about Ludgrove with stories of his own time at Cheam prep school and the fun he claimed to have had there. It should have been the prelude to a family weekend. He outlined his plans. They would include a picnic and a visit to some old churches in the area. The boys were enthusiastic. They saw less of their father than they would have liked and to be with 'Papa' was something of a treat.

The next morning, however, Diana whipped the boys off to a local fairground, leaving Charles behind. The prince subsided back into a gloom that only got worse when, early on Sunday, Diana suddenly announced that she was leaving and taking the boys with her. It was 11.30 a.m. and William was not due back at Ludgrove until much later that afternoon, but Diana simply could not face spending any more time with her husband.

The following month Diana again outmanoeuvred her husband. Without his knowledge she arranged to take William out of school to attend a St David's Day service at Llandaff Cathedral. It was William's first visit to the principality. It would have been politically damaging had the Prince of Wales not been there in these emotive circumstances and he had to rearrange his schedule in order to attend.

It was another skirmish Charles lost in the battle the Waleses were fighting over their children, and not even William and Harry's first skiing holiday was enough to bring about a truce.

During their half term vacation in March 1991, Diana took the boys to Lech, the picturesque Austrian resort much favoured by the Dutch royal family. They were accompanied by Diana's niece, Laura Fellowes, Catherine Soames and her son, Harry. Also in the party was Princess Margaret's young and energetic son, Viscount Linley, who the boys regarded as something of a daredevil.

Charles was not there. He remained behind at Sandringham. The choice of Lech had led to yet another row.

Charles had long been promising his sons that he would take them to the Alps. But he wanted to go to Klosters, his favourite ski resort in Switzerland. It was there, three years before, that the Queen's equerry and onetime admirer of Princess Anne, Major Hugh Lindsay, had been killed in an avalanche which Charles was lucky to survive. Diana roundly declared that she would never return to the scene of that tragedy. When Charles refused to budge, Diana got a sheaf of skiing brochures, decided she like the look of Lech and, on impulse, went ahead and booked the holiday.

As a capable skier himself, Charles had been looking forward to introducing his sons to the sport. He was furious that his wife had denied him that pleasure by picking a week when she knew full well he was hosting a long-arranged shooting party for eighteen people. 'Diana basked in his irritation,' her PPO, Ken Wharfe, recorded.

Even without their father, the princes enjoyed their first excursion onto the snow. By his second day six-year-old Harry, by now much the more adventurous of the two brothers, was in a downhill racer's crouch and skiing through the legs of his instructor. He laughed when he took a tumble and seemed to have no fear. 'He's a real snow bunny,' Diana said.

William was more circumspect. He found it difficult to maintain his balance and kept falling down. The fact that he was recovering from a bout of flu did not help. As Harry went shooshing by on the second morning, he was crying and complaining to his PPO, 'I feel sick.' He had to be taken back to the five-star Hotel Arlberg where the royal party was staying. Diana teased him out of his sulk and had him back on the slopes that afternoon. By the end of the week William was nearly as proficient as Harry and, in their youthful enthusiasm, they tried to find their own routes down the mountains. 'Whenever I said go right, they would go left,' Diana said. She added, 'They had a really good time.'

So had Diana. The Alpine sunshine had done wonders for her spirits and the princess was in exuberant humour throughout. The frowns that had become her perennial mask were replaced by bright smiles, and she chatted cheerfully with the photographers who followed her down the easier runs.

They were too polite to overtake her. What she could not outrun, however, were the rumours. With her marriage over in all but name, the presence of bachelor David Linley at her side invited salacious comment. When they returned to England they exchanged regular notes that Linley addressed to 'Darling Diana' and ended with the endearment, 'Masses of love, from David'.

Linley denied that anything untoward had taken place between himself and his cousin's wife. He later stated, 'I never had an intimate relationship with Diana. We were close friends for a period of time but nothing more than that.'

The boys were too young to take account of the stories swirling around his parents, especially Harry, who was far too busy making mischievous ones of his own.

At the Horse of the Year Show a colonel's wife asked him, 'What have you been doing?'

'What's it got to do with you?' he replied impudently.

One of his PPOs told him, in the manner of a drill sergeant addressing a new recruit, 'You're a rude, 'orrible little boy. What are you? You're 'orrible!'

To which Harry merely replied, 'Yep.'

He wasn't always cheeky – especially if a pretty girl had caught his eye, as it did one afternoon when he was with a group of friends in London's Chester Square gardens. Spotting a young girl sitting with her mother and baby brother a few yards away, the six-year-old Prince went up to her and asked her if she would like to play with them. The girl, who was called Sophie, shyly agreed and soon she was running and leapfrogging with Harry and his friends.

'When the games started to get a bit too boisterous Sophie came back to me and sat down on the grass,' recalled her mother, travel writer Louisa Lucie-Smith. 'The next thing I knew, Harry walked over with his arms full of yellow flowers – he must have picked an entire bed of them – and laid them down in front of Sophie.

"I'm sorry if we were too rough," he said. "I thought you would like these."'

As the 'spare', Harry was allowed greater licence than his older brother. He would stand behind visitors and pull faces. And he showed an early talent for mimicry which took scant account of the importance of the person he was imitating. Both Charles and Diana were more amused than annoyed by his antics. Even the Queen, so critical of William in his infancy, regarded him with grandmotherly tolerance.

Later events would suggest that more early discipline might have been helpful, but Harry wasn't going to be the one to complain when he was allowed to get away with his transgressions. He knew where he stood in the royal pecking order: at the age of nine he turned to his brother and declared, 'You're going to be king. It doesn't matter what *I* do.'

William, on the other hand, was increasingly weighed down by his situation. He became withdrawn and his head drooped in public. The sight of a camera made him uncomfortable. Arthur Edwards, a well-regarded royal photographer who had always got on well with Diana, noted at the time, 'If he is ever going to carry out the role he is destined to fulfil, somehow he must learn to live under the glare of the spotlight.'

Ken Wharfe held Diana at least partly to blame for the change in William. Notwithstanding the fact that the princess had gone out of her way to court the support of several influential members of the press, she kept telling her sons that they were 'bad, bad men'. She had implied much the same thing on William's first day at Wetherby when she had told him not to smile. Wharfe took the view that this was not wise advice to give to two young men who were going to spend the rest of their lives in the public eye.

Harry paid his mother little heed. William did. The matter-of-fact Harry was happy to get on with his life, taking the rough with the smooth without worrying too much about the consequences. William was different. As his introspection became more pronounced, he became more receptive to what their mother had to say. As is the way with children, the princes were establishing their own individual relationships with their parents, and while Harry found he had more in common with their father, William was becoming closer to Diana.

There was no marked favouritism involved. Charles and Diana were careful to dispense their affections equally and their sons responded in kind. When it came to activities, however, interest and empathy divided the family into two camps.

Taking over from where William had left off, Harry became fascinated with guns and all things military. He pestered his father into taking him to Salisbury Plain to review the Gurkhas stationed there. They travelled by helicopter. Both were wearing combat fatigues. Harry was delighted and declared that he wanted to be a soldier when he grew up. That was less an ambition than a foregone conclusion for the member of a family for whom military service was all but compulsory, but he was hardly to know that.

William, meanwhile, was quite content to spend his afternoons home from school curled up on the sofa in Diana's Highgrove sitting room watching television. Explaining the difference in their characters, Diana told me, 'William is very sensitive and Harry is very lively.'

She added, 'William wants me to be there for him.'

On the afternoon of 3 June 1991, that involved a high-speed dash down the M4 motorway from Kensington Palace to the Royal Berkshire hospital thirty-nine miles away in Reading. William had been hit on the head with a golf club at school and knocked senseless. Diana rushed to his bedside.

She had been having lunch at San Lorenzo when the news of the injury was beeped through on the pager to Ken Wharfe from William's duty PPO, Reg Spinney. They left immediately in Diana's green Jaguar.

Charles was at Highgrove. That morning Major-General Christopher Airy, the private secretary he had just dismissed after less than two years, had come to make his formal and strained farewell. When Charles was told of his son's injury he recalled, 'My heart went cold.' He grabbed his coat and set off for Reading in his blue Aston Martin.

'I worried all the way to the hospital,' he said.

What actually happened at Ludgrove that day depends on who is doing the telling.

It was William's first day back at school from his half-term break. In the official version he was accidentally cut on the head while messing about during supervised play on the putting green after lunch. According to Reg Spinney, a careless school chum raised his club to hit a ball and accidentally struck William on the forehead.

One of the boys who was there gave a more graphic account. 'We were all walking along swinging our golf clubs and the boy in front got William who was behind him. He fell to the ground with blood pouring from his head. The 'tec thought he was dead. There was a great panic.'

Buckingham Palace denied that the incident was anything other than an accident. A spokesman said that no action would be taken against the other boy, adding, 'The Prince and Princess of Wales both take the view that this was an accident of the "boys will be boys" variety.'

It wasn't the cause but the treatment that most concerned Spinney at that moment. William was carried back to the school's main building. The staff wanted to transfer him to the sanatorium and call a doctor. Spinney was having none of it. In language that reflected his background in the Marines he told one of the teachers, 'You're in charge of his education – I'm in charge of keeping him alive.'

At the PPO's insistence, an ambulance was called and William was driven to the Accident and Emergency unit at the Royal Berkshire fifteen minutes away. There were thirty other casualties there when William arrived – some had been waiting for up to an hour and half. The future king was examined immediately. 'There was no queue jumping – priority is always given to head injuries and young children,' claimed a spokesman for the NHS hospital.

When Charles arrived William was sitting up in bed. 'He was chatting away,' Charles said. 'Then I knew he was going to be all right.'

The doctors who treated the prince gave a more guarded prognosis. The injury, they said, was serious and on their advice William was transferred to a special brain unit at Great Ormond Street Hospital in London. Diana rode in the ambulance with William. Charles followed in his Aston Martin.

Tests confirmed that William had suffered a depressed fracture of the skull. At 9.30 that night he underwent a seventy-five-minute operation under general anaesthetic to relieve the pressure on the brain and check for bone splinters. Diana held his hand as he was wheeled into the operating theatre.

Reg Spinney's prompt action had probably saved the prince's life. It earned him the personal thanks of the Prince and Princess of Wales and a commendation from the Police Commissioner.

There were to be no plaudits for Charles. At 7.15 p.m. he left the hospital to attend a performance of Puccini's *Tosca* at Covent Garden. He explained that he was hosting a group of visitors from the European Commission in Brussels, that he had cancelled them once already and that it would have been impossible to do so again. The surgeons, he said, had assured him that while the injury was serious, the operation was routine and that there was no need for him to remain at the hospital.

In a further effort to justify his absence, his staff later said that he had a pager with him so that he could be summoned if there were any complications.

The excuse did not carry water. In the minds of many, Charles was again shown up to be cold and uncaring, just as he had been three years earlier when he had refused to break off his Italian holiday to be by Harry's side when he underwent a hernia operation. The fact that after the opera he had taken a train to Yorkshire to attend an environmental conference and had spent the night away from his son's bedside only increased the criticism.

Charles was horrified by the reaction. To his way of thinking, he was simply doing his duty. But as far as the public was concerned, his first duty was to his son. It was yet another public relations disaster – and one that Diana was quick to seize on.

To add to her husband's torment, she authorised her man of the moment to accuse him of being a rotten parent. Speaking on the princess's behalf, car dealer James Gilbey said, 'She thinks he is a bad father, a selfish father . . . He will never delay, cancel or change anything for their benefit. She can't understand her husband's behaviour, so, as a result, she just blocks it out.

'Diana said, "I know where my loyalties lie. With my son." '

There is no doubt that the princess had been badly shaken by William's injury and the subsequent operation. She told me later, 'I'll never forget the moment he went under the anaesthetic. His little body lay there so still. I cried.'

To use her boyfriend to attack her husband, however, was taking the battle to an extraordinary extreme. William quickly recovered from his injury – although it would be many years before he again wielded a golf club – but the Waleses' marriage did not. It was fast approaching its denouement.

There were some last-ditch attempts to hold it together. In August the Prince and Princess of Wales went on a cruise around the Mediterranean aboard an ocean-going liner masquerading as a yacht lent to them by John Latsis. And in October they went on tour to Canada with William and Harry, who arrived the day before with their nanny and PPO (the Queen had directed that, for the safety of the dynasty, her heirs should not travel on the same plane).

The boys enjoyed these jaunts. Latsis's *Alexander* had a room full of computer games which were forbidden them at home. 'I don't approve of the boys spending hours looking at a computer screen when they could be out of doors,' Charles told me. He added, 'William and Harry must be the only young boys without a computer.' Given this sudden free access, they went berserk. 'We couldn't even get them into the swimming pool – they preferred to spend all their time playing on those blasted machines,' said a senior member of staff.

In Canada they stayed on board *Britannia.* When the were taken aboard one of the escort frigates they were allowed to play at being sailors – and turned one of the warship's twin-barrelled guns on to a nearby police launch. They got up to more tricks when they went to see Niagara. They viewed the falls from the cruise boat *Maid of the Mist*, and took turns at the helm.

'The little guys wanted to take the boat right under the falls but I told them we'd never come out,' said skipper Richard Schuyler. Hyper and over-excited, they tooted the boat's horn all the way back to the quay.

The only sour moment, from William's point of view, came when Diana made him look at the camera for a souvenir photograph with *Britannia*'s crew. When he tried to hide his face, Diana tapped him smartly on his arm and told him off. Like his mother, William hated being reprimanded. Upset by the rebuke, he ran below deck. Charles had to chase after him to bring him back to wave to the crowds waiting to see them off.

But if William's humour soon revived, his parents' didn't. Diana had been miserable throughout the cruise on *Alexander.* She had spent most of it by herself, either in or beside the yacht's swimming pool, while Charles entertained their guests including Lord and Lady Romsey, a couple Diana had come to dislike intensely.

In Canada she had looked chic and elegant. But the couple were sleeping in separate bedrooms and Diana was preoccupied by the decision she had just reached to cooperate secretly with Andrew Morton on his book, which was destined to tear away the last shreds of discretion surrounding her marriage. Charles and Diana's only communication was through their private secretaries. 'Their lives are spent in total isolation,' Gilbey felt moved to observe.

That was no recipe for a festive Christmas. The gardener, Paddy Whitehead, had put up two trees. One was in the nursery, which the boys decorated themselves. The other was in the hall. To make it fit, Paddy had cut off the top instead of the bottom, much to the amusement of William and Harry, if not their parents who were no longer able to see the funny side of anything.

A week before Christmas Day they went to Althorp to see their grandfather, Earl Spencer. They were in boisterous form. Lord Spencer observed, 'They behave when they are on duty but not when they are off. They run up and down the corridors all day and all night. If I can't find them, I know where to look. There are some moveable steps in the library and that's where they are to be found – hanging upside-down on them. William frightened the life out of us by taking a toboggan to the top of the stairs and whizzing all the way down.'

The mood was very different at Sandringham where the Christmas court was now held. 'You could have cut it with a knife,' one member of the Royal Family said. All the outward forms of a Royal Family Christmas were dutifully maintained, however.

William and Harry arrived on the afternoon of Christmas Eve in their own chauffeur-driven car followed by a police back-up vehicle and a Land Rover filled with the presents Diana had helped them buy and wrap in brightly coloured paper. The boys rushed in ahead, leaving the staff to carry in the gifts and their personal luggage, which was taken upstairs to their nursery suite.

The Queen greeted her grandsons at the door. They bowed and then kissed her.

Following a tradition introduced from Denmark by the Queen's great-great-grandmother, Queen Alexandra, the presents were exchanged after afternoon tea, which was served at 5 p.m. All the parcels were placed down a side of a room on tables covered with white linen cloths and laid in order of precedence, with the Queen's gifts first, then Charles's, followed by William's and Harry's.

In the glow from hundreds of lights on a 20-foot Christmas tree felled in the nearby woods and topped with a large silver star, the family then embarked on the frenzy of present opening. The staff was left to clear the discarded paper but they also collected the labels as mementoes and for possible future sale. The Queen Mother, grand to a fault, resolutely signed herself 'Elizabeth R'. Everyone else lapsed into artful informality. The Queen signed her gifts, 'From Lilibet'. Princess Alexandra was either 'Pud' or 'Puddy'. William's were laboriously written in capital letters while Harry's were a wobbly scrawl.

That night the guests walked into dinner according to precedence. The atmosphere in the house was festering rather than festive and the Queen had spend days beforehand working out her *placement* so as to keep her two married sons as far apart from their wives as possible. Charles needed a couple of very large dry martinis before he could face the evening.

It was no better at lunch on Christmas Day. Everyone, with the exception of the Queen and the Queen Mother, wore paper crowns but there was no lingering over the turkey and the plum pudding. The food was gulped. Everyone was anxious to get away from the table as quickly as possible.

There was no improvement in the days that followed. At one dinner Diana decided that she wanted to discuss the future of the monarchy. What, she asked loudly, was going to happen to the Royal Family when Britain became a part of a federal Europe? She later recalled that everyone looked at her as if she was 'mad'. Then, after a moment's stunned silence, they went back to talking about the day's shooting and ignored her for the rest of the evening. On another occasion she fled the dinner table in tears and ran upstairs to her bedroom, much to the embarrassment of Charles.

Christmases can be a trial for any family. It was excruciating for the royals as they headed into what the Queen called their '*annus horribilis*'.

Fergie was smitten with the Texan oil man, Steve Wyatt, Diana was deeply unhappy with the Prince of Wales, and the two women spent long hours huddled together conspiring to make a spectacular joint exit from the Royal Family. The duchess, who had come to rely on the advice of a coterie of soothsayers, tarot card readers, astrologers and psychics, warned the princess that the Royal Family was doomed and that they had to make their escape before it was too late. A cousin recalled, 'They were saying quite awful things about their husbands and giggling.'

When the weren't plotting, they deserted the house party and drove to nearby King's Lynn to visit the Knight's Hill health club to swim in the 15-metre pool. William and Harry and Fergie's three-year-old daughter Beatrice accompanied them. It was a welcome break from the despondency enshrouding the 'big house', although, when everything was taken into consideration, the winter break was a lot more enjoyable for the princes than it was for their parents.

Both were given bicycles for Christmas and, with 20,000 acres of private estate to ride through, spent as long as they could pedalling furiously up and down the paths and driveways, oblivious to rain and wind whipping in off the North Sea. There were pheasant shoots from Boxing Day onwards, and the princes were allowed to accompany the guns as they moved from drive to drive. They also had the companionship of Princess Anne's children, Peter and Zara, with whom they were friendly.

It would have been remarkable, however, if what Fergie called the 'bad vibes' had not affected them in some way. William in particular was markedly affected by the dire situation they were an innocent part of.

Their mother had spent a good part of the holiday in tears and locked in her bedroom, listening to music or watching the rain run down the window pane. With the boys off playing with the other children, she had no one to talk to apart from Fergie and there was only so much scheming she could do before despair again overwhelmed her. One her staff said, 'It was grim for her the whole time she was there.'

She was still in tears when she got back to Highgrove on 10 January. Charles was not there, which gave her William and Harry to herself; they spent the afternoon watching a Mr Bean video. When he arrived home the following evening, however, the rows resumed.

Charles did not like his sons watching television during the day. Children always try and find a way round that ban and William and Harry were assisted by their mother, who let them sneak up the back stairs to watch the set in her bedroom. That only added to the arguments which now extended to include what to eat and where to eat it. On William's last night before returning to school, Diana refused to come down and he dined alone with his father.

It was a tense meal. William was dreading going back to school. He wanted to stay at home. Charles told his son that he knew exactly how he felt and that he, too, had hated going back to school at the beginning of each term.

It didn't help. William was in tears when he left Highgrove after lunch the following day. Charles gave him a hug. Diana rounded on her husband and said, 'He's under additional pressure because of who he is. It must be very difficult for him.'

Child psychologist David Fontana noted, 'Children who are exposed to these running battles, and to the uneasy period of truce which punctuate them, suffer greatly. For one thing, their loyalties are divided. They love both parents, so whose side should they be on? For another, they fear their parents may separate, breaking up the home and the life they know.'

Harry seemed more pliable. He was still living at Kensington Palace and making the drive to and from Wetherby every day. Charles made only fleeting visits to KP, which was now Diana's separate residence. When he wasn't there the princes was more cheerful, more at ease with herself, less prone to the bouts of tearful dejection that coloured their moments together, and that made it easier for the boy. He was popular at school and his good humour did not desert him when the quarrels flared. But as Fontana noted in *Your Growing Child*, 'Because the harm done to children isn't visible on the surface, it doesn't mean it isn't there.'

Harry's problems with alcohol and drugs would manifest themselves later. William had to confront his emotions then.

So, too, had their mother. In March 1992, when Charles and Diana got together long enough to take their sons on their second skiing holiday in

Lech, her father died. The news was telephoned through by her sister Sarah to her PPO, Ken Wharfe, who then broke the news to Diana. She burst into tears, crying, 'What am I going to do?'

Charles said immediately that he would accompany his wife back to England. Diana objected. 'It's a bit bloody late for Charles to start playing the caring husband, don't you think?' she complained. 'I don't want him with me.' Wharfe was called in to mediate and after yet another fraught exchange it was agreed that Charles would fly back to London with the princess, as protocol dictated he should.

It was Charles who told William and Harry that their grandfather had died. They took it in their stride, as children often do. Diana then decided that it would be better if they stayed on to complete their Easter vacation with their cousin, Laura Fellowes, Catherine Soames's son, Harry, and Prince Harry's friend from Wetherby, George Grumbar. Catherine Soames and Diana's friend Kate Menzies, an heiress to the newsagent chain, were left in charge of the skiing party.

It was a welcome interlude for the princes. The pistes were covered with spring snow, the weather was fine and the skiing conditions were excellent. There was great competition between them, but William had improved enough to beat his younger brother by a hair's breadth in a slalom race for beginners – much to Harry's annoyance.

There were other respites. Diana always made a great thing about the boys' birthdays. The previous year she had given Harry a party for twenty school friends at Kensington Palace themed around his favourite cartoon, *The Simpsons*. And when William celebrated his tenth birthday it was with a Cowboys and Indians extravaganza held at the Hampstead home of his godfather, ex-King Constantine of Greece.

Charles and Diana entered into the spirit of the occasion and buried the hatchet for the day. Harry and William wore cowboy outfits, while their mother went dressed like Doris Day in *Calamity Jane*. Charles, who is an honorary Indian chief and has the full regalia including the feathered headdress, confined himself to a stetson. Smarty Arty, the party's organiser and entertainer, recalled, 'You wouldn't have thought anything was the matter. They both joined in all the games, like running with a plate of water, and appeared to be enjoying themselves.'

This cowboy theme was continued later into the summer when William joined his school friend, Miles Duffy, and his father Simon, finance director of Thorn-EMI, in Montana at the E-Bar-L dude ranch.

William's day began with a tin cup of tea and bowl of porridge served from a chuck wagon. After a day of riding, swimming, fishing and square dancing, he joined the other youngsters on a hay ride into the hills. Out among the pines he proved himself quick on the trigger with his rifle, hitting the clay pigeon targets with aplomb. His gun skills attracted no criticism. In the United States firearms are an everyday fact of life.

One of the real cowhands said, 'He didn't make a big thing of who he was. He was really friendly to the other kids. Even though he could ride and shoot better than most of the adults he wasn't big-headed about that either. He enjoyed passing on his skills.'

William telephoned home and told his mother, 'This is the best holiday of my life.'

But no holiday, however exciting and untroubled, could disperse the black clouds of disharmony hanging over the family.

In January the Duke and Duchess of York announced their formal separation. Diana reneged at the last minute on her promise to join in Fergie's escape plan, leaving the duchess to face the brickbats of vitriolic denunciation on her own. She even seemed to take malicious delight in her sister-in-law's discomfort, which culminated in the infamous incident when she was pictured topless beside a swimming pool in the South of France having her toe sucked by her 'financial adviser' John Bryan. Diana called her 'the Redhead'. It was not a term of endearment. One courtier of long experience observed, 'The princess used the duchess to draw the poison.'

However, it was the Waleses' marriage that held the public spotlight. On 7 June, the *Sunday Times* began its serialisation of Andrew Morton's explosive book under the headline, 'Diana driven to five suicide bids by uncaring Charles'.

The copies of the first edition were wired through to Highgrove at 5.26 on Sunday morning by the Waleses' press secretary, Dickie Arbiter. When Diana came down to breakfast she found her husband reading the faxes that had been placed at the head of the dining room table. After a few moments of silence made even more excruciating by the presence of interior designer Robert Kime and his wife Helen, Diana fled back upstairs. After Charles had read the scathing demolition of his marriage he went on a short walk through the gardens with the Kimes who left immediately afterwards.

The prince then went upstairs to confront his wife. A few moments later the princess ran out of the house and headed back to London, her eyes brimming with tears. The utterly bewildered Harry went with her. She had known full well that this was going to be a dreadful weekend and had brought her son with her for emotional protection.

Diana's initial reaction to the crisis was to deny that she had played any part in the preparation of Morton's damning annihilation of a royal marriage. That was a blatant lie, as soon became transparently obvious.

Even at this catastrophic juncture the Queen refused to confront the reality of the situation. Desperate to preserve the façade of regal unity, she urged the couple to stay together. It was a facile hope. If further evidence were needed to illustrate just how empty it had become, it came with the publication that August of the transcript of the so-called 'Squidgygate' tapes in which Diana disparaged the Royal Family and exchanged sexual innuendoes with James Gilbey.

No marriage could survive such a public hammering – and no marriage could be expected to. The end had come and on 9 December 1992, Prime Minister John Major informed the House of Commons that the Prince and Princess of Wales had decided to separate.

William and Harry knew well beforehand. In September Charles and Diana had taken Harry to Ludgrove when he followed his brother to boarding school. They returned separately a few weeks later to tell their sons that the family was splitting up. Buckingham Palace confirmed that the princes had been 'kept informed' of developments that affected them so directly.

The meetings with the princes took place in the headmaster's sitting room overlooking the front drive to the school. Diana and Charles sat in turn on the soft, chintz-covered sofas and told their sons that it was all right, that they really did love them and that the break-up would not change that. Diana told them that, 'although I still loved Papa, I couldn't live under the same roof as him, and likewise with him'.

All that William could bring himself to reply was, 'I hope you'll both be happier now.' An extremely mature remark for a ten-year-old to make.

There was no doubting the princes' anguish, however. Late in November William wrote a very personal letter to Nanny Olga Powell saying how sad he was. She wrote back to him on 28 November, sharing his feelings.

But while the news was heartbreaking, it was hardly unexpected. For the distressing truth was that William and Harry had been forced to contend with their parents' misery, both as onlookers and pawns in that vicious marital battle, for most of their lives.

NINE

Difficult Times

Harry was only two and William four when James Hewitt became a regular guest at Highgrove. He would keep coming for the next five years.

Prince Charles was never at home when the young army officer came to stay. He was there at the personal and intimate invitation of Princess Diana.

He got on well with the little princes. During the day he would sit chatting with them in the main kitchen. In the evenings he would join the detectives in the violent pillow fights that raged up and down the nursery at bedtime. Hewitt enjoyed those raucous romps. He would later recall sending the future king sprawling with one particularly violent blow that reduced William to tears.

'But he soon recovered and told me not to worry,' he said.

Once the exhausted boys had finally been settled into bed he would join the princess and the other members of the house party for an informal supper in the dinning room. Hewitt was assigned the blue bedroom, which has its own en suite bathroom. He did not remain there long. Once the staff had cleared away and the house had settled down for the night, he would tiptoe across to Diana's room on the other side of the landing wearing nothing but a silk dressing gown.

The princess's bedroom was on the first floor overlooking the gardens. It adjoined Charles's dressing room, the door to which she kept locked from her side. There was a table under the windows with a sofa in front of it covered with soft cuddly toys. In winter a wood fire burnt romantically in the fireplace.

The bed was a four-poster. It stood against the wall – directly underneath the nursery floor where her sons were sleeping.

Hewitt remained there until dawn, when he would make his way back across the landing. He recalled, 'Diana even came into my room one morning to make sure I'd ruffled my bed sufficiently so it looked slept in. She was careful and even calculating in the ways of deception.'

No one was fooled by the subterfuge. The other house guests often included Diana's old flatmate, Carolyn Bartholomew, and her husband William and they certainly knew what was going on. So did the staff and the police officers who were in constant, twenty-four-hour attendance. They passed no comment on what might have been taking place in the princess's bedroom.

'I wasn't there to make a moral judgement, only to look after her,' her PPO Ken Wharfe told me when I raised the matter with him.

Diana would later argue that she had done nothing wrong: that if Charles was off 'doing whatever he was doing with that woman' (she was referring to Camilla Parker Bowles), she was surely entitled to the same independence. It was nonetheless an act of exceptional recklessness on the princess's part to conduct an illicit affair in her own bed in her marital home with her sons asleep upstairs.

It was also a quite extraordinary backdrop against which to bring up a future king and his brother.

Royal morals have always been questionable. However, for the better part of the twentieth century the sanctity of the family reigned supreme, and no breath of scandal ever attached itself to George V and Queen Mary in their married life, or to George VI and his wife, later the Queen Mother. And despite the whispers of innuendo that were directed at Prince Philip over the years, the Queen always stood above reproach. All in their way and according to the ideas of their time endeavoured to bring up their children in a safe, respectable and, above all, stable environment.

The Prince and Princess of Wales broke that mould. Charles continued to keep in touch with Camilla Parker Bowles, herself a married woman, and while he insisted that nothing untoward took place until his marriage had 'irretrievably' broken down, their relationship had a devastating effect on his marriage.

Diana chose to believe that Charles's association with Camilla absolved her from the wedding vows she had made before a worldwide television audience of 700 million people.

In 1985, when Prince Harry was less than a year old, a rumour did the rounds of royal circles that Diana was having an affair with Barry Mannakee. As her Personal Protection Officer, Mannakee was always at her side.

After a senior member of Charles's staff allegedly discovered the princess and the policeman in a compromising situation on the eve of the wedding of the Duke and Duchess of York in July 1986, Mannakee was moved to other duties. He died in a motorcycle accident a year later. According to one of the Royal Family's senior PPOs, Charles was 'utterly shocked by the Mannakee affair. He turned to Camilla and sought her advice. She saw her chance and moved in. She was his emotional bedrock at a very difficult time.'

Diana told Mannakee's eventual replacement, Ken Wharfe, that the stories were totally without foundation. However, James Hewitt would recall how, when he asked the princess why Mannakee had given her a large stuffed brown bear which was propped up in pride of place on the lace-edged pillows of her four-poster bed, she replied matter-of-factly, 'He was my lover.'

There were no question marks over her relationship with Hewitt. In her *Panorama* interview in 1995, the princess was to declare, 'Yes, I adored him. Yes, I was in love with him.'

That passion was enough to keep the affair going until 1991, and during that time the roguish Life Guards officer developed a close bond with William and Harry. In her television interview Diana accused Hewitt of betraying her trust by writing about their affair. She told me afterwards, however, that she regretted mentioning Hewitt because it had upset her sons – and besides, 'he was always so good with the boys'.

She had taken them to stay at the Devon home of his mother. And when they were at Highgrove he had helped hone their riding skills, joined them in games of football and cricket on the lawn and sat watching television with them in their mother's sitting room.

'Diana encouraged me to read them stories,' he remembered. 'My preference was *The Wind in the Willows* but William's favourite was always *Winnie the Pooh*.'

In the beginning both boys were still going through their military phase and he took them to the barracks at Windsor and dressed them in little army uniforms he had specially made for them by the regimental tailor. Hewitt helped them adjust their berets in order to look like proper soldiers. 'They climbed all over the tanks and other armoured vehicles and appeared to have the times of their lives,' he recalled.

When Hewitt went on active service to the Gulf in 1990 following Iraq's invasion of Kuwait, Harry took a personal interest in his welfare. He would sit cuddled in bed beside his mother watching the news reports on television – wearing the uniform Hewitt had had made for him.

'I was never trying to be their father,' Hewitt would later insist. 'They had a perfectly good father of their own.'

There were occasions, though, when it was Hewitt who appeared to have the greater run of the house. When Charles returned to Highgrove after an official engagement he discovered that the water in the fountain near the front of the house was dirty. 'What's been going with that fountain?' he demanded to know. 'It's all murky.'

The answer was that Hewitt's labrador, Jester, had been swimming in it but no one was daring enough to tell the prince that. Even William and Harry kept quiet. They had been well schooled by their mother in the art of diplomatic silence.

There was only so much that Diana could conceal from her husband, however. Just as he had found out about Mannakee, so Charles eventually came to learn of her affection for Hewitt.

He also discovered that his sons had grown very fond of the red-haired Life Guard, which, given the nature of his association with their mother, Charles had good cause to regard as thoroughly inappropriate. It was not an example he chose to follow. No doubt wary of his wife's temper, he did not invite Camilla to stay at Highgrove until after the separation. Indeed, according to both his and Camilla's accounts, they had no call to be alone together. Camilla told Diana as much at a party given by financier Sir James Goldsmith's wife Lady Annabel in 1989 at her home on Ham Common in Surrey.

Diana had confronted her rival while she was talking to Charles in the children's playroom in the basement and said, 'I know about you two.'

Recalling the meeting, Diana said she told Camilla, 'I'm sorry I'm in the way, I obviously am in the way, and it must be hell for both of you. But I do know what's going on, don't treat me like an idiot.'

She then stormed out – but not before Camilla fired off a riposte. The princess later recounted to her clairvoyant, Debbie Frank, how Camilla told her, 'Don't think it's my fault. Charles and I had a pact that I wouldn't contact him for five years after the wedding.'

That would appear to date the resumption of the prince's love affair with the woman Diana called 'the Rottweiler' to 1986, the year Mannakee was dismissed – and at around the same time that Hewitt claimed he began his liaison with the princess Camilla nicknamed 'Barbi'.

'I first met Diana in May 1986 in a corridor at Buckingham Palace,' he recalled. 'I was in a scarlet army tunic and she made a joke about my "nice outfit". The next time I saw her was at a drinks party at St James's Palace in September. That was when she asked me to teach her to ride and it was from there that our affair began.'

Brother officers in the Life Guards recall a different timetable. They remember a notice going up on their board at Knightsbridge Barracks in 1984, asking for an officer to volunteer to teach the Princess of Wales to ride. 'Hewitt was the one who put himself forward,' said one former serving officer from the same regiment who was at the barracks with Hewitt. Prince Harry was born on 15 September that year.

It was this confusion over dates which gave rise to the calumny that would dog Harry into adulthood. 'He's my little Spencer,' his mother said, referring to her son's red hair. It did not escape cynical notice, however, that Hewitt also had red hair.

Hewitt eventually felt compelled to declare, 'I must state once and for all that I am *not* Harry's father. There really is no possibility whatsoever that I am Harry's father. Harry was twenty months old when I first exchanged pleasantries with his mother and past his second birthday when the affair started. When I first met Diana, Harry was already a toddler. Harry was already walking by the time my relationship with Diana began.'

That superficial similarity of the hair colour dissolves in close up. As well as his father's ears, Harry has close-set eyes like both his father and Prince Philip. Also, the affection and easy camaraderie that has always existed between Charles and his younger son gave visible confirmation to what Hewitt was saying. But the very fact that Harry's paternity could ever be called into question provided a sorry commentary on the state of his parents' marriage. With Charles and Diana living virtually separate lives from 1986 onwards – he with Camilla, she with Hewitt and, between 1989 and 1991, simultaneously with James Gilbey – even the most outrageous tittle-tattle carried the weight of possibility.

There was no way William and Harry could be sheltered from their parents' indiscretions. Their butler Paul Burrell was told not to bring the newspapers into the house so as to spare the sensibilities of the boys. All too often, though, the papers were there, spread out on the dining room table. Charles would profess not to read them but Diana knew that he did. 'I'd come down in the morning and usually discovered he had refolded them,' Diana told me. 'He was trying to pretend that he hadn't read them, but I knew that he had.'

So did William and, as he grew older, so did Harry. Slowly it dawned on them what was going on and that was a disturbing thought for two boys on the threshold of adolescence. Hewitt had been a regular visitor to their home and Mrs Parker Bowles was only a short drive away over the county line in Wiltshire. As Diana's friend Vivienne Parry, who ran the Birthright

Charity when the princess was patron and later became a trustee of Diana's memorial trust, observed, 'Children don't want to know – and they certainly don't want to know that their parents are doing it. It's out of the question. So when it's obvious that your parents *are* doing it – and with different people – it's a bit disturbing.' Mrs Parry was referring to sex.

It wasn't so much what Diana and Charles got up to when they were elsewhere as how they behaved when they were all together that caused their sons such anguish, however. In the battle of the Waleses, William and Harry were used by Diana as both weapon and shield and they became the unwitting pawns in a disruptive power play that no one could fail to notice.

If Charles wanted to eat outside, as he often did in summer, Diana would loudly insist on dining indoors with the children. When the prince wanted to take their sons out for the day, she would often say, 'No, you can't – I've already arranged for them to do something else.'

The boys always got excited when they saw their father getting dressed to go and play polo, and pleaded to be allowed to accompany him. Charles wanted them to go with him, on the condition that they behaved. Some days Diana would agree, even though she detested polo. All too frequently, however, she would find an excuse to keep them home.

In the evenings, when Harry had gone to bed and Charles was expecting to have dinner on a card table in the sitting room, he would ask, 'Where's the princess – and where's William?' only to be told, 'They're in her bedroom.' Charles would enquire, 'Are they coming down?' Back would come the embarrassed answer, 'No, sir, they're not.' And there Diana and William would remain, watching television and eating their supper off trays that the princess had ordered earlier.

'It was humiliating for him,' a member of staff said. 'Charles would end up looking like a fool.'

Diana often spent her evenings in tears, cuddling up to William. 'It must have been very difficult for the boy,' their housekeeper Wendy Berry observed. 'He was at that certain age and imagine being closeted in a bedroom with the meals coming in and his mother crying.'

William was very concerned by his mother's unhappiness. He would put his arms around her and say, 'Don't cry, Mummy.'

One day William found Diana in tears on the back stairs leading up from the kitchen. When Charles suddenly appeared he turned on his father and said, 'Why do you make Mummy cry all the time?' He ran off into the garden shouting, 'I hate you, Papa.'

As tensions rose, Highgrove came to embody not the happy home life that had anchored the Royal Family's image for the better part of a century, but a scene from *The Lion in Winter*, James Goldman's play about the dysfunctional relationship between the medieval King Henry II and his queen, Eleanor of Aquitaine. Even something as natural as their sons' growth became a source of insult. When William started shooting up, Diana remarked, 'He's getting very tall, don't you think – and we all know which side of the family that comes from.'

A former staff member recalled, 'The doors at Highgrove were very thick and you couldn't hear the screaming matches unless you had your ear to the keyhole.' There was no need to go to such lengths. As the marriage deteriorated, Charles and Diana abandoned their attempt to present a united front and all too often the rows were conducted in full view of their staff and children. Shouting matches would erupt without warning in the sitting room, in the corridors and on the staircases. When Diana dissolved into yet more tears, Charles would wring his hands with exasperation. When he flew into one of his sudden rages, she would retreat into a sulk. 'He would always apologise to us afterwards,' the staff member said. 'She did not.'

So frequent were the arguments that, in the words of one member of the household, 'It just became a way of life. In the end William became so used to seeing his mother in tears that he accepted it as an everyday fact of life.' He became adept at handing her tissues.

Yet notwithstanding those occasional outbursts against his father, William, like his brother, tried to avoid taking sides when their parents started screaming at each other. Too young to control their own environment, they had no alternative but to deal with it as best they could. That was difficult. Harry somehow managed to remain happy-go-lucky as the rows raged around him, but William's face betrayed his hurt. The sense of security so vital to a child was being undermined. Each morning brought the fear of being witness to another clash of temperaments. Given these dismal circumstances, it was not surprising that he became old beyond his years. One of Charles's friends observed, 'William was very grown up for his age.'

He also became skilled at hiding his feelings. The misbehaviour that had marked his infancy was replaced by a mask of surliness. When William and Harry were away together on holiday – they paid regular visits to the Scilly Isles in the company of a chef, a nanny and their PPO – they behaved, one observer remarked, 'just like any other little boys. They could be themselves. They would play on the beaches and go for rides in motorboats and enjoyed lots of barbecues. But as soon as they went back on public show they turned into little actors.'

Charles and Diana would join them, arriving separately and only staying for a couple of days before flying off again. Too preoccupied by their own troubles, neither was able to relate to their sons in the free and relaxed way they would have wished. William and Harry were not unhappy to see them leave. They enjoyed their breaks away from their parents' endless bickering. It was the increasingly morose atmosphere they encountered at home that was becoming the norm, however.

In 1991 Diana finally ended her affair with James Hewitt when he refused her pleas to opt out of serving in the Gulf War. Ken Wharfe was not surprised. He told me, 'She was only in lust with him. But because of her naivety she didn't know how to get rid of him and it dragged on longer than it should have done.'

That change in her romantic circumstances brought no improvement to her marriage. For the sake of show, the Waleses continued to weekend together and Diana later claimed that, in her attempt at reconciliation, she asked Charles for another baby. 'Getting baby three on board,' she said, might have saved the marriage. She told me, 'I would have loved to have had a daughter. How lovely it would be to have a little girl that wants to be with Mummy all the time.'

The prince rejected the suggestion. Diana recounted, 'Charles said, "Oh no, there are far too many children in the world already." '

Wounded, hurt and out of love with the wife he believed had betrayed him, he informed her that 'Sundays are for Camilla.' Before driving off for his tryst he would take a leisurely bath and then dress in blazer, open-necked shirt and cravat in the style favoured by the comedian Terry-Thomas, although he thought he looked rather more dashing than that. By the time he left, Diana was long gone, usually in tears.

The Queen and Prince Philip were well aware of the deteriorating situation and on their insistence they continued to keep up the veneer of appearances. Philip wrote kindly to his daughter-in-law, acknowledging the difficulties of her position, recounting the difficulties he had encountered early on and urging her to tough it out, for the good of the institution she had married into and for the well-being of her sons.

It was sound and well-meant advice, but it was too late to save a marriage that in its tangle of broken promises, distrust and dangling spars of loathing had become an emotional shipwreck. Attempts to seal the breaches only succeeded in punching another hole in their floundering relationship.

Diana accompanied her husband to the Trooping of the Colour in 1992, as protocol dictated she should. But by unfortunate coincidence, it was held just six days after the *Sunday Times* began its serialisation of Andrew Morton's exposé and the princess was extremely nervous. Rather than face the frosty glares of her in-laws, she slipped away before the balcony finale and was observed by the Queen's lady-in-waiting, Lady Abel-Smith, doing cartwheels on the Buckingham Palace lawn.

Lady Abel-Smith was appalled. Diana was thirty years old and Lady Abel-Smith took the view that this was no way for a Princess of Wales to conduct herself on one of the great occasions of state. She was not the only one to take exception. While the picture of the troubled Diana coupled with her concern for the sick and deprived won her great public sympathy, her own caste was less understanding. To many in the royal circle and among the aristocracy beyond, she was a simply a loose cannon who did not know how to behave.

Charles was little help. Led by her feelings, Diana was not only vulnerable but also very defensive and refused to respond to his attempts to re-establish some kind of rapport, pulling her head away whenever he tried to kiss her. Unable to deal with her emotional demands, Charles went into his royal shell and acted as if nothing was wrong. That only made the situation worse.

The cruise aboard Latsis's yacht that summer certainly did not improve matters. A fortnight before they sailed, Diana suddenly informed Charles that she wasn't going and would stop William and Harry from joining him. According to Wharfe, 'In fact, she had every intention of going on the cruise but took considerable pleasure in unsettling her husband.'

She very quickly came to wish that she had carried out her threat and stayed at home. The party was much the same as previous years and included ex-King Constantine, the Romseys and their children, and Princess Alexander and her husband, Angus Ogilvy. When Diana went into one of her sulks, they ignored her. 'They think I'm mad, but they've no idea what I'm going through,' she complained.

When Charles started telephoning Camilla on the ship-to-shore radio, Diana announced that she was leaving the yacht. She said that she was going to disembark at Cyprus and board a cheap holiday flight back to England. It took all Wharfe's powers to talk her round. He reminded her of the publicity such an undignified exit would generate and the distress it would cause William and Harry.

By this stage, of course, the princes had grown accustomed to their mother's erratic behaviour and got on with enjoying their holiday. One day Harry leapt the thirty feet off the back of the yacht and into the sea. Not to be outdone, William felt compelled to follow suit. Wharfe plunged in after them – and was promptly dunked under the sea by the two princes.

Charles was horrified by the escapade. Diana predictably chose to praise the boys for their daring and courage. But it did lighten the mood aboard the *Alexander* and the rest of the cruise passed off without any more unseemly spats.

The pattern set by disharmony was quick to reassert itself once the family were back on shore, however. On 25 August the transcript of the so-called 'Squidgygate' tapes were published, which laid bare in embarrassing detail Diana's affair with James Gilbey (by vicious irony, they were recorded by a radio ham working with a grant given him by Charles's Prince's Trust).

Diana was profoundly upset by the dent this made to her image of injured innocence. So was her eldest son. William was still finding it difficult to settle down at school, and Harry's arrival at Ludgrove only seemed to make matters worse. While Harry went about the bewildering business of adjusting to being a boarder, William started showing off and became involved in a numbers of scrapes.

Diana and Charles, meanwhile, continued to battle it out. Everyone who could intervene had tried to do so, but after the Queen and Philip's failure there was no one left with the authority to impose even an uneasy peace. The final straw came during William and Harry's autumn exeat from Ludgrove.

Charles had arranged a shooting party at Sandringham for 20 and 21 November to coincide with the boys' half term. As she had done so many times before, Diana suddenly declared, 'I'm not going – and nor are they.' She wrote a letter to Charles explaining that the atmosphere in Norfolk would not be conducive to a happy weekend for the children and that she would either go to Windsor or remain at Highgrove.

Charles had usually backed down when confronted with his wife's intransigence. Not this time. When Diana refused to change her mind, he telephoned the Queen and told her that it was impossible for him to carry on with his marriage. 'She's mad,' he told his mother.

On Friday, 20 November, the thousand-year-old Windsor Castle caught fire. Charles rushed back from Sandringham to watch that seemingly indestructible symbol of royalty consumed by flames.

Diana stayed at Highgrove. The next day she arranged for William and Harry to go go-karting at Highgrove with Nicholas and Alexander, the sons of her butler, Paul Burrell. They raced round in the pouring rain, churning up Charles's prized garden.

On the following Wednesday a meeting was held at Kensington Palace, where the princess was told that Charles was demanding an immediate legal separation.

Afterwards Diana and Charles sat on the sofa in the first-floor salon of Kensington Palace. The princess told me, 'We asked each other why this had to happen.' Overwrought, they embraced and sought comfort in each other's tears. They talked of the affection they had once had for each other. 'Charles absolutely loved me,' she said to me.

But it was far too late for second thoughts. The names of solicitors had already been exchanged and on 9 December 1992, Prime Minister John Major rose to inform the House of Commons that the fairytale was at its end.

TEN

The End of a Marriage

Separation, royal-style, is not easy. Diana couldn't simply pack her Louis Vuitton bags and head off with her sons to start a new life.

The Queen would not allow that. William is the second-in-line to her throne and his future lay with the Royal Family.

That had been spelt out, clearly and incontrovertibly, in the terms drawn up by their lawyers. In the agreement hammered between her legal representative, Paul Butner, and the royal solicitors, Farrer and Co., acting under Lord Goodman, she was given the day-to-day care of the boys. She would have the apartment at Kensington Palace to herself and was spared the weekly trek to Highgrove in Gloucestershire.

What she did not have was the right to cut them off from their royal heritage. During one particularly ferocious outburst, she declared, 'I would hope that my husband would go off, go away with his lady, then leave me and the children to carry the Wales name through to the time that William ascends the throne.' She would, she said, do her utmost to ensure that William and Harry had what she called 'an appreciation of the tradition into which they were born'.

She was never going to be given the chance. It was going to be the Royal Family – and not the woman who with black humour now described herself as a 'semi-detached' royal – who would interpret what that tradition was.

That was made patently clear to her that first Christmas apart from her husband. She initially wanted to take the boys away on holiday. She was firmly informed that was out of the question.

The Queen had been badly shaken by the separation and her staff noted that she was more partial than usual to her pre-dinner Martini. Even at this late stage she was still hoping that her son and daughter-in-law might yet reconcile their differences and get back together, if only for the sake of their children. She was sympathetic to Diana's plight and made time in her schedule to listen to the princess pouring out her woes.

What she was not prepared to countenance, however, was the sight of her grandsons cavorting on a Caribbean beach during the religious festival of Christmas. Their place was with the rest of the Royal Family.

That was the last place Diana wanted to be. The Queen, unwilling to break with long-established tradition, had invited her to join her sons at Sandringham. The princess turned it down flat and refused to go.

It was a snub that struck at the heart of the Royal Family.

From the reign of Queen Victoria onwards, Christmas represented the joys of settled domestic life which the Royal Family had come to personify. And if their celebrations were more extravagant than most of their subjects could afford – the Queen's uncle, the Duke of Windsor, described royal Christmases as 'Dickens in a Cartier setting' – they still contained the same essential ingredients shared by millions of ordinary people. Victoria called it a 'most dear happy time' and with her husband, Prince Albert, coupled with the literary inspiration of Charles Dickens, was instrumental in making children central to a festival that hitherto had primarily been an adult feast.

They helped popularise the fir tree introduced to England in the 1780s by George III's German-born wife, Charlotte. They donated them to schools and handed them out to soldiers in their barracks. They took great delight in decorating their own tree and started the custom of laying out the presents they had bought for each other around its base. And when in 1848 the *Illustrated London News* published a picture showing the Royal Family gathered round a tree, the fashion quickly spread.

That link between the Royal Family and Christmas was soldered by the Christmas broadcast. First delivered on radio in 1932 by George V, it is continued by his granddaughter, Elizabeth II, and remains an important part of the British Christmas. By this seamless display of stability they put themselves forward as the formal embodiment of continuity to become the monarchy of family.

That was what made Diana's action so radical and subversive. By her refusal to join the Royal Family at Christmas she had broken the continuity and exposed the human frailties behind the carefully polished image.

The Queen was aghast at this damaging departure from carefully honed tradition, while Prince Philip categorically denied that he sent Diana a letter calling her a 'harlot' and advising her to stay away from Sandringham, as she hinted he had. Both wanted her at Sandringham, if only for appearances' sake. But the princess was not to be swayed. She declined the invitation her mother-in-law sent her, and took herself off to Althorp, her own family's home a hundred miles away in Northamptonshire, where she spent a most unfestive few days with her brother, the new Earl Spencer, and their sisters, Jane and Sarah.

She spoke to William and Harry on the telephone on Christmas morning, but instead of sharing their excitement as they rummaged through their stockings, the only glimpse she got of them was on television, along with the rest of the nation. She saw them wave as they went to church and smile as they helped the Queen and the Queen Mother gather the flowers presented to them by well-wishers.

There were 800 people outside the Sandringham church of St Mary Magdalene that year, and most were critical of the princess's behaviour. One woman handed William and Harry a bar of Toblerone chocolate each and then gave voice to the many when she remarked, 'I feel very sorry for them. I never thought Diana would leave her children on Christmas Day.'

The service was relayed to the people outside through loudspeakers. They heard the rector, Canon George Hall, offer prayers for the Queen and add, 'Bless Queen Elizabeth, the Queen Mother, the Duke of Edinburgh, Charles the Prince of Wales . . .' and then pause for a long moment before adding, 'the Princess of Wales . . .' Even the Established Church of England, it seemed, was disestablishing her.

It was harrowing for a young mother so devoted to her sons. Her friend Vivienne Parry recalled, 'She talked about them incessantly.' A family member said, 'It is heart-wrenching.' William and Harry were equally upset. They kept saying, 'I wish Mummy was here.'

They had little opportunity to mope, however. Sandringham house parties are frenetic affairs conducted around a full timetable of meals and outdoor pursuits and evenings of board games. The adults have to change their clothes up to five times a day and even at their young age the princes were required to dress appropriately – jeans for riding their bikes, jodhpurs when they rode their ponies, tweed when they followed the guns on the shoots and well-pressed trousers and jackets for tea. It was all part of their royal training and because that was the way everyone around them behaved they took it for granted.

There were also the endless practical jokes which the Royal Family is so fond of. One particular trick of the Queen's was to put her own box of chocolates and fudge on the piano in the salon and then surreptitiously peek down from landing above to see who would sneak one. William and Harry were caught regularly, amid much laughter.

It might not have been what Diana wanted for her sons, but this was a part of their royal inheritance and they were starting to revel in it. One of her relations said, 'She is not happy with the arrangement, but she accepts that this is the reality of separation.'

Diana was on surer ground when William and Harry were delivered back to her care on the fifth day of Christmas. It was now time for the Caribbean break she had set her mind on. Travelling first class and at a cost of £7,000 in airline tickets, the princes and their mother flew to the island of Nevis via Antigua. Accompanying them were Catherine Soames, her son Harry, and four Personal Protection Officers from Scotland Yard.

The princess was thrilled to be reunited with her sons and, without Charles there to upset and irritate her, the holiday was a great success. While the Prince of Wales was braving the freezing cold to go out painting on the Sandringham estate and attending services at the local church, his sons were climbing palm trees and swimming in the tropical sea.

They were installed in the Montpelier Plantation Inn, a former slave plantation set in sixty acres. Diana mixed informally with the other guests, joining them for barbecues and evenings lubricated by rum punches.

It was the daytimes that gave her most pleasure, however. They were spent on a deserted beach, with a picnic lunch prepared for them by the hotel. William and Harry quickly made friends with the owners' children. They played cricket and splashed around on their boogie boards, the half-sized surf boards she had bought for them at Harrods.

One day Harry discovered some giant toads lurking in the undergrowth and, having caught a dozen of them, devised a game of toad racing. A course was made out of sticks and palm leaves, the children were each given one to hold, and the creatures were let loose, urged on by screams of laughter.

In the fine royal tradition of the turf, William and Harry insisted on betting on the outcome with the money their mother had given them to buy drinks with. But there were no rich pickings to be had in the Nevis Derby. As soon as they were released, the toads unsportingly hopped back into the bushes.

Diana was too squeamish to handle the toads, but that did not detract from her fun. This was exactly the kind of holiday she wanted after the traumas of the past few months. The only sour note, as far as the princes were concerned, were the photographers. Every morning Diana held a twenty-minute photocall, having been persuaded by her bodyguards that there was really no alternative but to cooperate if she was going to have any chance of being left alone for the rest of the day. William and Harry were learning that being around their mother was one long photocall.

Wherever they went, there were always the cameramen, and often as many as a hundred were waiting for them. They were there in March when Diana again took them skiing in Lech.

And they were out in force at Thorpe Park, the Disneyland-style funfair just off the western section of the M-25 motorway that rings London. William and Harry, dressed in jeans and baseball caps and with butler Paul Burrell's sons in tow, were taken for a spin in a giant teacup, went rushing down Thunder River in dinghies and buried their faces in their hands as they careered down Loggers Leap, one of Britain's highest flume rides.

The pictures of a water-drenched Diana were among the most enchanting ever taken and this appearance of normality, of the two princes out with their mother and enjoying themselves just like millions of other youngsters, was regarded as a great public relations coup for the princess. The fact that they were filmed and photographed throughout, however, indicated just how far removed they were from the normal experiences of childhood. They were royal showpieces, forever the centre of attention. But that, too, was part of their training, albeit of a very different kind from the one they received at Sandringham.

There was no respite for Diana, either. If anything, the separation had only increased the interest in her, with a heavy emphasis on her romantic entanglements. With Hewitt and then Gilbey out of the way, she took up with Oliver Hoare, a dealer in Oriental art and a married man. To little credit but great embarrassment, it was discovered that she had made hundreds of nuisance telephone calls to his home after he ended their affair in order to save his marriage.

The relationship would have another, fatal consequence for the princess. For it was Hoare, worried that his visits to Kensington Palace were being logged by Scotland Yard, who put the idea into her head that she would be better off without her official bodyguards. Had they still been employed, these highly trained police officers might very well have prevented the tragedy in Paris. Ken Wharfe called it 'a decision which, I truly believe, resulted in her death'.

At the time, though, Diana saw their dismissal as a way of reclaiming the freedom she had surrendered when she married Charles. It was a false hope. There was no chance of a normal life for the most famous and photographed woman in the world and no sanctuary for her to retreat to – her brother, Earl Spencer, refused her the house she wanted on the Althorp estate because he didn't want his own family disrupted by the Diana circus.

When she took William and Harry to theme parks – Thorpe Park, Alton Towers and Disney World in Florida – the visits were well-planned operations which did away with queuing or any need for preparation on her part. And when she tried to do something on a whim it usually ended in farce.

On the spur of the moment Diana once announced that she wanted to go to Marseille 'the ordinary way'. She told Wharfe, 'I want to queue with my passport – and no SOA for me.' SOA is the Southside Of Airport at Heathrow reserved for VIPs and private jets.

Her PPO explained that they would have to be at the airport an hour and a half early. She agreed. But as their departure time approached, Diana said that she was having her hair done at three and couldn't leave when they had planned. Wharfe said, 'But you wanted to be ordinary.' She replied, 'I must have my hair done.' He said, 'We'll miss the plane.' They ended up SOA-ing it. Wharfe commented afterwards, 'So much for living like the rest of us.'

On a holiday in the Bahamas Diana objected to her PPOs having a better villa than the one she was staying in with Kate Menzies. 'Who's paying for this – it's the taxpayer, isn't it?' she furiously informed her bodyguards. As politely as possible, they pointed that they were only there because she was there. But what really annoyed her was that William and Harry and their friends, Andrew Charlton and Harry Soames, much preferred to be off playing with the PPOs than sitting around on the beach watching their mother sunbathe. A further cause of irritation, according to Ken Wharfe's interpretation, was that the cameramen had managed to get a picture of the princes but had failed to spot the princess 'who was lying on the beach practically naked, hoping for a photo to be taken'.

There is no doubt that William and Harry enjoyed their holidays with their mother. They told their friends so afterwards. But they found the constant conflict between the private and the public and the way their mother veered between the two perplexing and at times perturbing. After a spell with Diana they were always glad to get back to the seemingly immutable routine of royal life. William, especially, soon made it clear that he preferred the protective peace of Balmoral and Sandringham to the flash of places like Disney World. That brought him more into his father's orbit.

Never able to hold his own in the rough house of emotional combat, Charles had been reduced to a state of near collapse by the break-up and in a fit of incapacitating self-pity told his lawyer, Lord Goodman, 'I have nothing to live for.' The first thing he did after the separation was drive to Highgrove. Diana had declared, 'My main concern is for the boys. As far as possible I want everything to seem the same when they come here.' The prince was having none of that. He barred from the house those members of staff, including Paul Burrell, who were going to work for her at Kensington Palace. He then shovelled all her possessions into one of the spare bedrooms and locked the door.

Within a month he had stripped out the decor chosen by Diana assisted by the South African Dudley Poplak, and replaced it with a scheme designed by Robert Kime. When Diana came to collect her things in early January, Poplak went with her. They looked at the new decorations and remarked, 'You can see this is an old man's room.'

Others saw it differently. With all trace of Diana expunged, down to the last photograph, an ageing weight was lifted from Charles's spirits. Having his sons to himself from time to time certainly helped. A member of his staff observed, 'Before, the princess took the boys over totally and Charles never got a chance to get a relationship with them as she manipulated their time.' That situation had now been resolved. As a part of the deal thrashed out at the separation, Charles was now able to spend more time with his sons and he delighted in the opportunity. His valet, Michael Fawcett, told the Highgrove staff over dinner one evening, 'Prince Charles is doing really well and is very positive. He feels that now that he has the boys to himself it is much better and he is getting on really well with them. And they are getting closer to him.'

At last able to set his own agenda and carry it through without being made to change it at the last minute, he set about introducing first William and then Harry to the works of Shakespeare, of which he is such a fan.

'Shakespeare,' he explained, 'had this incredible insight into the human psyche. He confronts us so often with such eternal truths, such blunt reminders of the flaws in our personalities, and of the mess which we so often make of our lives.

'Time and again in Shakespeare's characters we recognise elements in ourselves. Othello's jealousy, Hamlet's indecision, Macbeth's ambition are all horribly familiar.'

They were characteristics that Diana had recognised in Charles. But it was Henry V, another much criticised Prince of Wales, that Charles most closely identified with. 'For someone in my position it's someone closer, perhaps, than other characters in Shakespeare. '

Trying to persuade his sons to share his enthusiasm was not easy, not in the beginning. He tried to make them watch a video of Kenneth Branagh's *Henry V*, 'but they were only keen to replay the gory bits, such as the Duke of York's death', he complained.

Slowly he managed to win them round. In 1993 he took the eleven-year-old William to see a Royal Shakespeare Company production of *The Tempest*. Charles recalled, 'That was his first and I was really worried about how he would take it. The thing is to choose the right play and *The Tempest* was by far the best – he enjoyed it enormously because it has such wonderful special effects. And the great thing was that the school had got him going on it so that he knew much more about it than I did.'

That same year he took Harry, then aged eight, to see *A Midsummer Night's Dream*. 'I was thrilled that he enjoyed it as much as William did,' he said.

As a further addition to their education, he invited the poet, Ted Hughes, to Highgrove. 'I have a Poet Laureate who I'm very keen on, a marvellous man,' he said.

That Hughes was suspected of driving his first wife, Sylvia Plath, to the grave was something the prince chose to ignore. He was interested only in the poet's talent, not in a private life which in those troubled times might have been seen as a metaphor for his own. As Charles recounted, 'He had a wonderful poetry reading session the other night. William has got a marvellous feel for language. He's very good at English and reads poetry quite beautifully without quite realising it – absolutely intuitively. I find it very moving listening to him. By the end of it you're begging him to read more.' Many boys of that age would have resented having culture rammed down their throats in such a way, but William enjoyed the experience and the attention his father was giving him.

This was an area in which Diana could add very little. She had once declared, 'I want them to lead from the heart, not the head,' and what she excelled at was giving comfort and affection. She was deeply angered, therefore, when she learnt how close her sons were becoming to another woman.

It wasn't Camilla who so exercised the princess, not in this instance. Diana had made it quite plain that she would not countenance a relationship of any sort whatsoever between Camilla and her sons. Charles acquiesced to her demand and stuck to the agreement until 1997. It would have been a disastrous PR move to have done otherwise. He was in trouble enough as it was when, in January, 1993, the transcript of a taped telephone conversation he had had with Mrs Parker Bowles was published. Promptly named 'Camillagate', it exposed the prince's risible wish to become a tampon. Diana was shocked and told her private secretary, Patrick Jephson, 'God, Patrick, a Tampax, that's sick.' Most people agreed with her, and Camilla's son Tom had to face a gauntlet of taunts at Eton from boys reading extracts from the tapes in silly voices. It was a forerunner of what William would have to endure two years later after Diana's *Panorama* interview.

But that was for the future. What concerned Diana then was the arrival of Tiggy Legge-Bourke in her sons' lives. She felt that her maternal role was being usurped.

Charles hired the jolly twenty-nine-year-old with a voice like a hunting horn a few days after William and Harry returned from Disney World in the summer of 1993. She was ostensibly employed as a £20,000-a-year aide to Charles's private secretary, Commander Richard Aylard, but her real duty was to help look after the princes when they were staying with their father.

Diana's private secretary, Patrick Jephson, recalled how Tiggy 'immediately became an object of curiosity and suspicion for the princess and of course an innocent target for much of her unhappiness about the rest of the world'. She was furious when Harry was photographed sitting on Tiggy's knee. All her fears seemed to be confirmed when Tiggy tactlessly said that William and Harry 'regard me as something of surrogate mother'. Diana complained to friends that she didn't need a stand-in father to help her when her sons were with her, 'So why does he need a substitute mother when they are with him?'

She fired off a series of angry letters to Charles, demanding a clarification of Tiggy's role and what the nature of her contact with the boys would be. That William and Harry were clearly very fond of a girl one of the Highgrove staff described as 'a thumping great Sloane' only exacerbated Diana's belief that her estranged husband was deliberately trying to push her into the wings, and she ended up convincing herself that Tiggy and Charles were having an affair.

Tiggy was initially indifferent to the princess's hostility. Her family home was Glanusk Park in Wales. Her maternal grandmother, Peggy, was married to Viscount De L'Isle, who won the Victoria Cross for bravery in the Second World War and served as Governor-General of Australia. Her brother, Harry, was a page-of-honour to the Queen, and both her mother Shan and aunt Victoria had served as ladies-in-waiting to Princess Anne. Those aristocratic connections ensured that she was comfortable in royal circles and, like so many of her class, regarded Diana with suspicion. As far as she was concerned, her job was simply 'the nursery maid, guv', and Diana could think what she liked.

At Balmoral and Sandringham she brought a breezy bounce to the often stifling proceedings, climbing trees, wading through mud, always laughing and forever popping out for a cigarette with the estate secretaries. Refreshingly free of any airs and graces, she turned down the Queen's invitation to stay in the castle when she visited Balmoral and opted instead for a cottage on the estate. William and Harry had never had a nanny like her before and one courtier observed, 'They absolutely adore her.' She had once owned her own nursery school called Mrs Tiggywinkle's after the character in the Beatrix Potter books (hence her nickname), and was the only person who seemed to be able to impose any discipline on the ever more impish Harry. When she went to visit him at Ludgrove he would run down the drive and leap into her arms.

Unlike William, Harry had adapted well to the school's routine. Like all the boys, he was allowed to create his own garden and his was a spectacular confection of shells brought from Highgrove and which is still there. He was not overly academic, as the exam marks that were put on the notice confirmed. But he was in all the sports teams, which ensured his popularity, and he soon formed his own gang of friends who included Charlie Henderson and Ed Birrell, whose father worked in the City.

When Diana turned up to watch him play football, the other parents made a point of treating her like any other mother. On one occasion, however, she rather spoilt the pretence by striking up a conversation with one of the fathers on the touchline and telling him, 'All Charles's friends are terrible snobs,' adding that she was going to the opera that evening 'to watch a story about another stupid prince'.

She was careful, though, not to make that kind of disparaging remark within earshot of her sons. Like Charles, she was anxious not to add to the problems the separation had already visited on them. Both parents wanted to bring at least a semblance of harmony back into their lives.

Harry proved the more resilient of the brothers. Possessed of a natural equilibrium, he seemed better able to ride the shock waves. After the confusion of being away from home for the first time had passed, he had quickly settled in. Settling down was another matter. On one night he got into a fight in his dormitory. While trying to thump his adversary, he inadvertently hit his security bleeper. His PPO, convinced that a kidnap attempt was in progress, burst in brandishing his gun. 'We loved that,' a contemporary remembered. 'It was the talk of the school.'

It was a rare incident. Harry was one of those children who had the happy knack of not being found out and, apart from being caught talking in chapel and being punished by being deprived of his 'grub' for a week, he had a more or less trouble-free time at Ludgrove. One of Harry's chums summed him up. 'He's quite cheeky, quite different from his brother, not so polite, but rather more fun.'

As that comment suggested, the mischievous exuberance that had been a mark of William's infancy had been worn down by the battles he had witnessed between his parents. He became alternatively attention-seeking, then quiet and introverted. At Kensington Palace he would shout at the staff to do things for him and then go and lock himself in the bathroom, sometimes for hours.

That mixed-up attitude did not make him popular at school and he became involved in a number of fights, not all of which he won. Repeating what he had said at Mrs Mynors', he threatened one opponent, 'If you give me a hard time, I'll get my dad to cut your head off.' After a fight in the lavatories with a boy he accused of sneaking on him to the teachers, he was hauled up before the headmaster and warned as to his future conduct.

More usually, though, it was the search for comfort rather than the prospect of punishment that brought William and Harry to Gerald Barber's study. The headmaster and his wife, Janet, were well versed in dealing with their pupils' domestic problems. The Duchess of York's half-brother, Andrew Ferguson, had also been caught up in a family scandal while he was at Ludgrove when their father was discovered to be attending a sleazy massage parlour. His mother, Sue, said, 'The Barbers are marvellous. They treat all the boys like one big family. They are very supportive.' Harry, in particular, liked popping in to see them, if for no other reason than to play with their Springer spaniels, one of which had only three legs.

There was a limit to what the school could accomplish, however. No teacher, no matter how sympathetic, could resolve the problems William and Harry were facing. That was up to the boys and their parents and, given the lingering hostility between Charles and Diana, that was no easy matter.

In her resolve to give her sons as rounded an upbringing as possible, Diana took William on a visit to a shelter for the homeless in London. He had seen their plight on television when he was curled up in bed beside his mother at Kensington Palace and asked, 'Why don't they have a house and bed like us?' She now deemed it time to see the squalor and misery at first hand. It was important, she explained, that he saw a different side of life and learnt that 'not everyone is rich, has four holidays a year, speaks Standard English and has a Range Rover'.

Her friend Vivienne Parry explained, 'Diana was brought up in the tradition of noblesse oblige, and with an aristocratic upbringing comes an obligation to do a bit of good. She was determined that William and Harry shouldn't have a life of total privilege and should see the other side of life, pretty sanitised, but vital experience all the same.'

The Royal Family did not approve. To them it carried an eerie and unwelcome echo of the visit paid by the Prince of Wales, later the Duke of Windsor, to the unemployed steel-workers of South Wales during the Great Depression when he famously declared, 'Something must be done.' He abdicated a month later, pitching the monarchy into crisis and disrepute.

Diana was about to perform an abdication of her own. On 3 December 1993, she announced that she was withdrawing from public life. It was a decision forced on her by her brother-in-law, the Queen's private secretary Robert Fellowes, who did not want her doing and saying things that might rebound on the Royal Family.

Taking herself out of public life did not take her out of the public eye, however, and once again it was her behaviour, rather than anything the Queen said in her Christmas broadcast, which dominated the Yuletide news.

Diana had learnt from her mistake the previous year and had written to the Queen, asking to be allowed to join her sons at Sandringham 'for a couple of days'. The Queen agreed.

It proved to be an unhappy decision. Diana arrived on Christmas Eve and spent most of that first night in Charles's suite of rooms, which he had vacated to make way for her while he was put up in a small bed in the old nursery. On Christmas morning she dissolved into tears, which greatly upset William and Harry.

After morning service at St Mary Magdalene church and before the traditional Christmas lunch, she suddenly decided she couldn't stick it any more and dramatically announced she was leaving. That provoked yet more tears from William and Harry. As she drove away, Princess Margaret remarked witheringly, 'She'd better put her foot down and get through those gates before the Press leave or they won't see her go.'

No one was sad to see the back of her. With Diana gone, the tension lifted. And while this was definitely not the kind of Christmas they wanted, even her sons were able to enjoy what was left of their 'family' holiday once they had got over the bitter disappointment of her departure.

It was nevertheless a worrying pattern that was being imposed on their lives and the Queen was growing ever more concerned at the effect it was having on her grandsons. She complained to Charles that she was not seeing enough of them and that they would benefit from spending more time with their royal relations. The prince agreed and they started making more trips to Norfolk and Scotland, where they took over Birkhall when the Queen Mother was not in residence. They also spent a lot of time with Hugh van Cutsem and his wife, Emilie, on their estate near Sandringham. Their son, Edward, although nearly a decade older, became a valued companion of the princes, taking them out on the rabbit shoots they so enjoyed. A member of the household said, 'They would have liked their mother there, but as that wasn't possible they had no alternative but to make the best of the situation.'

They soon discovered that there were certain compensations to be had from having separated parents. It meant they got to go skiing twice a year, to Lech again with their mother, and then back to Klosters with their father. In the summer they went to Spain with Diana and then up to Scotland with their father.

This four-holidays-a-year lifestyle was reflected in their toys. With their interest in mechanised speed whetted by their trip to the European Grand Prix at Donington with Diana, they acquired RAC national karting licences and their own 50 mph Zip Karts, costing £1,104 each. Their father also bought them Yamaha mini motorbikes. But no matter how fast they drove, they could never outpace the scandal following in their wake.

In 1994 their father was back on the front pages after he admitted to adultery in an interview with Jonathan Dimbleby. Then James Hewitt gave a lurid and over-romanticised account of his affair with their mother in a book entitled *Princess in Love*, written by Anna Pasternak.

'I was absolutely devastated when this book appeared because I trusted him and because, again, I worried about the reaction on my children,' Diana said. 'And then, when it did arrive, the first thing I did was rush down to talk to my children.' At Ludgrove William presented her with a box of chocolates and said, 'Mummy, I think you've been hurt. These are to make you smile again.'

It was William who was finding it hardest to muster a smile by this stage. Diana had been to Ludgrove to try and explain 'without resentment or any anger' why his parents' marriage had collapsed, but as she admitted, 'He's a child that's a deep thinker and we won't know for a few years how it's gone in.'

The staffs at Highgrove and Sandringham were quicker to draw their conclusions. They were becoming increasingly concerned by William's behaviour. One senior member of the household said, 'He is petulant and moody, while Harry is happy and laughing. It's a bit of a worry.'

In his final year at Ludgrove he became a monitor and, to add to the salver he had won for the clay pigeon shooting, he got his colours for representing the school at cross-country running. He also did well enough in his Common Entrance exam to pass into Eton. But trying to carry his family's distress on his young shoulders was a weighty burden. It was not a responsibility he wanted.

ELEVEN

Life at Eton

Prince William got off to a difficult start at Eton.

On the day he arrived at the College in September 1995, the front pages were picking over the revelation that the England rugby captain Will Carling had followed Hewitt, Gilbey and Hoare into his mother's private quarters at Kensington Palace.

Two months into his first 'half', as Eton call their terms, his mother gave her explosive interview to the BBC's *Panorama* programme. In it she admitted her affair with Hewitt, made her comment about 'three people in this marriage' and then questioned his father's ability to live up to his future role as king.

To crown it all, by term's end his about-to-be demoted mother was at war with his royal grandmother, the Queen.

No wonder that within a few months, as the family rows became increasingly heated and his mother ever more distressed, William would be questioning whether he wanted to be king at all.

On top of all that, he had the problem of settling into a large and intimidating school where even the pedigree of princes is treated with a haughty irreverence refined over five centuries. He was a new boy in a school of 1,200 pupils who were either very clever or very well connected and often both.

No special concessions were made for this confused thirteen-year-old. In his first fortnight he had to learn the names of all the housemasters and the complex workings of the school where tradition is part of everyday ritual. He had to adjust to wearing a morning coat and master the rudiments of Eton's unique argot in which teachers are called beaks, punishments are peonas, and those who play cricket are known not as batsmen or bowlers but 'dry bobs'. At the end of his first fortnight he was tested on his knowledge of these arcane rites by the senior boys.

It is a bewildering experience and William made a hash of it. He had signed his name in the wrong place in the entrance book. Then, as he looked at the form, the confused future Defender of the Faith and titular head of the Church of England had been forced to ask his father, 'What religion?' The Prince of Wales replied firmly, 'C. of E.'

He was not the only new boy to make such mistakes, but history has a way of detailing such minutiae when the miscreant is a member of the Royal Family.

What made it especially gruelling for William was the spotlight of unwelcome attention his parents commanded. It made him the butt of any number of sly comments from the older boys, for whom the tribulations of the Waleses had become a source of ribald humour. No boy likes to be singled out, but it was impossible for him to escape into the shadows of anonymity.

'Eton was not like Ludgrove,' Prince Charles admitted to me. 'At Ludgrove everyone had been very protective.'

At prep school the newspapers had been banned and the headmaster, Gerald Barber, had on one occasion ordered the school bus through country lanes to spare William the sight of newsagents' billboards. No such consideration was afforded him at Eton. There was no way the College was going to attempt to isolate 1,200 well-educated young men, some of them nineteen years old, to protect the sensibilities of one lowly 'tit', as new boys are traditionally called. The papers were widely available and all too often they were dominated by the latest episode in the ongoing saga of Di and Charles.

In a rare show of unity, he was delivered to the school that September day by both parents and his brother. It was the relationship between

Carling and Diana that was making the news, however. Carling would later admit, 'I did love the princess. I was flattered by the princess's attention. I'd defy any man to say he wouldn't be.' At the time, though, he was steadfastly insisting that nothing untoward had taken place. His wife, Julia, formed her own opinion and left her husband later that month.

No young man in the throes of adolescence would welcome such attention and there was worse to come in November, after Diana's *Panorama* interview. It was watched by over twenty million people, including most of Eton. In it she expressed her doubts about Charles's ability to deal with the demands that would be placed upon him if he became king. It was a salvo aimed at the foundations of hereditary monarchy. By implication, she was suggesting that the throne should skip a generation and pass to her elder son. That was a responsibility that the untried William Wales, at the bottom of the pecking order in a new school, was nowhere near confident enough to endorse.

Diana had been secretly planning her broadcast since August, when she had taken William and Harry to Colorado to stay in the house owned by film star Goldie Hawn and go white-water rafting on the appropriately named Roaring Fork River. What she had not done was tell her elder son what she had in mind. She also went to great lengths to conceal from the Palace what she was up to. It was Diana herself who opened the Kensington Palace door to her private apartment to the four-man television crew on 5 November – the 390th anniversary of Guy Fawkes's gunpowder plot to blow up the Houses of Parliament and the Queen's predecessor, James VI and I. For all her determination to go ahead regardless, she was fearful of what the reaction would be, particularly on the part of William. Her qualms were well founded.

William was at Eton when the story of the forthcoming interview broke in the newspapers. His housemaster, Andrew Gailey, telephoned Diana and told her that it was imperative she came to the school to explain to her son, face to face, what she was intending to do.

She refused, asking, 'Is that really necessary?'

The next day Gailey telephoned again and more or less ordered Diana down the M4 motorway to Eton to see her son. The princess agreed reluctantly but the meeting proved to be a very short one. She told William that it would contain nothing controversial and that he would be proud of her. Before he had a chance to ask any embarrassing questions she left. Their conversation lasted barely five minutes.

William watched the broadcast in his housemaster's study. He was utterly distraught by what he saw and heard.

He viewed it as an unwarranted attack on his father with whom he was now far closer than he had been in the bad days leading up the separation. He was also incensed by her admission of her love for James Hewitt, which went against the code of royal discretion which had been drummed into him since he was little.

Diana later shamefacedly told me, 'I shouldn't have brought it up, I should have just left it, but Martin Bashir [the BBC interviewer] insisted.'

It was an excuse that did not impress William. A wedge had been driven between mother and son. One of his Eton school friends recalled, 'He was absolutely furious with his mother. He couldn't believe what she'd done. He wouldn't talk to her for days afterwards.'

Adding to his discomfort was the reaction of his fellow Etonians. Some came from families who knew the Waleses personally and made it clear where their loyalty lay, which was usually with Charles. Most had watched the broadcast and many started imitating Diana's doe-eyed performance, fluttering their eyelashes and inventing their own monologues laced with crude schoolboy humour as they talked into make-believe cameras. The school that has produced eighteen prime ministers was giving what Old Etonian Alan Clark, diarist and one-time Defence Minister, called 'an early introduction to human cruelty'.

Harry was spared the worst of such problems. He was still too young to take in the full implications of what his mother had said and Ludgrove, where Diana had been to see him before the broadcast, provided him with a protective cushion. Eton was a different matter. William had no alternative but to stand up for himself as best he could.

Echoing her husband's concern, Diana later told me, 'I don't think William is finding Eton that easy.' For that she must shoulder much of the responsibility.

It had been Diana's initial suggestion that William and his brother be sent to this most venerable of British boarding schools, and Charles had agreed. 'It was very much a joint decision, one we sat down and talked about and took together,' she told me.

As far as Diana was concerned, this was the most natural of educational progressions. Her brother had been to Eton, and so had her father.

For Charles, however, this was a departure from what had become the royal norm. Like his father before him, he had been educated at Gordonstoun, the robust establishment in the north of Scotland. Noted for its cold showers and early morning runs, it was the very antithesis of the cultural and social refinement of Eton.

Philip, an exiled European princeling without funds, had been among its first dozen pupils when it was founded 492 years after Eton in 1934. He had thrived in its Spartan outdoor environment, rising to head boy, and felt that Charles and, later, Andrew and Edward, would benefit likewise. Philip explained, 'When Charles first went to school, one of the problems we were confronted with was, "How do you select a prep school?" In the end he went to Cheam, where I had been.'

For that same, reason Charles had then been dispatched to Gordonstoun. 'But this is something better understood in this country than almost anywhere else – that people frequently do what their fathers have done. People say, "Oh, he's gone because his father went," and there's no further argument.'

The explanation was nowhere near as straightforward as Philip tried to make out. From the moment of his marriage to the future Queen, Philip had been thwarted at every turn by Palace courtiers who regarded him as a bumptious upstart who the Queen Mother's niece, Mrs Margaret Rhodes, described as 'a foreign interloper out for the goodies'. He was even denied the right to call his children and their descendants by his own surname – as a result of an order issued by the then Prime Minister Sir Winston Churchill,

William is called William Wales and not William Mountbatten. His attempts to modernise the Royal Family were treated just as dismissively by the old guard. And most of them, as Philip sourly noted, were Old Etonians.

Not surprisingly, Philip quickly developed a dislike bordering on loathing for the well-educated, coolly arrogant men wearing Eton's black and pale blue striped old school tie who had reduced him, as he bitterly observed, to a 'bloody amoeba'. The perennial outsider, he made no effort to ingratiate or integrate – calling one Eton-educated civil servant a 'silly Whitehall twit' was hardly likely to win him friends or influence. Nor was he prepared to send his son to the College that had produced so many of his Palace enemies.

The Queen's great-aunt, Princess Alice of Athlone, had observed, 'I'm sorry the prince isn't going to Eton. He would make many more contacts there, which would stay with him through life.' The Queen Mother agreed. She came from a family of Etonians and was herself an honorary Old Etonian. But when she voiced her opinion that Charles would benefit from being at the school just across the River Thames from the family home at Windsor it only served to harden Philip's resolve. The two never hit it off (the Queen Mother often referred to her son-in-law as 'The Hun') and he had no intention of being dictated to by a woman he regarded as a meddlesome busybody.

It was therefore for reasons less to do with education than with Philip's disdain for the Etonian caste system that Charles was dispatched into windswept isolation on the coast of the Moray Firth.

It proved to be a thoroughly inappropriate choice. Even Dr Kurt Hahn, the Jewish educationalist who founded Gordonstoun after fleeing the persecution of Nazi Germany, had nursed doubts as to whether his school was really suitable for Charles and he was proved right. Introverted and over-sensitive, the prince had a sorry time of it. He was lonely, out of place, homesick and bullied. He later declared, 'I had a dream that I was going to escape and hide in the forest, in a place where no one could find me, so I wouldn't have to go back to school. I hated the institution, just as I hated leaving home. When you lead a perfectly agreeable existence you don't want to go back to cold showers at seven in the morning and a quick run before breakfast.'

Years later the merest mention of Gordonstoun was enough to make him shudder. Diana recalled, 'All I had to do was remind him of all those ghastly cold showers.' He had no intention of inflicting a similar unhappiness on his own sons.

The person who finally persuaded Charles that Eton would be the best alternative was Dr Eric Anderson. He had been a tutor at Gordonstoun when Charles was there and was one of the few teachers with the perception to appreciate that there was more to the timorous Prince of Wales than an ancient title. He ran the small discussion group where Charles first learnt to express his opinions – something Philip rarely allowed him to do at home. He was also responsible for casting Charles in the title role of Shakespeare's *Macbeth* in the school play. Philip was dismissive of his son's performance but most people agreed with Anderson's assessment that Charles had acquitted himself with distinction.

Always in search of an older mentor he could turn to for encouragement and guidance, Charles continued to seek his advice in the years that followed. (It was Anderson who Charles called in as a mediator in the last desperate days before his separation from Diana.) With a detour via Fettes, the Scottish public school where he was charged with the education of the future prime minister Tony Blair, Anderson had gone on to become a successful headmaster of Eton. And when he told Charles that Eton, with its outstanding academic record and its broad base of societies and clubs that catered from everything from hunting with beagles and cheese tasting to jazz and Japanese, would be ideal for William, the prince was convinced.

Diana was delighted. So, naturally enough, was the Queen Mother. The Queen was quietly supportive. She had never been fully convinced by the Gordonstoun experiment and, despite having agreed to send her three sons to her husband's alma mater, much preferred the company of Etonians. Prince Philip harrumphed his disapproval but Charles took no notice. There was little empathy between them – when Charles was younger he had kept a photograph on his desk in Kensington Palace on which was written, 'I was not made to follow my father's footsteps.' William accepted with the stoic fortitude of youth a decision he had no say in.

On Anderson's suggestion, William's name was put down for Manor House, which according to Eton's esoteric rules is known as ALHG after the initials of its housemaster, Dr Andrew Gailey. An Ulsterman with a passionate interest in history, he had graduated from Queen's University and then completed his postgraduate doctorate at Cambridge. In 1987 he had published a book about his troubled homeland entitled *Ireland and the Death of Kindness*, which Charles had found 'thought-provoking'. Anderson called him 'young, bright and a real live wire'.

Manor is situated in an old Georgian building. The Iron Duke of Wellington was educated there and a portrait of the victor of Waterloo still adorns the main hallway, despite the half-hearted protests from the parents of two French boys who were there with William. As heir-in-line to the throne, William was in a unique position, even by the lordly standards of a school founded in 1440 by King Henry VI where the black coats the boys are required to wear date from the funeral in 1820 of its benefactor, King George III.

Gailey was determined, however, to grant him no special favours. He held the firm belief that the prince must be allowed to develop in his own way and at his own speed, without any obvious helping hand from his housemaster. That extended to his very presence at the school where parents had to stump up £12,500 a year in fees, not counting the extras that always seemed to run into several thousand more. Under Anderson's reforms, neither wealth, a long family association with the College or ancient lineage was enough to gain admission. Academic competence was now an essential requirement and William had had to pass the competitive entrance examination like every other applicant. And once there, he had to fall in with the conventions and routines like everybody else.

His typical day began with breakfast in the house dining room at 7.45 a.m., followed by chapel on Mondays, Wednesdays and Fridays – the half-hour service was C. of E., as William quickly learnt – beginning at 8.30. Lessons were from 9 a.m. through until 'chambers' at 11.20, when boys

Diana and seven-year-old Harry come down the Depth Charge –
a hair-raising ride on inflated rubber rings at Thorpe Park (*UK Press*)

A winter walk for William in Kensington Gardens, with Nanny Barbara Barnes pushing a disgruntled Harry wearing William's cast-off playsuit (*Rex Features*)

Playing soldiers: (above) Harry, daubed in camouflage paint, rides in a light tank during a visit to the barracks of the Light Dragoons in Hanover, Germany, in 1993 (*PA Photos*); (below) William, dressed in camouflage, cheekily takes aim during a visit to the Royal Windsor army barracks (*Rex Features*)

William getting a piggyback ride from Tony Blackman,
one of his first personal protection officers (*Rex Features*)

(Above) William sharing a joke with protection officer Ken Wharfe during a visit to Thorpe Park (*UK Press*); (left) William, now a schoolboy at Eton but still with the ever-present protection officers. This time, Christopher Tarr (*PA Photos*)

(Above) Tiggy Legge-Bourke laughs as Harry films her with a video camera at Cirencester Park Polo Club in 1997 (*PA Photos*); (below) Harry and Mark Dyer watch an air display while brother William hides his face from the cameras on the day that the report into the death of their mother in France was published (*PA Photos*)

Harry with family friend Tara Palmer-Tomkinson in Klosters, Switzerland, during a half-term break with his father and William in February 1994 (*Alpha*)

Harry holding on to his father's hand while looking at the floral tributes outside the gates of Balmoral, four days after their mother's death in 1997 (*PA Photos*)

could go and wait outside School Hall if they needed to see one of the beaks about their work. More lessons followed at 11.45 and continued until lunch back at Manor, where he sat with boys from his own year with the housemaster looking down from the top table.

After lunch came games on the playing fields where the Duke of Wellington said the Battle of Waterloo was won. Eton is a football school (the word 'soccer' is derived from As*soc*iation, which is what Eton calls its first eleven) and William was a keen if not exceptionally talented player. There was another period of lessons in the late afternoon, followed by the 'quiet hour' which, in the contrary way typical of Eton, lasted for an hour and a half between 6.15 p.m. and 7.45. Boys who left their house during that time to go to the library or to a tutorial had to sign out. The in-house supper was served at 7.45, followed by prayers at 8.30, when hymns were sometimes sung and any dissertation on religious matters that a boy might have written would be read out. After that came the society meetings (William joined the agriculture one).

In the evenings the boys were allowed into Windsor, but only out of school uniform and never on Saturdays. Fights between 'town and gown' – the local toughs and the Etonians – had long before become too serious for the provocative flaunting of the traditional morning coat.

By 9.30 p.m. William had to be back in his single room. His spare clothes were kept in the ottoman his parents had bought him and which every Eton schoolboy is required to have. He had brought his own curtains, linen and duvet covers. His books were placed on the wooden desk called a 'burry'. His walls were decorated with posters, including one of model Claudia Schiffer. He had little time to look at them. As he admitted, he found the first few weeks 'exhausting', not least because, in keeping with Eton's arcane traditions, the timetable varied slightly each day so that the prince often found himself running around the town in the effort to keep to his schedule. There was no excuse for slacking. The pressure was applied right from the beginning.

That left him little time to worry about the state of Diana's mental health. In this all-male and highly academic society, 'rips' (when the top of the page is ripped to show bad work) and 'showups' (meaning good work to be shown) took priority over his mother's tears. There was also the business of making new friends to keep him occupied. Several of his contemporaries at Ludgrove had gone on to Eton but they were all in different houses. William nevertheless managed to stay in touch with Andrew Charlton and Edward Corry-Reid. Another good friend from his Ludgrove days was William Rickards, the son of an Old Harrovian banker. Rickards's mother, Harriet, had once been the girlfriend of Mark Birley, owner of Annabel's in Mayfair, the only nightclub the Prince of Wales has ever visited. They formed the nucleus of William's circle and, like young men everywhere, their minds (when their work load allowed them the chance – and sometimes when it didn't) were becoming increasingly preoccupied with girls.

When Charles was at Gordonstoun he was allowed no contact whatsoever with members of the opposite sex. To keep the royal virtue intact, the usual sources of female companionship were deliberately closed off. There were no dances with the local girls' schools, and upon his arrival the number of parental visits allowed in the year was deliberately reduced to limit the opportunity for meeting younger sisters. He managed to slip under the wire only once. On a rare and heavily supervised excursion into the nearby town of Elgin to take part in a concert, he met and developed a crush on one of the local girls. Charles called her 'my *first* girlfriend', but the romance never progressed beyond a furtive kiss; when Charles suggested that she be allowed to play the part of Lady Macbeth in the Gordonstoun production of the play, the idea was promptly vetoed by the headmaster, Robert Chew.

It was an old-fashioned, repressed and, by modern standards, unnatural upbringing which explains why, in the years to come, Charles was so ill at ease in the company of women from outside his immediate family. The prince recognised the fault and resolved that no such restrictions would be forced on his sons. A traditionalist in so many other things, he wanted them to learn to mix with women in a normal way, and on his first 'long leave' (Eton-speak for half-term) William was allowed to attend the Fiesta Ball at the Hammersmith Palais in west London.

This gathering of well-heeled youngsters from the top fee-paying schools in the Home Counties had been started by Bedales-educated Justin Etzin, whose American father founded the Brother international industrial empire. Etzin called it 'an unrivalled but most importantly safe end enjoyable party for the fashionable young of today'. No alcohol was allowed, but most of the youngsters had managed to imbibe something before they arrived. Those who were there that October night remember it as a 'giant pulling ground', where dozens of mini-skirted girls and young boys gauchely puffing away on the cigarettes they had smuggled in tentatively circled each other before piling on to the dance floor in a pulsating frenzy of pubescent hormones.

Charles had paid the £20 for a ticket for his son, who turned up wearing black tie, only to discard his jacket and pull his shirt tails out of his trousers as was the fashion at the time. A host of girls made a predictable beeline for the prince, offering to join him in the balcony for a 'snog'. William had two Police Protection Officers with him, but they were under instructions not to interfere with his enjoyment and simply let him get on with it.

Reporters from the *Sun* had managed to infiltrate the party and reported that William kissed a string of mini-skirted girls who queued up to embrace him and that one had sat on his lap. The following day the newspaper ran an advertisement inviting anyone who had kissed the prince or knew anyone who had to telephone them with the information.

Charles was very upset by what he regarded as this intrusion into his son's private life. He told me, 'William must be allowed to develop without having to look over his shoulder all the time to see if he's being spied on.'

He might almost have been talking about himself, for it was Charles's marriage and his relationship with his estranged wife that continued to attract the largest share of press attention. It wasn't only William who was upset by the *Panorama* interview. So was the Queen. What appalled her most was the criticism Diana levelled at Charles. She saw it as a direct challenge to her dynasty and that, notwithstanding the sympathy she felt for her anguished daughter-in-law, was something she was not prepared to tolerate.

Immediately after the interview Diana flew to Argentina on precisely the kind of ambassadorial role the would-be 'Queen of Hearts' had claimed for herself in the interview. She then went to New York to collect a humanitarian award from America's former Secretary of State, Henry Kissinger.

On her return she was greeted by a stinging letter from her former ally, Princess Margaret, accusing her of letting everyone down and being 'incapable of making even the smallest sacrifice'.

There was worse to follow. In the week before Christmas 1995, she received a handwritten missive from the Queen. It was hand-delivered to Kensington Palace. A similar letter was dispatched to Charles at Highgrove. In these, the Queen expressed her anger and frustration and spelt out her demand 'for an early divorce'.

A Buckingham Palace spokesman stated, 'The Queen has written to both the prince and princess after considering the present situation. It is her view, which is supported by the Duke [of Edinburgh], that an early divorce is desirable. The Prince of Wales has also taken the view that an early divorce is desirable and has made this known to the princess. Obviously the Queen and the Duke will continue to do all they can to support the princess and particularly the children.'

The letters were written in confidence but were leaked almost immediately. Diana took Harry, then aged eleven, to see his hero James Bond in his latest outing in *Goldeneye*. When she returned home to Kensington Palace and turned on *News at Ten* on television she was aghast to see the headline. In a show of family solidarity, the following day she took Harry and William to the Harbour Club in Chelsea to play tennis. But the PR game, with Charles and Diana scoring ever more destructive points against each other, was about to end. The Queen had had enough.

Since the separation Diana had insisted that she had no wish for a legal end to her marriage. That decision had now been taken out of her hands. Faced with the Queen's ultimatum, Diana went to pieces. She couldn't sleep at night and started taking strong sleeping pills. The tears that had never been far from the surface now flowed constantly.

It was while in this unstable state that she rounded on Tiggy Legge-Bourke at the Waleses' staff Christmas party and told her, 'I'm so sorry to hear about your baby,' implying that her sons' companion had been pregnant by Charles.

This was the moment that Tiggy's sang-froid deserted her. Outraged by the insult, she dispatched a solicitors' letter to the princess, requesting an immediate apology and a withdrawal of her 'false allegations'.

Given these untoward circumstances, it was not surprising that Diana felt incapable of facing Christmas with the Windsors. Once again, and despite all the problems of previous years, she was invited to Sandringham. Once again she accepted, only to change her mind a few days later. 'I would have arrived in a BMW and left in a coffin,' she remarked. She chose instead to spend Christmas Day at Kensington Palace, by herself and in tears, before flying off to the K Club in Barbuda in the West Indies with her secretary, Victoria Mendham. William and Harry chose to spend the rest of their holiday in Norfolk.

By then William was running short of patience. He had reached the age when children, in the first stirrings of independence, start to become judgemental of their parents and, when his mother went into one of her moods, courtiers noted that his face took on what they called a 'here we go again' look. The sad truth was that Diana was becoming an embarrassment.

Diana said, 'I keep telling them how lucky they are to have me as a mother,' but admitted, 'They don't seem to appreciate it.' It was meant as a joke, but William wasn't finding it easy to laugh. His first end-of-term report had been approving. The Queen was delighted by his results. She told her husband how intelligent he was, to which Prince Philip snorted, 'He doesn't get that from his mother, does he?'

It was clear, however, that the traumas engulfing his parents were affecting William. The withdrawal into himself, which had been noticed at Ludgrove, was becoming more pronounced. And while he had at last acquired the good manners that his grandmother had so sternly demanded of him when he was little, he was nowhere near as genial or easy-going as he had once been.

Harry, too, was starting to be affected by the emotional cauldron their parents' battles had cast them into. Hardly a day passed without some new snippet of information and misinterpretation making its way into the gossip columns, and even something as simple as the holiday in Klosters where Charles took William and Harry in January was billed as an 'escape from the controversy of the marriage'. According to Diana's friend, Elsa Bowker, 'William and Harry loved Diana very much but they also loved their father and they loved the Queen.' To be tugged, first in one direction, then in another, as they tried to maintain some semblance of balance between the warring parties was causing them enormous strain.

What particularly upset William were the demands his mother was making on his time and attention. Her friend Rosa Monckton, whose lawyer grandfather, Walter, the first Viscount Monckton, had played a pivotal role in the abdication of William's great-great-uncle King Edward VIII, explained Diana's approach. 'She told Prince William, in particular, more than most mothers would have told their children. But she had no choice. She wanted her sons to hear the truth from her, about her life and the people she was seeing, and what they meant to her, rather than read a distorted, exaggerated and frequently untrue version in the tabloid press.'

It was a terrible responsibility to burden a youngster with, no matter how fond of his mother he might be. Vivienne Parry, another friend of Diana, noted, 'I'm not sure she was right to confide in him that way. She probably over-relied on him. He was always pretty level-headed, but it must have been very difficult for him.'

It was with this very much in mind that the Queen had come off the fence and written the letters to Charles and Diana, demanding an end to the marital crisis that had reached a point where it was threatening the future of the monarchy William had been born to inherit.

In February the negotiations at last turned serious. On the 15th Diana had a meeting with the Queen at Buckingham Palace. The Queen, who had never heard of bulimia when she was first told that this was what Diana was suffering from but had since made a detailed study of the ailment, insisted that her deputy private secretary Robin Janvrin be there to take notes because, as she explained, 'bulimics rewrite history in twenty-four hours'.

It proved to be a wise precaution. According to Diana, one of the central questions was whether she would be allowed to continue to call herself 'Her Royal Highness'. She told friends that the Queen wanted her to surrender her honorific, 'and you don't say no to the Queen'. The truth, as it turned out, was quite different.

On 28 February the two women held another meeting, this time with Charles there. The discussions were supposed to be private, but immediately afterwards Diana issued a statement saying that she had agreed to the divorce, that she would continue to be involved in all decisions pertaining to William and Harry – and that under pressure she would be giving up her HRH.

The Queen was furious and immediately countered with a statement of her own. Her press secretary Charles Anson announced, 'The decision to drop the title is the princess's and the princess's alone. It is wrong that the Queen or the prince asked her. I can state categorically that is not true.'

To head off any counter claim by Diana, who had become adept at using the Press she professed to despise to propagate her own version of events, Anson added, 'The Palace does not say something specific on a point like this unless we are absolutely sure of the facts.'

In effect, the Queen was calling her daughter-in-law a liar, which stands as a measure of just how exasperated she had become with the princess's machinations.

Another indication came a few weeks later when Diana telephoned and asked if she could bring William and Harry to tea at Windsor Castle. By carefully arranged agreement, the Duchess of York rang up a few minutes later and asked if she could bring her daughters, Beatrice and Eugenie.

It was the day after the Queen had visited the Scottish town of Dunblane, where sixteen children and their teacher had been shot dead in their classroom by a deranged gunman. The Queen had been deeply moved by the tragedy and had wept when she met the grieving parents. She was in no mood to fall in with what she regarded with good cause as the cynical ploys of her daughters-in-law, and Diana most especially. She agreed to Fergie's visit, because, as she said, 'At least she behaves herself when she is with me.'

Not so Diana. The Queen instructed one of her pages, 'Call back the Princess of Wales and tell her the boys can come – but she cannot.' The Sovereign was at the end of her tether. As one of her courtiers recounted, she said, 'I just can't face Diana. I don't know what she is going to do or say.' She added, 'I just can't take it any more.'

That afternoon the Queen entertained William and Harry, along with Fergie and her two daughters, to tea in the Oak Drawing Room of the ancient castle. Diana was not there.

Nor was she invited to the Queen's seventieth birthday party which, in a break from tradition, she had decided to celebrate with a dinner not at Windsor Castle but at the Waterside Inn in nearby Bray. The story was leaked. The Queen blamed Diana, when the party then had to be moved to Frogmore, a house on the Windsor estate. She angrily declared, 'Thank you, Diana, for ruining another day for me.'

It was against this increasingly bitter background that Diana entered her final divorce negotiations. Dealing with the Royal Family in matters of this sort is never easy. With the weight of the Establishment behind them, they are usually able to outmanoeuvre their adversaries, as the Duchess of York was about to discover. Unable to support her profligate lifestyle and with her in-laws adamant in their refusal to bail her out, she eventually ended up some £4 million in debt. Diana's lawyer, Anthony Julius, used her case as a guide and referred to Fergie as the 'yellow canary', a reference to the birds that coal miners used to take with them underground to give warning of any poisonous gases.

Diana had no intention of being pushed around, however. So emotional in other matters, she revealed a cunning grasp of legal tactics. She sought the advice of Princess Anne's former husband, Captain Mark Phillips, and the Earl of Snowdon, once married to Princess Margaret, both of whom left their marriages with settlements that were less than generous.

'They both told me to get the money first,' Diana explained to me.

'They were both treated very badly. That's why I held out. I was determined that was not going to happen to me.'

She opened with a demand for a lump sum of £46 million. The Royal Family were horrified, as Diana knew they would be. She said, 'I knew Charles didn't have that kind of money.' It nonetheless proved to be an effective bargaining position. She heeded Lord Snowdon's advice and refused to accept Charles's offer to pay her bills for the rest of her life. By digging her heels in, she finally got the Royal Family to agree to a one-off payment of £17 million, paid out of the loan Charles was forced to raise from the Duchy of Cornwall's bankers. It was a demeaning experience for a family whose accounts had for the better part of a century been immune from public scrutiny.

What Diana failed to win for herself was the right to retain the HRH. The Queen had steadfastly maintained that, even in divorce, Diana should be treated with the dignity befitting 'the mother of the future king'. That included the use of the titles she had acquired on marriage. The HRH was the most important. For without it Diana would be reduced to the ranks and henceforth would be required to curtsey to those with it, including Fergie's daughters, Beatrice and Eugenie.

It was not a prospect that appealed to the princess. But by declaring unilaterally, as she had done during that meeting in February, that she no longer wanted the HRH, Diana had overplayed her hand. When she refused to give an undertaking to work in cooperation with the Palace, insisting that she had the right to set her own schedule, the Queen's advisers responded that they had no alternative but to take away her title.

Now it was Diana's turn to be horrified. She tried appealing directly to the Queen over the head of her courtiers, led by her own brother-in-law Robert Fellowes. The telephone conversation was short. Diana pleaded to be allowed to remain Her Royal Highness. Her mother-in-law replied that this would be 'very difficult'. It was her way of saying no. Diana had sealed her own fate. As the Queen later remarked, 'She wanted to give up the title – so give it up she will.'

This was not the way Diana chose to present her humiliation. The mistress of propaganda quickly leaked the story that she had been stripped of her status by a Royal Family who, by inference, were cold, ruthless and heartless. It is a version of events her brother would later refer to with such dramatic effect during his address in Westminster Abbey.

Even more poignantly, Diana said that when she asked William if he minded that she was losing her royal status, he replied, 'I don't mind what you're called – you're Mummy.'

Charles preferred to keep his thoughts – and those of his son – within the confines of the Royal Family. Diana's stream of pronouncements and leaked quotes went against the royal grain and he found them distasteful. For all his differences with his father, he subscribed to Philip's view that 'the children soon discover that it is much safer to unburden yourself to a member of the family. You see, you're never quite sure – a small indiscretion can lead to all sorts of difficulties.'

Keeping matters in a family she had come to despise was not Diana's way. With no intention of retiring from public view, she threw her considerable energies into the causes she espoused, and the campaign against land mines in particular. Given her immense popularity and the genuine concern she brought to the projects she involved herself in, this offered her the opportunity to become a force in her own right. In the minds of millions, she was already a far more sympathetic figure than any of her in-laws.

Yet despite her remarkable talent for reaching out to people which Rosa Monckton astutely called 'genius', she was never quite capable of discarding the consuming resentment she felt towards the Royal Family. It kept bubbling to the surface in quotes and comments that served only to draw attention back to the troubles of a marriage that had officially ended on 28 August 1996.

In conversations with the Queen, she constantly declared that she would never do anything to harm the Royal Family or the monarchy. She once told me, 'I wouldn't do anything to harm what is essentially part of William's heritage.' She said that she was determined that her elder son should grow up to appreciate the duties and responsibilities that come with his position.

She was just as keen that Harry, too, should play his royal part in the future of the monarchy. 'She was very conscious that both had a role to play,' Rosa Monckton recalled. 'She was grooming Prince Harry to be of support to his brother.'

Asked on *Panorama* about the damage she may have caused the monarchy, she replied, 'Why would I want to destroy something that is my children's future?'

When the question of the future of the monarchy was raised in a televised debate in January 1997, however, she could not contain her vitriol. She watched the programme in her sitting room at Kensington Palace with William and Harry at her side. When viewers were asked whether Charles should be by-passed in favour of her elder son, she allowed William to register his No vote.

'I'm not sure he will ever accept it. It's everything he doesn't want to do,' Diana told Simone Simmons, who was at the other end of the phone.

When the programme's host, Sir Trevor McDonald, posed the question, 'Should the monarchy be abolished?' Diana's composure deserted her. She angrily exclaimed, 'They have to learn what it is like for ordinary people. What on earth would they think if there were a revolution? They don't know what hard work means.'

Diana was one of the first to vote Yes. Throughout the evening she kept pressing the redial button on her phone to register more than 250 votes in favour of the abolition of the monarchy.

'William was more interested in how much money we were wasting on the calls,' Simone told me. 'He counted up the number of times we had called and said, "Haven't you got anything better to do with your money?" '

Afterwards Diana tried to justify herself. She told me that she was merely trying to illustrate to William that when he became king 'he will be in a position to modernise the monarchy'. She went on to say that that was why she kept taking her sons to visit the homeless and the sick 'so they could see first hand their suffering and learn to appreciate what they could do to help'.

That was not how her son saw it. In a cry of desperation he declared, 'I don't want to be king!'

His dread was understandable. He had seen what being a member of the Royal Family had done to his mother. He was frightened that the same thing would happen to him. Diana tried to explain it away to me by saying that he did not like the endless attention that went with his position, that he was shy and sensitive, that he found the pressure of being who he is difficult to deal with. The break-up of the marriage, she said, had much to do with that. And she was honest enough to acknowledge that she had been partly to blame for his anxieties.

She tried to make light of his concerns. She told me, 'Harry loves soldiers and castles and all that pomp and ceremony and is always teasing William by saying, "Don't worry, if you don't want to be king, I will be." '

She went on to insist that, given time, William would 'grow out of it'. And she was adamant that he would have to learn to live to 'shoulder his responsibilities'. I replied that she never had. Diana replied, 'William was born to it, so has been used to it right from the beginning. I wasn't.'

That was hardly reassuring to a fifteen-year-old looking down the long barrel of his future and hating what he saw. All he really wanted to do, he confided to friends at Eton, was run away and hide.

It was a problem that was affecting his school work. Under the Eton system the people charged with dealing with any troubles the boys may encounter are his housemaster, his dame and his tutor, and William was well served by all three. The house dame, as Eton calls its matrons, was Elizabeth Heathcote, the daughter of an Old Etonian who had been at the school for over thirty years. She was remembered by the boys in her care as considerate and friendly, especially to the homesick juniors. The tutor in his first two years was C. A. Stuart-Clark, a well-regarded English teacher who was there to provide friendly counsel if the boy's relations with the housemaster proved difficult. That did not apply in William's case, as he got on well with Dr Gailey, but his calming advice was certainly welcomed by William in those early weeks.

There was only so much they could tell a young prince, however. The old adage about not worrying because problems always blow over was no comfort to a prince caught in this emotional maelstrom. As the Duke of Windsor had noted, members of the Royal Family were 'always on parade' and it had broken him. Now William was bending under the pressure.

'It was very hard for him,' one of his contemporaries recalled. 'You had to feel sorry for him, but that didn't help because the last thing he seemed to want was people feeling sorry for him. He was very royal in that respect.'

His parents did what they could, but they too were limited in what they could achieve. Charles, for all his heartfelt concerns for his son's predicament, has always found it difficult to confront problems, while Diana's influence was now being seriously undermined by the courtiers she both disliked and feared. Her private secretary, Patrick Jephson, noted, 'It was no secret that towards the end of her life reactionary elements in the royal establishment were questioning her desirability as a mentor in the art of kingship.'

The one person who could help was the Queen. She knew only too well what pressures William was facing. She told her advisers that she was worried that he might 'crack up' like his mother had. Her natural inclination was to let the situation ride in the hope that somehow the problems would melt away but Prince Philip, ever vocal, pointed out that this wasn't going to happen. He insisted that the situation Diana had created had to be confronted – and with Charles too wrapped up in his own concerns, the Queen had to step in to encourage and comfort her grandson.

On Sundays all the Eton boys are allowed out into the town. For William that came to involve a short walk, his detective Graham Cracker at his side, down the High Street and across the bridge to Windsor and then up the slight hill to the castle. He would sometimes join the Queen and the Duke of Edinburgh for lunch. Afternoon tea was just for the sovereign and the sovereign-to-be.

They met in the Oak Drawing Room overlooking the quadrangle. They talked over their week. William would tell 'Granny' what he had been up to and she would give an account of what she had been doing. For much of his young life she had maintained a somewhat distant relationship with her grandson. But the traumatic events of the previous few months had sharpened her focus, and this most formal of ladies lowered the curtain of majesty to embrace him.

'The Queen was so thrilled to see him,' a courtier recalled. 'One of her sadnesses was that, up until the separation, she had hardly seen him. Then she was at last able to see him on a regular basis and form a proper relationship.'

In this quiet intimacy the Queen was able to impress upon William that the institution of the monarchy was something to be upheld and respected, and was worth preserving. It was his birthright, after all, as much as it was hers.

TWELVE

Eton Revisited

W illiam was confirmed on 9 March 1997. He was fourteen years old. In the eyes of the Church of England he had entered into adulthood.

It should have been a joyous family event. Instead it turned into a series of running skirmishes that dragged the reluctant prince back into a spotlight of controversy that was destined to grow ever brighter.

William had been prepared, along with thirty other Eton communicants, by the Reverend Tim Mullins, a College chaplain. What the clergyman could not do was prepare his future Supreme Governor for the secular fuss that marred what should have been an occasion of solemn spiritual significance.

Even the choice of who would preside over the ceremony had been a source of acrimonious comment. By royal tradition, the task should have fallen to the Archbishop of Canterbury. But Charles disdained the liberal views of the current incumbent of the ancient see, Dr George Carey, leading light in the 'happy clappy' evangelistic wing of the Established Church. He opted instead for his Cambridge contemporary, the Bishop of London, the Right Reverend Richard Chartres, a traditionalist who supported the near-abandoned sixteenth-century Book of Common Prayer and was opposed to the ordination of women priests and homosexual clergy.

William was not involved in these arcane discussions but Diana was happy to go along with her ex-husband's decision, albeit for more mundane reasons. She had come to dislike Lord Runcie, the Archbishop who had married her at St Paul's Cathedral where he coined the ill-starred phrase 'fairytale marriage' but who had later implied that she was a 'schemer' and an 'actress' whose eyes clouded over at the merest mention of any abstract ideas. She was equally out of tune with his successor, Dr Carey, who, much to her irritation, had tried to give her spiritual counsel prior to the separation. By then her own religious ideas had moved away from the faith of her childhood into the world of astrologers and spiritualists. The sententious pronouncements of an Anglican priest, however well intended, no longer carried weight with a woman who had even started flirting with Islam, an upshot of her infatuation of two years with Pakistan-born heart surgeon Dr Hasnat Khan.

What did concern the princess was the guest list. In January Charles had telephoned to ask her who she would like to invite. She replied that she would think about it. When she received a print-out of the people on her ex-husband's list she flew into a rage. For there, among the predictable complement of royals and godparents, were the names of a number of members of staff she had fallen out with over the years, including her former butler, Harold Brown, her first chef, Mervyn Wycherley, and her old nanny, Barbara Barnes.

They were there, Charles explained, because they had known William since his infancy and it would be churlish and unChristian not to invite them. Diana acquiesced. There was one person she was not going to allow into St George's Chapel, Windsor, and that was Tiggy Legge-Bourke.

By then Tiggy was employed only on a part-time basis, but Charles had made the tactical mistake of asking her to help him with the arrangements for the confirmation. When Diana found out that it was Tiggy who had sent out the invitations without consulting her, she made it plain that she would not attend if 'that woman' was there.

Faced with such extreme hostility, Tiggy felt she had no alternative but to withdraw from the proceedings. 'I'm Tiggy-in-the middle,' she said. 'What can I do? If I go, all hell will break loose. And if I don't, there will be uproar.'

It was a no-win situation, with Tiggy cast as the loser. It didn't do much for William's sense of spiritual well-being, either. He had thoughtfully decided that his confirmation should be held not at Eton with his fellow communicants, but at Windsor, in order not to overshadow the event for everyone else. As a youngster he had rarely been taken to church and when he arrived at Eton was not even sure which denomination he belonged to. Compulsory attendance at Eton's chapel had changed that. He was now going through a religious phase and had been looking forward to the ceremony.

His godfather, Norton Knatchbull, was there, but his wife Penny, was not. Prince Philip wasn't there either. He had chosen this, of all days, to take himself abroad for the World Wildlife Fund. It was not that he was without faith. 'Without the chance of receiving the message of religious thought, the most well-meaning, energetic and intelligent human is really no more than a bumble bee trapped in a bottle,' he had once declared. But the prince who had so nonchalantly changed denomination from Orthodox to Anglican to marry the future Queen had little enthusiasm for the formal rituals of his adopted creed, and at Charles's confirmation had spent the entire service reading a book. ('Bloody rude, that's what I call it,' the presiding Archbishop of Canterbury, Dr Michael Ramsey, remarked afterwards.)

More hurtful was the absence of William's maternal grandmother, Frances Shand Kydd. Having succeeded in getting Tiggy excluded, Diana then played no further part of note in the event. She had been asked to invite forty guests of her own. She invited no one, not even her own mother, with whom she was having yet another feud. Mrs Shand Kydd, who had recently converted to Roman Catholicism, was instead reduced to placing a notice in the newsletter of Oman Cathedral. It read, 'For my grandson William on his confirmation day, love from Granny Frances.' Asked why she was not at the service, she replied sadly, 'I'm not the person to ask.'

The Queen tried to make light of these dark undercurrents, smiling, laughing and even making jokes. It was difficult to draw Diana into the proceedings. After the service the guests were ushered into an ante-room where the Queen, Charles, Diana, William and Harry had gathered. 'It was like a cocktail party, but without the cocktails,' a guest recalled.

The princess stood at the side of the party, a lady alone, hardly speaking to anyone. It was the last time many of them saw her.

But if the mood of his mother was conspiring against William on what was supposed to be one of the most propitious days of his life, the prince was making a gallant effort to rise above them. He was nearly fifteen and already six feet tall and he was starting to exert his own authority. He was learning the painful lesson of princes throughout the ages, made more urgent by the advent of the camera lens – to watch himself being watched. He was, after all, a king-to-be and while that was not a position he would have chosen for himself, it had bred in him a self-assurance that no amount of squabbling could entirely blunt.

He was standing with his mother outside the chapel when Nanny Barnes came into view. Diana looked away in embarrassment. Without seeking his mother's permission, without so much as a glance in her direction as far as anyone noticed, he walked over to Barbara and gave her a hug followed by a kiss on the cheek. It was the first time he had seen his nanny since she had left royal service a decade earlier, but he still remembered her with an affection that the years had not dulled.

He also acknowledged the other members of staff. 'Diana didn't say a word to us, but William came across and spoke to us all,' one recalled.

He would show the same resolute independence at the Eton open day in June.

Tiggy Legge-Bourke had been pencilled in to accompany William and Harry a few days later on the East African safari their father had organised for them. After the furore over the confirmation, Charles had second thoughts and decided that, for the sake of 'the quiet life' he was always so anxious to preserve, it would be better if she stayed at home. It was the second time in less than a month that Tiggy had been excluded.

Harry, still only twelve years old, was very upset and kept asking, 'Why can't Tiggy come?' His elder brother knew the answer and kept quiet. Like his father, he was reluctant to incur his mother's increasingly unpredictable temper. But when it was time to issue an invitation of his own, William felt himself old enough to make his own decision.

Eton's '4th of June' celebrations, called Founder's Day, commemorate the birthday of George III, although, as with so many of the College's other arcane customs, they are rarely held on the 4 June, but either a few days earlier or later; that year, it was 29 May. Notwithstanding confusion over the date, they are the social highpoint of the College's calendar. Parents gather to picnic on the playing fields and watch a ceremonial procession of flower-bedecked boats row down the Thames to the accompaniment of the 'Eton Boating Song', while the boys go about their youthful business of chatting up their school friends' sisters.

Diana always felt uncomfortable at these gatherings. After one visit to the school, she told me, 'William has some really wonderful friends at Eton. How sophisticated they are. The worst thing about Eton is all the fawning parents. It's not the boys, it's the parents who stare at you all the time.' She stood and showed me how people bowed and curtsied before her. 'I call them the nods and bobs,' she said. It is not a description of themselves that many Etonian parents would recognise. Diana, it seemed, was becoming terrified of her own celebrity.

What she either did not realise or refused to admit was that William now felt equally uncomfortable in the company of *his* parents. According to Kate Figes, author of the best-selling *The Terrible Teens*, children's 'inexorable drive towards independence means that they are reluctant to rely on their parents for support'. In William's case that natural development was heightened by his dislike of the attention Charles and Diana inevitably attracted, and he told them that he did not want them to attend. Instead he invited Tiggy to join him for the afternoon's revelry.

She arrived bearing a bottle of chilled wine and a hamper of sandwiches which she placed on a rug on the playing field known as Agar's Plough. She came with William's friend, William van Cutsem, a pupil at Ampleforth, the Roman Catholic public school. They were joined by a bevy of mini-skirted girls. After their al fresco lunch the two boys went for a stroll through the field of parked cars, chatting amiably with friends, leaving

Tiggy to clear away the debris. William then returned to his house before setting off to join his mother at Kensington Palace for the start of his summer holidays.

It was an afternoon without incident which would have passed off without comment but for Diana's reaction. Upon his return to Kensington Palace, William found his mother in tears. He asked her, 'What's the matter, Mummy?'

She replied that she was upset that he had invited Tiggy and not her. Over a cup of morning coffee some time later when we were discussing the incident she asked me, 'What mother would like that situation?'

Instead of regarding it as a sign that her son was growing up and treating the incident with the feigned indifference Charles adopted, she took it as a personal slight.

It was an illustration of the intensity of their relationship. Her friend and confidant, designer Roberto Devorik, observed, 'Diana had a mother and son relationship and a mother and husband relationship with Prince William.' What she could not abide was the thought of another woman coming between them. That night Michael Gibbins, the private secretary who had succeeded the disillusioned Jephson, issued a statement in which Diana was said to have described Tiggy as 'thoughtless, foolish and idiotic' in accepting William's invitation.

Within forty-eight hours, however, Diana was backtracking, wrongly blaming Gibbins for exceeding his responsibilities. She insisted, 'I didn't know anything about Tiggy going to Eton but I wasn't cross about it, if that was what William wanted.'

All that did, of course, was attract yet more of the unwelcome attention William had been so anxious to avoid. For that he blamed his mother. He told his Eton friends that he was 'fed up' being treated as an appendage incapable of making a decision for himself. Like any normal boy approaching his fifteenth birthday, he wanted to cut free from his mother's apron strings.

Her friend Vivienne Parry observed, 'Diana was probably a better mother for children under twelve than, perhaps, she was for teenagers.'

In the attempt to heal the breach with her son, Diana tried to make her peace with Tiggy. She told me, 'For William's sake I invited Tiggy to lunch. For William's sake I wanted to be friends with her.' Not surprisingly, Tiggy refused to go.

As usually happens in households with children in their teens, the argument soon blew over and for a while life at Kensington Palace settled into a routine that might almost have been called ordinary. William and Harry were becoming adept at circumventing their mother's moods and Diana, for her part, was having to learn to accommodate their desire to be allowed out on their own, without her in constant and (to their way of thinking) suffocating attendance. William had shot up and Harry was also growing quickly, and at this stage they were not as instantly recognisable as they would soon become. She allowed them to join their friends in cafes around Kensington High Street just as short walk away from their mother's apartment in Kensington Palace. William was becoming increasingly interested in fashion and with his mates would pop into the stores to rifle through the racks of the latest clothing. There was always a bodyguard in attendance somewhere in the background, but by princely standards this was about as normal as life could get. And that was what Diana had always professed she wanted for her sons.

The Queen was delighted. She told her courtiers how pleased she was that 'Diana has gone so quiet. She seems to be coping rather well and adjusting to her new life.'

What neither the Queen nor the Prince of Wales knew was that Diana's way of coping with her new life encompassed more than just ensuring her sons had the freedom to go shopping with friends. Her butler, Paul Burrell, would later record, 'The Princess would send me out to buy top shelf magazines for William, who was very interested in them, notwithstanding his early age.' The pornographic magazines showed naked women in a variety of erotic and often obscene poses. One carried a section of photographs entitled Readers' Wives. Some of Diana's staff were understandably horrified that a woman who complained that she was being exploited should tolerate and indeed encourage her son to look at pictures of women being sexually exploited in such a graphic fashion. Others saw it as a means, albeit an extraordinary one, of maintaining a maternal control over her son as he was trying to break free from her and strike out into adulthood.

Diana, however, maintained that the first she knew of the magazines was when she discovered them hidden under William's bed. 'You'd think he would have found a more original hiding place. It was so obvious!' she told her friend Simone Simmonds.

Simone also says that Diana never actually went to meet Dr Hasnet Kahn wearing only a fur coat and jewellery, as has been claimed. It was a light-hearted idea which she had no intention of carrying out, but she loved to tease those around her with outrageous suggestions.

In public Diana was still managing to maintain her image of wounded innocence. It was a commodity which she was able to turn to good purpose. Despite the tribulations of the divorce and her increasingly obsessive relationship with her elder son, Diana remained committed to her good works. She realised the power of her presence and, in the case of land mines, she travelled to the places concerned to see at first hand what the problem was. But she also wanted to contribute in other ways – and it was William who showed her the best way of doing so.

Through her friendship with the American-born, London-based Marguerite Littman, she had become enthusiastic about the work being done by the Aids Crisis Trust. Her ability to make a financial contribution was severely limited, however.

'I looked at my divorce settlement and I realised I wasn't allowed to sell my jewellery, or the furniture or anything,' she told me. 'It was William who came up with the answer.'

In her determination to show her sons the rougher aspects of life outside the gilded circle, Diana had continued to take them to see the terminally ill in hospices and the dispossessed in shelters for the homeless. The visits had made a vivid impression, especially on William, who started to question the need for the opulence that continues to be a mark of royalty. He pointed to Diana's bulging cupboards of clothes and declared, 'You don't need all those.'

Diana agreed. To get rid of them, she reasoned, would be a cathartic break from the past. She called in Christie's who sent along their expert, Meredith Etherington-Smith ('*très formidable*' was Diana description of that effervescent lady) to help her select the dresses that would be suitable for sale.

It was William, however, who often made the final decision. He was ruthless in his selection, overruling his mother on several occasions. 'This one's ghastly – and so is this one,' he told her, as he rummaged through the collection of some of the most photographed gowns of the twentieth century. Her butler Paul Burrell was delighted to see them go. 'He was always complaining how heavy they were and how they took up so much room,' Diana said.

One frock that she wanted to keep was the long strapless sheath dress and jacket by Victor Edelstein made of oyster duchess satin and embroidered with pearls and beads. 'It was my favourite,' she admitted to me. 'It is the frock I always dreamed of having and it was really hard for me to part with that one.'

But William was insistent. 'You're not going to wear it again,' he told her firmly. It sold at auction in New York for $90,500, which converted to £54,436. The total proceeds amounted to $3.26 million, or £1.86 million. The catalogues alone raised $2.5 million (£1.49 million). William said that, since it had been his idea in the first place, he was entitled to 10 per cent – but that was a tease.

There was another joke to come out of the sale, although the Royal Family wouldn't see it that way. In the 2002 trial of Diana's butler Paul Burrell, it was alleged that a number of her frocks had ended up being worn by men at gay parties. Diana had foreseen that possibility and professed to find it amusing. 'I don't care if lots of transvestites buy the frocks – as long as they can fit into them,' she told me.

The sale was held on 25 June 1997. Fourteen days earlier Diana had written to Mohamed al Fayed, the Egyptian owner of Harrods and the Ritz Hotel in Paris, to accept his invitation to join him and his family in the South of France. He had invited her and the princes over to Paris on several occasions before to see the house where the Duke and Duchess of Windsor lived in exile and which he then owned. Wary of his buccaneering reputation, she had always declined. 'He probably even bugs the soap,' she joked.

But she was now a newly single woman and that, as far as Diana was concerned, gave her the liberty to choose her own friends. She said to me, 'I don't want to take favours from anyone by using their place to go with my children. But I like Mohamed. His language is so naughty – and so is he. He has promised to tell me all about the Duke of Windsor. He tells me the Duke was gay and that he has the proof.'

Fayed had been very generous to her charities. Another deciding factor was that he was employing Raine Spencer, the stepmother Diana had once hated and called 'Acid Raine', but with whom she was then on the best terms. 'I prefer to communicate with Raine than with my mother,' she told me. She added, 'I hate my mother.'

It was a chilling insight into the love–hate relationship between mother and daughter. Mrs Shand Kydd had sparked that latest outbreak of hostilities by selling an interview to *Hello!* magazine in order to raise money for a religious sanctuary on the isle of Iona. The fact that her mother, a convert to Roman Catholicism, had also taken exception to her affair with the Muslim Hasnat Khan only served to exacerbate matters. It meant that the lady called 'Gran Fran' by William and Harry saw little of her grandsons. It wasn't the remote west coast of Scotland Diana headed for that last summer, but the sybaritic heat of the South of France.

Diana arrived at the Fayed villa in St Tropez on Friday, 11 July, with William and Harry and their two police bodyguards. This was not the boys' first visit to the Riviera. They had been there the previous summer with their mother and Fergie and their cousins, the princesses Beatrice and Eugenie. William had hated it. The villa they were staying in had been surrounded by the paparazzi and William had spent much of his time hiding indoors.

It was supposed to be different with Fayed. With his own Gulf Stream IV jet, his heavily fortified villa and *Jonikal*, the £14 million yacht he bought the day after Diana accepted his invitation, he promised the royal party the one thing they craved, which was privacy.

It didn't turn out that way. The beach was public and the area was crawling with photographers who even went to the length of chartering a helicopter to buzz over the villa. Diana became increasingly fractious and one morning took a boat out to the lurking press launch to admonish them for ruining her holiday. 'William is freaked out,' she shouted. 'My sons are always urging me to live abroad to be less in the public eye and maybe that's what I should do – go and live abroad.'

To have taken her children with her would have been an impossibility. The Queen was of the strong opinion that William and Harry should see as much of their mother as possible, but under no circumstances would she give her permission for the second and third in line to the throne be allowed to leave Britain to be brought up in America or France or anywhere else. The Queen was not trying to deny Diana her maternal rights. She was simply protecting her dynasty.

Besides, abroad was the last place William and Harry wanted to be at that juncture. They *were* abroad and things were not going at all well. They were finding it difficult to deal with the glitz and extravagance of the Riviera lifestyle, with its hectic schedule of restaurants and nightclubs and funfairs. What they decided they were missing was the peace and quiet afforded them on the royal estates back in Britain.

One morning Harry became embroiled in a fight with Fayed's youngest son Omar. According to Trevor Rees-Jones, bodyguard to Fayed's film producer son Dodi, 'Omar wanted his own way and Prince Harry argued back. Omar went for him, so Harry gave him a good "scutching". All the bodyguards said, "Yes! Prince Harry's kicked his arse!" '

Diana was getting on a whole lot better with Fayed's eldest son, Dodi. It was on this trip that they began their fatal romance. According to the bodyguards, William and Harry regarded the producer of the Oscar-winning *Chariots of Fire* as 'a bit of a poseur'. For all that, they quite liked him. He was playful and fond of gadgets and went out of his way to be friendly towards them. When he started hurling fruit at a passing boat of photographers they gleefully joined in. As one previous girlfriend observed, 'His charm was like a flame thrower.'

There was a limit to their affection for the amiable Dodi, however. William in particular was always extremely circumspect in the company of his mother's paramours.

On Diana's insistence, Charles had always been careful to keep Camilla in the background. On the day before Camilla's fiftieth birthday on 18 July, Diana had staged a spectacular diving exhibition and made sure that she was pictured riding behind Harry on his jet ski. But that was for her own satisfaction. Her sons were not allowed into the ploy. Indeed, they knew so little about her that when, during the televised debate on the future of the monarchy, Trevor McDonald asked the audience to vote on whether Camilla should be Queen, Harry had piped up, 'Who's Camilla?' Diana had immediately ushered him from the room.

She was a lot more open about her own relationships. They had made a point of bringing James Hewitt into their lives. She had also gone out of her way to introduce them to Dr Khan.

That meeting had not been a success. William had said, 'If it makes you happy, Mummy,' but the remark that did not carry the weight of truth. He disliked intensely the idea of his mother being involved with anyone other than his father. Harry was always more open-minded. Diana told me shortly before she died, 'He's always asking me to have another baby, as he's fed up with being the youngest. I keep telling him, "But I'll have to get married first." I told him that that was not that easy because I've got to marry someone who's prepared to cope with me.' Harry was persistent. Diana recalled, 'He kept on saying, I don't want to be the youngest. Just hurry up and get married.'

William took an altogether different view. 'He wants me for himself,' Diana admitted.

On Sunday, 20 July, the princess and her sons flew back to England. Two days later Diana flew to Milan for the funeral of designer Gianni Versace, who had been murdered a week earlier in Miami Beach. She returned to London and then flew off to Paris for a clandestine weekend with Dodi.

It was now Charles's turn to have the boys and royal duty called. They attended the Queen Mother's ninety-seventh birthday lunch at Clarence House and joined the Queen and Prince Philip and the younger members of the Royal Family, including the yet-to-be-married Prince Edward and his girlfriend Sophie Rhys-Jones, for the last ever cruise of the Western Isles aboard the *Britannia*. William and Harry left the Royal Yacht early with their father and travelled on to Balmoral for their Scottish holiday, drawn by the lure of the grouse shooting. They were glad to get there. They told the staff at Balmoral that they had had a difficult summer with their mother.

Diana meanwhile had moved on to Greece for a cruise around the Aegean isles with Rosa Monckton. She tried to telephone William and Harry but could rarely get hold of them. 'They're out killing things,' she said.

On 20 August she returned to London, only to fly out the next day to Nice to join Dodi for her third Mediterranean holiday in five weeks. On 30 August the lovers returned to Paris.

The following day was a Saturday. William called her on her mobile phone and told her that he was unhappy because he was been required by Buckingham Palace 'to perform'. They wanted him to carry out a photocall at Eton where he was about to start his third year in four days' time. What troubled the prince was that the spotlight was shining on him, to the exclusion of Harry. She told him not to worry, that she would sort it out and that she was longing to see him the next day when they were all due back at Kensington Palace.

William and Harry would never speak to their mother again.

THIRTEEN

Death in Paris

William and Harry were woken at 7.15 a.m. on the morning of 31 August 1997.

They knew that something was wrong the moment they saw their father. Charles's face was drawn, his eyes were red-rimmed and he looked far, far older than his forty-eight years.

He had been up for most of the night, speaking to the British Embassy in Paris, calling his advisers in London, consulting with his mother, praying all the while that the news coming through from France that his former wife and mother of his children had been involved in a fatal accident wasn't true, that it was an exaggeration, that somehow Diana would manage to pull through.

The first reports were that Dodi had been killed but Diana had walked away almost unscathed. Then it was being said that she had suffered brain damage.

At 3.45 a.m. the Queen's assistant private secretary, Robin Janvrin, who was in attendance at Balmoral that weekend, took the fateful call from the Embassy. He immediately called up to the Prince of Wales and said, 'Sir, I am very sorry to have to tell you, I've just had the ambassador on the phone. The princess died a short time ago.'

Charles's composure collapsed. All that held him together was the desperate needs of his sons. He asked his mother, 'Shall I wake them?' The Queen said, No, that it was better to let them sleep while they dealt with the unfolding dramas.

Like everyone else in the family quarters on the first floor of the castle that night, the Queen was in a state of shocked confusion. She walked up and down the tartan-carpeted corridor outside her bedroom, dressed in her old-fashioned dressing gown, talking to Prince Philip, consulting with Prince Charles and drinking endless cups of tea brought her by her page. 'She was so young,' was one of her heartfelt comments. Charles, still in his pyjamas, kept asking, 'Why, why?'

But what to do? Charles was determined to go to Paris in a plane of the Queen's Flight. Janvrin counselled against that, but when they learned Diana was actually dead the argument was abruptly ended. There was now no question but that a plane be made available to the prince.

But first and foremost and by far the greatest concern was how to break the news to William and Harry. And who was going to do it? Charles knew that he had to be the one and he was dreading the task.

It was a moment of crisis of a kind the prince had never been good at confronting, and he called on his religious faith. It is his genuinely held belief that death is 'the next great journey of our existence'.

That is what he tried to explain to his sons on that bleak morning. He held them close. There was to be no shame in their tears. To see a parent cry, as they had often seen their mother, can strike deep at a child's sense of security. But in grief it is Nature's way of releasing a surge of emotion that would otherwise be almost unbearable.

By the most terrible of coincidences, it was the day that William and Harry were due to return to London to spend the last few days of their holiday with their mother. Instead they were locked in anguish in a castle that had suddenly become laden with despair. But they were not without comfort. Tiggy Legge-Bourke was there and she was a consoling presence, especially for Harry. So was Charles's old nanny, Mabel Anderson, who the boys were very fond of. And as soon as he heard the news, Princess Anne's son, Peter Phillips, who they so admired, had flown to Scotland to be with his cousins. His support would prove invaluable in the days ahead.

They also had the Queen and Prince Philip to turn to. Diana had always found them cold and distant but that was not how they were perceived by her sons. They had been the one stable backdrop in William and Harry's all-too-disjointed lives and they provided the continuity and security their grandsons needed. It was the Queen, her self-possession restored, who said that the family must go to church that morning. She always attends the nearby church at Crathie when she is at Balmoral, but this Sunday the service would have a special meaning. As she told William and Harry, 'We are going to pray for your mummy's soul.' William agreed. He told his grandmother that he wanted to 'pray to Mummy'.

There was no overt display of mourning at the church other than the black dress of the Queen and the black ties worn by the men. No statement was given and no tears were shed. To their way of thinking, grief was a private matter. It was an old-fashioned view and one that was perilously out of step with the feelings of the nation, as they would soon discover. On the Sunday morning, however, they behaved as they thought was right and proper and William and Harry saw no reason to question that royal tradition. The last thing they wanted, as they told their father before he left for Paris, was to go on public show, and it required a great deal of coaxing before they agreed to appear outside the castle gates for the photocall the following morning. They looked at the floral tributes that had started piling up and Harry, clutching the hand of his father who had just returned to Balmoral, bent down to read some of the messages of condolence on the cards.

But what they wanted, more than anything, was to be left alone to find their own accommodation. Together, sometimes with Peter Phillips for company, they spent long hours wandering the hills around Balmoral, talking to each other, sharing their memories, finding solace in each other's company. It seemed to help, for the castle staff was struck by how composed the two boys were. That is not to suggest that they were not profoundly distressed by the death of the mother they both adored, yet it was noticeable (and was duly remarked on) how composed they appeared to be.

The nation, which had once prided itself on its self-control and reserve, threw off its restraints. Flowers left at the gates of Buckingham and Kensington Palaces grew into fields of cellophane. Notes, gifts, teddy bears, photographs and handwritten verses of poetry were pinned to railings. In a display of anguish urged on by mounting anger, the country rose up to demand a show of public grief from their Royal Family. Suddenly the old rites and protocols no longer held true. The Prime Minister, Tony Blair, whose attempts to take charge of the funeral arrangements so irritated the Queen, had called Diana 'the people's princess' and it was the people who now took charge of events. On their insistence the flag over Buckingham Palace was lowered to half mast. And they demanded that the Royal Family return to London to share in their lamentations instead of being allowed to mourn in the privacy of their Highland fastness.

The Queen was shaken by this surge of rage directed against her family. In her opinion Diana had been a source of endless trouble. What she failed to appreciate was the deep affection in which she was held by the majority of her subjects. Even with the mob baying at the gates of Buckingham Palace, she still could not fully grasp the enormity of what was happening.

'I can't believe it – they didn't even know her,' she told a member of her staff. 'It's like one of their own family has died.' That was precisely the point, for to millions Diana *was* part of their family.

That was as surprising to William and Harry as it was to their grandmother. To them Diana had been a mother who could be loving, affectionate, consoling and, always, great fun, a sort of royal Jim'll Fix It who arranged for them to throw a ball around on the hallowed turf of Twickenham, to play tennis with Martina Navratilova and to sit in world champion Nigel Mansell's racing car, and introduced them to Cindy Crawford and Claudia Schiffer, the supermodel whose poster William had pinned up in his study at Eton. But she could also be emotionally demanding. William, in particular, had become very worried about the direction in which her life seemed to heading and the possibility, however remote, that she might marry the Muslim Dodi had caused him great concern. It is unlikely they remembered her as a saint.

Faced with a public that was becoming so irate that the very future of the monarchy was being called into question, however, the Royal Family had no alternative but to submit. They returned to London and William and Harry went on walk-about through the sea of flowers that had sprung up outside their home at Kensington Palace. Again William was a reluctant participant but, as Prince Philip reminded him, 'If you are really going to have a monarchy, you have got to have a family and the family has got to be in the public eye' – and never more so than now.

If William had had his way, that brief walk among the cellophane-wrapped flowers in Kensington Gardens would have been his last public appearance that autumn. What he did not want to do was play any prominent part in the funeral itself. It would be but one of many rows that day.

The Queen said, 'We must have a private funeral.' It was her wish that Diana be buried at Frogmore, the traditional resting place for members of the Royal Family with the exceptions of sovereigns and their consorts. Close to Windsor, it would enable her sons to visit her grave whenever they chose. But Diana was no longer royal, as her brother, Earl Spencer, made brutally plain. She had been stripped of that rank on her divorce. He insisted that she be buried instead at Althorp, the Spencers' family home in Northamptonshire. The Royal Family, forced on to their back foot, felt they had no choice but to agree. What they would not submit to was his demands for the funeral service itself.

Spencer objected to his nephews being asked to walk behind the gun carriage bearing their mother's body to Westminster Abbey. 'I thought it was unfair on them, they were so young,' he explained.

Form, however, dictated that they should and in the high emotions of the occasion, form was all the Royal Family had to hold on to. But trying to persuade William to do what was expected of him proved to be very difficult. At first he flatly stated that he wouldn't do it. He hated the idea of thousands of people staring at him. Charles Spencer supported his nephew's stance. 'I genuinely felt that Diana would not have wanted them to have done it,' he said. A distraught Charles told his son, 'It can't just be me and Harry – you have to do it, too.'

There then ensued an argument which was only resolved when William said he would make that long walk down the Mall and on down Horse Guards' Parade to the Abbey, but only if 'Grandpa' joined him.

Diana had become very suspicious of Prince Philip. She complained to William that he was always shouting at his staff and told him, 'You must never do that. You must never shout at people who cannot answer back.' But children have a way of forming their own opinions and her sons were close to their grandfather. He took them shooting at Sandringham, and one of the activities they most looked forward to was being taken by him in the early mornings into the marshes to hunt for duck. To their young minds he was sturdy, reliable and manly. He returned their affection and, when William delivered his ultimatum, he readily agreed and declared, 'If I walk, we all walk.'

Philip talked to his grandson under his breath throughout the procession in the effort to keep him calm. As the cortège trundled under Admiralty Arch he put a comforting arm around William's shoulder.

As it turned out, it was Charles who needed the greater reassurance. He had received a number of death threats in the days following Diana's death and was convinced that someone was going to take a shot at him. Before he set out, he had even gone to the length of writing farewell letters to his mother and two sons.

Charles Spencer had his own recollections of that walk. 'It was just awful,' he recalled. 'It was something I would never wish on anyone. You could not look to either side, you were just walking through a tunnel of grief and it was a very odd feeling because you could feel the depth of the despair coming in waves from either side. I still have nightmares about that. I can hear the bridles and all the metalwork on the horses and their hooves and the wailing of the crowd. I have never been in such a nightmarish place in my life.'

He admired the way William and Harry conducted themselves. 'I think it was an almost impossible task but they both did it brilliantly,' he said. 'I imagine they just blocked off what was going on around them and got on with it.'

That did not lessen his anger towards the Royal Family. Years later he would still be complaining about the way they had been made to walk behind their mother's coffin. 'I thought that was where tradition and duty went too far against human nature,' he said.

His disregard for his royal in-laws was given immediate vent in the address he delivered in Westminster Abbey. In barely veiled phrases, he admonished the Royal Family for the appalling way he believed they had treated his sister. He said, 'She needed no royal title to continue to generate her particular brand of magic,' ignoring the fact that it was Diana herself who had first suggested giving up the HRH. He closed by saying, 'She would want us today to pledge ourselves to protecting her beloved boys, William and Harry, from a similar fate and I do this here, Diana, on your behalf.

'And beyond that, on behalf of your mother and sisters, I pledge that we, your blood family, will do all we can to continue the imaginative way in which you were steering these two exceptional young men so that their souls are not simply immersed by duty and tradition but can sing openly as you planned.'

He would recall, 'I don't remember actually giving the speech. I remember the first bit and stumbling over a word quite early on, then an immense calm coming over me until the part where I was talking to William and Harry across their mother's coffin and that was incredibly difficult. My throat was so tight I almost broke down.'

Time would not be kind to Spencer. A few months later the earl who had admonished a prince for his treatment of his wife walked out on his own spouse and their four children. During the Burrell trial in 2002 it was revealed how he had refused to give Diana the sanctuary of a home on the family estate.

Nor were his remarks well received by the Church of England. The Anglican funeral service has no place for the settling of scores. Quite the opposite; it is a ceremony of remembrance intended to bury the woes of the past alongside the body. Spencer had refused to show his address to anyone beforehand. After his outburst the Established Church, which still includes prayers for the Royal Family in its Sunday services, changed its rules and now demands that anyone making a funeral address must first let the officiating priest know what they are intending to say.

His pledge to William and Harry also started looking rather thin. Contact between the earl and his nephews has been intermittent, although Spencer insists, 'It was a vow made to two boys and they are two young men now. They are two young men who have very full social diaries and an active life with their father's family and I understand all that. I was not saying I was going to nanny them; I was just there to protect them and give them a different direction if they needed it. William and Harry always know we are there and willing to help, if need be.'

On that day, though, his words caught the mood and his speech was greeted by a huge cheer that started in the Abbey and was taken up by the multitude thronging the streets beyond. More than a million people had poured into London to pay their farewell to a woman who, in death, really was 'the people's princess', and watch her cortège as it bore her body up the M1 motorway to its lonely resting place on an island in the middle of a lake on the Althorp estate.

William and Harry were there to watch her coffin, covered in the Spencer and not the royal standard, as it was lowered into the earth. It would be a year before they again visited her graveside. Five years on, Charles had still not been there.

It had been a terrible, draining experience but their life had to go on – and they had to learn how to cope with it without the support and encouragement of the mother they loved.

FOURTEEN

After Tragedy

Charles was transformed by Diana's death. Overnight he turned into a 'proper father' to William and Harry.

That was the considered judgement of the policemen and staff who worked for him at Highgrove in the weeks and months following the funeral.

His inherent insecurity had only been made worse by the collapse of his marriage, and he had taken refuge in the fastidious detail of his princely position. He would pick up on the slightest mistake, be it a picture out of place, bath water at the wrong temperature, or food that was not served exactly to his taste. Memo writing had become an obsession. Even a tasty helping of prune ice-cream would warrant a note of thanks to the chef.

'I always have my best thoughts in the bath and as my memory is appalling I have to write everything down,' he explained to me. 'And I keep small cards in my left-hand pocket so when I remember something I write it down immediately.'

It was more than just a memory aid, however. It was a way of communicating without having to actually speak to the people concerned, and there had been times when that extended to his sons.

That changed the moment the call came through informing him that Diana had died. A member of his staff recalled, 'He took charge of everything. It was the only time I saw him take an interest in everything that was going on. He cancelled all his engagements and really went for it, taking total responsibility for his sons. He made sure he was with the boys all the time.'

After the funeral William and Harry returned to Highgrove with their father. He gave instructions that everything should carry on as normal. The in-house staff that week included two butlers, a housekeeper, a chef, his valet Michael Fawcett, Tiggy Legge-Bourke and Mark Dyer, the former Welsh Guards captain who had enjoyed a brief romance with Tiggy and during that time had forged a close friendship with William.

No reference was made to the terrible events of 31 August or its emotionally fraught aftermath. Instead, the routine of the house was maintained. The princes' conversation with staff who had given loyal service for several years never ventured much beyond, 'What would you like for lunch, sir?'

'The normality was almost shocking,' said another member of the staff. 'Everyone went around saying, "Aren't they doing marvellously", but never mentioning anything like that to their faces.'

The only mention of what had happened was made on the Monday after the funeral when Tiggy drove William and Harry to follow the Beaufort Hunt which was out cubbing in the fields of Gloucestershire. The master was Captain Ian Farquhar and just before he led the hunt off, Farquhar lent down from his saddle and said, 'Good to see you, sirs. I just want you to know that we are all very, very sorry about your mother. You have our deepest sympathy and we were all incredibly proud of you on Saturday. That's all I'm going to say. And now we're going to get on with the day.'

'Thank you,' William replied. 'Yes, we all need to get on with the day.'

The weather that week was fine but, in one break from habit, the princes abandoned the barbecues that had always been a feature of Highgrove. Instead, Charles and his sons preferred to eat indoors in the main dining room or the smaller sitting room where William and Harry used to watch television with their mother.

The television was rarely turned on. Never a fan of the 'idiot box', as he called it, Charles had even less wish to watch it then, when so many of the programmes were devoted to dragging over the details of Diana's life.

For that same reason the newspapers were also banned, and for once the prohibition was observed. The staff was buying all the papers, but was careful not to leave one lying around the house. It was the continuation of a rule that had been in force for most of the summer.

'Prince Charles had had no desire to see photographs of the mother of his children cavorting around the South of France with Dodi Fayed and equally had no desire to see photographs of his sons walking behind her coffin,' a staff member recalled.

The emphasis was on the outdoors. Deprived of the diet of television soap operas they had watched with their mother, the young princes spent much of their time out on the estate, marching along the hedgerows looking for rabbits, William's labrador Widgeon at their side. As Diana had once observed, 'They are never happier than when they have a gun in their hands.'

It was all very casual and low key and deliberately so, and if William chose sometimes to take himself off to his room to lie on his bed, alone with his thoughts and listening to his music, Charles accepted that as part of the healing process.

Of Camilla there was not a sighting. In the weeks leading up to that fateful night in Paris, she had been a regular visitor to Highgrove. On her fiftieth birthday, which Diana had tried to upstage with that diving display in a leopard-patterned swimsuit in the South of France, Charles had given her a party in a marquee on the lawn. Diana had been deeply upset by his display of commitment towards the rival she so disliked.

She had told me, 'It wasn't Camilla who really, *really* destroyed our marriage. It was the people around us. They didn't give us a chance.' When she learnt about the party, however, she went into a funk. Her astrologer, Debbie Frank, said, 'All the hurt came to the surface again. I think that was why she was able to move from Hasnat to Dodi so quickly. It seemed to me she was substituting them for Charles.'

With Diana still quick in his memory, Charles took the prudent decision that this was not the time to introduce William and Harry to Camilla. Public anger had turned again, welling against the mistress so many blamed for the breakdown of the Waleses' marriage, which in turn had led to her death. And while that was not entirely borne out by the facts, it was nonetheless a potent force which it would have been foolhardy to ignore. The Royal Family's popularity was at its lowest ebb and in the interests of discretion and safety Camilla removed herself to the sanctuary of her own home in the quaint village of Lacock, twenty-five minutes' drive away in Charles's Aston Martin.

They kept in touch by telephone. Charles's dependence on Camilla was such that he could hardly make a decision without consulting her first, and he desperately needed her then. He called her frequently to pour out his woes, ask her advice and take comfort in her replies which were always supportive, never critical.

He also made sure that her refrigerator was kept well stocked and her cellar full of fine French wines. One of Camilla's relations recalled, 'He sent his policeman over with delicacies from his gardens. Some nights he even sent over a "takeaway" dinner which he'd had specially prepared for her.'

His sons knew nothing of this. A member of staff remembered, 'It was all very cloak and dagger.' A few months earlier Charles had tried to broach the tricky subject of Camilla with his sons but they were unreceptive. He later told Tiggy that William in particular had shied away from the very mention of another woman in their father's life. Their attitude had not changed. Tiggy was another matter. They knew that their mother had objected to her presence at their side (she had often asked them what she was like) but they were fond of her and it was with Tiggy that Harry and William chose to spend much of the daytime hours, dressed in open-necked shirts and chino trousers, kicking a ball around on the lawn or playing cricket and rounders. 'The best thing Charles ever did was get hold of Tiggy,' Fergie's father, the late Major Ronald Ferguson, said.

It was to their father, however, that they confided their real feelings. Tiggy was a friend. She was not an intimate confidante. Any discussion about the cause of Diana's death and their own reactions to what had happened was kept between the three of them.

Charles was careful to shield them from the endless stream of telephone calls. They were also spared the task of opening the eighty sacks of letters and parcels that arrived every morning. They were being dealt with by Clair Southwell, Charles's former masseuse who became their Swiss liaison and helped organise the Waleses' skiing trips to Klosters. Straightforward and discreet, Clair became friends with the boys and was asked to work as an archivist for William and Harry, compiling detailed records of their school life for the Royal Archives. The day after Diana's death she took charge of the operation to deal with the gifts, flowers and letters to the princes that flooded into Kensington and St James's palaces from all around the world. She would first read all the letters addressed to William and Harry to spare them any distress.

Gifts had come in from stars including film director Steven Spielberg and Sir Elton John, who rewrote his song 'Candle in the Wind' in Diana's honour and played it at the funeral. William insisted on giving most of them away, including the latest high-tech tennis racquet from the United States. 'I've got one racquet, what do I need two for?' he explained. His mother would have approved.

Harry was keen to open the parcels himself and was eventually allowed to open one. When it turned out to be a 'hideous' tea cloth with Diana's face on it, he lost interest and declined to open any more. But like his brother, Harry politely helped organise the replies. 'They chose their own private words of thank you in response to the letters,' Clair said. They would sometimes top and tail the letters with personal observations.

Joint letters of thanks were signed by Charles's private secretary, Stephen Lamport. They read, 'I am writing on behalf of The Prince of Wales, Prince William and Prince Harry to thank you most warmly for your kind letter of sympathy.

'Their Royal Highnesses have asked me to say how touched they were that you should have taken the trouble to write as you did. They greatly appreciate your kind and sympathetic thoughts.'

Charles was impressed by the way his sons handled themselves during this critical period. Charles gave his own interpretation of his sons' resilience. On 19 September, in an address to a meeting of business and community leaders in Manchester, he said, 'As many of you will know from the experience of family loss in your own lives, it is inevitably very difficult to cope with grief at any time. But perhaps you might realise it is even harder when the whole world is watching at the same time. I am unbelievably proud of William and Harry. They're coping extremely well, but obviously Diana's death has been an enormous loss as far as they are concerned, and I and they will always feel that loss.'

Like their counterparts in Scotland, the staff at Highgrove was struck by how well William and Harry appeared to be handling their loss. Even Prince Philip was moved to remark how stoic they were.

But while that reaction was notable, it was neither out of the ordinary nor callous. Sudden and unexpected bereavement produces several predictable clinical responses, according to Brett Kahr, senior research fellow in psychotherapy at the Winnicott Clinic, Regent's College in London.

The first reaction, he said, is shock and numbness. 'The numbing can easily last for a week or longer. It is a denial of reality. You become internally frozen and comatose. You feel in a very odd physical and psychological state. The best analogy I can give is that you feel like a piece of cork floating on a turbulent wave. This is our body and mind's own internal defence mechanism to protect us from being absolutely shattered as human beings.'

This reaction would be followed by feelings of anger and rage. For William and Harry that would be directed at their mother, for allowing this to happen, and against the paparazzi who at that early stage were being held responsible for the crash.

'The third category is absolute grief-stricken sobbing,' said Kahr. 'Sometimes these states can co-exist and a bereaved person can wax and wane. It can take a good few months, even for a relatively healthy adult, to register the reality of the horrific finality of death.'

Charles's interest in psychoanalysis had often made him a figure of fun. In these abysmal circumstances, however, it proved extremely useful. The prince is the patron of the Royal College of Psychiatrists, and had no qualms about seeking professional assistance for his sons. Both William and Harry underwent bereavement counselling.

What they didn't do was show the kind of public emotions that Diana had been so keen they should learn to express. For them, the grief had to be expressed in private. That was a lesson they had learnt earlier on in their lives. Diana had made emotional drama an everyday part of their home life, but the royal influence had been equally pervasive. They had seen how the Queen and Prince Philip conducted themselves, soaked up the imperial grandeur of the Queen Mother and admired the sturdy resilience of their cousin, Peter Phillips. They had heard Philip say, 'If you have a headache, take an aspirin'; the Queen Mother advise, 'Never look at your feet'; and the Queen's stern warning, 'Never show emotion in public.'

It was everything Diana had set her face against but it was the royal way of doing things and they had grown up with it. They had been taught that they had to set their faces and carry on, no matter what their private feelings might be. For William and Harry that meant returning to school. On Wednesday, 10 September, only four days after their mother's funeral, Charles took William to Eton and Harry to Ludgrove.

At Eton William was able to discuss what had happened with his friend, William Rickards, who had lost his mother some years earlier. He also had the support of the College. When he got back to his room in Gailey's house there were more than 600 letters waiting for him. Over half the school had written to him, offering their condolences but with the firm instruction that there was no need for him to write back. 'It was simply a show of solidarity,' a member of his house said.

Less welcome was the opinion poll conducted by Gallup published the following day. It showed that more than half the country wanted the crown to miss out Charles and pass to William. This was not a responsibility the fifteen-year-old prince was ready to shoulder. He had found the strain of being on show during the funeral a disturbing experience and was still harbouring serious doubts as to whether he wanted the throne at all. As he kept saying, 'All I want is to get on with my life at Eton.'

The reaction that greeted Harry at Ludgrove was more circumspect. 'We were told not to talk about what had happened,' one of his classmates recalled. No newspapers were allowed, television was even more closely monitored than usual, 'and we were asked not to mention cars or mothers'.

A few days later William joined the rest of his class on an outing to London to see George Bernard Shaw's play, *Pygmalion*. He appeared to enjoy himself.

The past can never be neatly closed off, however. The reminders were always there, waiting to pounce. It was Harry's thirteenth birthday on 15 September. At Ludgrove parents are allowed to come to the school for tea and share a slice of birthday cake with their sons. That year his aunt, Lady Sarah McCorquodale, stepped into the breach left by Diana and drove to Ludgrove in time for tea. As soon as she walked through the door Harry, who had been watching out for her from the window, ran to greet her as he used to do with his mother. As she hugged the newly teenage prince, she gave him a carefully wrapped gift.

It was the computer PlayStation his mother had bought for him in Paris.

FIFTEEN

A New Role for Camilla

It was Diana's heartfelt wish that Harry should follow his brother to Eton. 'If he doesn't go there everyone will think he's stupid,' she told me.

The younger prince had a number of abilities. He was an excellent horseman, a good shot, and a passable footballer and cricketer. 'He's very artistic and sporty and doesn't mind anything,' Diana said.

Academic flair was not among his more notable gifts, however. Geography was a struggle, and he used to be tested by his father on the world's capital cities and rivers on long car journeys. Mathematics was also something of a mystery, although in that he was only following in the tradition established by Charles, who needed three attempts before he passed his 'O' level in the subject.

Charles was worried that Eton's demanding intellectual standards might be beyond Harry, and at one point Diana agreed with him and they started considering a number of alternative public schools, including Radley in Oxfordshire and Milton Abbey in faraway Dorset.

It was William who finally settled the matter by telling his parents that Harry would be happiest at Eton with him. He told them he knew he was right – because Harry had already told him so.

That still left the problem of the entrance exam, which Eton was not prepared to relax, even for a prince. Additional tutoring was needed and parties had to be curtailed. It also meant that Harry had to stay on at Ludgrove to swot his way through an extra year.

There was some carrot to go with the educational stick. To encourage him and boost his confidence, his father took him on a tour of southern Africa on his first half-term break after the death of his mother.

Charles was there on official business. He went to Swaziland to meet the Sherborne-educated King Mswati, who already had six wives and would continue to add to his marital harem by exercising the royal prerogative which allowed him to take his pick of his nation's virgins. Charles then went on to the coronation of Lesotho's Ampleforth-educated King Letsie III.

While his father did his round of Africa's English public school-educated autocrats, Harry was out game spotting in the bush of Botswana accompanied by his friend at Ludgrove, banker's son Charlie Henderson, and the ubiquitous Tiggy Legge-Bourke. Charles was becoming increasingly concerned by her ability to put her foot into any hole that presented itself (she allowed herself to be photographed in a car, cigarette drooping from her mouth, with Harry hanging out of the back window blazing away at rabbits with his shotgun). But when he tried to talk to her, she responded by bursting into tears which baffled him. Besides, Harry adored her and, as Charles said, someone had to look after the prince while he was busy performing his official duties.

Father and son were reunited in South Africa for one of the most extraordinary royal engagements on record. At the presidential mansion on a hill-top overlooking Pretoria, they met Nelson Mandela – and were joined by the Spice Girls who were on tour. At an age when he was still more impressed by fame than lions and elephants, Harry said afterwards that his encounter with the feisty all-girl quintet was the highlight of his trip.

Indeed, Harry was so impressed that he insisted on attending the premier of the Spice Girls film along with William and his father shortly after their return to England. The girls were later invited to afternoon tea at Highgrove, where they were given a conducted tour that included the boys' quarters where they bounced on their princely beds.

At the Queen and Prince Philip's golden wedding ball at Windsor Castle in November, William had been seated near his extremely attractive cousin, Princess Victoria of Sweden, then aged twenty-four. He spent so much time talking to her that Zara Phillips started teasing him ruthlessly and he started to blush. He was made to blush again when the Spice Girls came to visit. Emma Bunton, who went under the name of Baby Spice, asked William. 'It's been in the press you have a picture of me on your wall.' William replied, 'Yeah.' Emma enquired, 'Is that at Eton?' The tongue-tied prince nodded that it was. Posh Spice, who married the Manchester United footballer David Beckham, was quick to observe, 'He does fancy Emma.'

The encounter wasn't quite the unqualified success it might have been, though. As Charles remarked subsequently, 'After all the trouble I go to, to arrange the Spice Girls to come round to tea, they change their minds, fickle little devils. They've now gone on to the All Saints.' In Charles's lexicon that would have been an ancient church. To his sons it meant another all-girl pop group.

The fact that the meetings took place at all was indicative, however, of the way that the Prince of Wales was trying to modernise the royal image. Like the Queen, he had been badly shaken by the public hostility towards his family which Diana's death had exposed. And bearing the brunt of this antipathy was Charles himself. His advisers told him that if he was going to reclaim the esteem so necessary for his future, he was going to have to try and shed his stuffy reputation and become more attuned to popular culture. Bathing in the reflected celebrity of people like the Spice Girls was one way of doing that (he called them 'Great fun, actually') and, while the ploy was an obvious one, it did signal a break from the formality of his mother's court. Involving William and Harry in the process helped to heighten the impression, which was the intention.

There was nonetheless only so much glitz Charles was prepared to tolerate. He had no intention of allowing his sons to be hijacked by the celebrity culture. The tour of southern Africa was intended as a holiday for Harry after the traumas of the autumn, but he wanted his son to derive some educational benefit from the trip. After the meeting in Pretoria he took Harry to Rorke's Drift where, in 1879, 139 British red-coated soldiers had withstood an attack by 4,000 Zulu warriors, winning eleven VCs, a record unsurpassed for a single engagement.

Charles was moved to tears by the description of the battle given by a local guide, David Rattray. His thirteen-year-old son was gung-ho. He had watched *Zulu*, the film of the encounter starring Michael Caine, on video and took the delight of a young man fascinated by soldiers and tales of derring-do, recreating the battle in his imagination as he walked around the old mission station. It was history brought alive.

'I'm a great believer in learning from the past,' Charles said. There was a personal point to his comment; his English history master at Gordonstoun once rebuked him, 'This is, after all, the history of *your* family.' It was advice that he passed on to the next generation and was one of the reasons he had taken Harry to Rorke's Drift.

The effort paid off. As often happens after the death of a parent, the loss of his mother had given Harry the determination to do his best and he succeeded in passing his Common Entrance in history, science, English, French, religious education and, trickiest of all, geography and mathematics. It secured him the place at Eton his mother wanted for him. Poorly educated herself – 'brain the size of a pea, that's what I've got', Diana once famously remarked – like every mother she had been anxious for her children to do well at school.

It was while Harry was doing his last-minute cramming for his exam that the meeting Diana had been dreading finally took place. On Friday, 12 June, Camilla Parker Bowles met Prince William at St James's Palace.

Since Diana's death Charles had been true to her memory and carefully arranged his schedule so that Camilla was never around when William or Harry were at home. It was a game of subterfuge that he was prepared to continue indefinitely. He didn't want to upset his sons by forcing the issue.

Nor did Camilla. She told relations that she was 'dreading' meeting the princes. Divorced from Andrew Parker Bowles in 1995 and with limited financial resources of her own, she was now almost as dependent on Charles as he was, in a different way, on her. But Charles's overriding commitment was and had to be towards his sons and she was very concerned that they might take against her, thereby driving a damaging wedge of contention between her and her royal lover. 'After all, all they've heard about me from their mother is bad things,' she said.

As it turned out, the boys proved to be a lot more mature in dealing with the situation than the adults. One day when Camilla was riding out with the Beaufort Hunt she got to Highgrove where she kept her horse, only to realise that she had left her hunting hat at home. She got back into her car to drive back to fetch it. As she rounded the bend, William came roaring by on his quad bike. The prince saw her and spent the next couple of hours following the hunt on his bike to try and catch a glimpse of his father's mistress. That proved to be impossible. Camilla, now in her hat, was unrecognisable from all the other riders. He quickly concluded that this was a ridiculous way to behave. A friend of William's recalled, 'He said that since eighty per cent of the boys at Eton came from broken homes or had stepmothers it would be odd if he was not allowed to meet Camilla. He thought that would be an insult to both him and her.'

The statistic may have been wildly wrong (the parents of Etonians are no more likely to divorce than anyone other social grouping) but the sentiment was accurate enough. He told his father as much.

As a first step William and Harry had been introduced to Camilla's children, Tom and Laura, who had been invited to spend a weekend with Charles and his sons at Birkhall during the Easter break. Despite the age difference (Tom was twenty-five, Laura nearly twenty), they got on well, which led William to conclude that if they were nice and reasonable people, it was quite possible that their mother wouldn't be the ogre Diana had painted.

On Friday, 12 June, William came to London and called by St James's Palace to change his clothes. 'It was sheer coincidence that Camilla was there,' an aide said. That was merely an excuse which would have allowed William to shy away if he suddenly got cold feet. He didn't and at 3.30 that afternoon Charles brought Camilla up to his son's suite of rooms in York House which is part of the Palace, introduced them and then left them to it.

Camilla dealt well with the situation. She was not over-effusive – that is not her style – and Diana was not mentioned once. Instead she confined herself to simple remarks on subjects she knew they had in common, such as hunting and how he was getting on at Eton, where her son, Tom, had also been educated. Afterwards Camilla said, 'I need a drink,' and poured herself a large gin and tonic. It was still only mid-afternoon, but the ice had been broken. Shortly afterwards the young prince and Camilla met again for tea and, as if to put the final seal on his approval, she was invited to join William and Prince Charles for lunch.

A few weeks later it was Harry's turn. They met at tea time at Highgrove on a Sunday afternoon. On this occasion Tom and Laura came too, but once again what might have been a contentious introduction was cordial and passed off without incident.

That left the Queen. She was fond of Camilla and had often dined with her and her husband. In a counter to Diana's vitriol, she had called her a 'much maligned woman'. It was not until 2000 that she agreed to formally meet her son's mistress at the sixtieth birthday party Charles hosted at Highgrove for his cousin, ex-King Constantine of Greece. However, her attitude towards Camilla would remain ambivalent. A firm believer in good housekeeping, at one juncture she felt that marriage would be the best way out of a messy domestic dilemma. But she became more cautious in her opinion when Charles's then private secretary Mark Bolland, whose methods she was extremely wary of, took Camilla over and organised a campaign to sell her to a sceptical public, worrying that he was pushing her forward too hard and too fast. What she was adamantly against was Camilla taking on any royal duties, official or otherwise.

The princes were too young to become embroiled in matters of such constitutional importance. For them it was simply a case of getting to know someone they knew their mother hated and they took a sensible attitude born out of necessity. They told their father that they didn't mind if she was around and, with relations established, Camilla was no longer required to organise her love affair with Charles around his sons' exeats and holidays. She was able to visit his homes in Gloucestershire and London without first checking to see if they were there, and when she stayed a night at St James's Palace shortly afterwards, William joined her and his father for breakfast the following morning.

What Camilla wisely never did was try to pick up where Diana had left off. She made a point of never interfering with the way Charles was bringing up William and Harry, other than to use the experience garnered with her own children's adolescence to point out why they sometimes behaved the way they did. That would prove invaluable when Harry suddenly went off the rails and started dabbling in drugs. In those early days, however, she preferred to keep in the background, following her own schedule, not imposing on theirs, but all the while building up a steady and tolerant relationship.

Both William and Harry's views of their father's paramour were mixed, as they were bound to be. Sometimes they liked her. At other times they found her presence irritating and absented themselves when she was around. She was a more untidy and a lot less tactile than their mother, and whereas Diana, on a good day, had always been full of bounding energy, Camilla was very much the countrywoman – matter-of-fact, straightforward, indifferent to how she looked and unconcerned about the impression she made.

That, in a way, was in her favour. A close friend of Camilla observed, 'Someone younger and more glamorous would have been far more threatening in their lives.'

Harry would probably have liked it if she had been more overtly affectionate – more like Tiggy. William saw her presence from a different perspective. He shared her love of hunting and, like Camilla, viewed with anger his grandmother's Labour government's plans to abolish the sport.

'William is very anxious about Tony Blair and the proposed anti-hunting law,' Diana once told me, and he often had heated debates with Lady Annabel Goldsmith's Green-minded sons, Zak and Ben. 'He gives the pro-hunting movement some cred,' said one of his closest friends.

For reasons of politics, both Camilla and William declined to join the pro-hunting march through London organised by the Countryside Alliance in 2002. But the prince delayed returning to university in order to be on the roof of St James's Palace to watch the marchers and used his mobile telephone to call through his support to his friends among the 500,000 people in the streets below. For her part, Camilla flew down from Birkhall that morning to attend the post-march party organised by novelist John Mortimer's wife Penny. She had a pro-hunting sticker on her shirt front, and I asked her if she had given any active support to the campaign to save hunting. She told me, 'I'm on the periphery.' She then left to join William at St James's Palace.

Camilla's friend explained, 'She worked at her relationship with the boys by not working at it. She just let it develop at its own pace. And she let them make the moves of friendship in their own time. She felt there was no point in pushing it.'

The first indication that William and Harry had accepted her into their lives came shortly after those first meetings in 1998 when they had insisted on inviting her to the surprise early fiftieth party they organised for their father at Highgrove on 31 July. The high point of the evening was a sketch based on the *Blackadder* television comedy, co-written and starring Rowan Atkinson who had figured prominently in their childhoods in the *Mr Bean* videos they used to watch with their mother. This one-off performance featured actors Stephen Fry and Emma Thompson alongside Atkinson and included walk-on parts for William and Harry. The *Blackadder* series had poked fun at such past monarchs as Queen Elizabeth I, and George IV as the Prince Regent. This time the jokes were aimed directly at their father, who William had become very adept at imitating, twisting his mouth and fiddling with his shirt cuffs.

William and Harry had arranged the seating plan. They put Camilla in the front row next to their father. It was their way of acknowledging her importance in his life.

The princes were back on stage again at the party for Charles's actual birthday in November. Like the previous bash, it was held in the Orchid Room at Highgrove and this time it was Camilla who did the organising. The Orchid Room has a stage and that night it was used by William and

Harry to give their interpretation of *The Full Monty*. There was some joshing between the two before they started their act. 'You go,' William told his brother. 'No, you go,' Harry replied. After a few moments of nervous indecision, they took the stage together.

Unlike the characters in the film, however, the princes did not shed all their clothes. William took off his dinner jacket and then his shirt. Harry did not get any further than a few shirt buttons. Charles looked on in mock horror and then joined in the laughter and cheering.

Afterwards William and Harry, well-fuelled from the bar, slipped outside for a cigarette. Diana had never smoked and Charles told me that, as a boy, he had sneaked out for an occasional puff 'behind the chicken coops at Sandringham, but I gave it up when I was eleven'. With the example of his grandfather, George VI, who had died of lung cancer, as a warning, Charles had subsequently become fervently anti-smoking. He made no concession for Camilla. She was getting through twenty a day, but he insisted that she had to do her smoking out of doors, even if it happened to be raining. When he discovered that his sons had also taken up the habit, he was furious.

It wasn't the smoking that would bring him the greatest distress, however. That was caused by the drugs that followed shortly afterwards.

Harry had settled well at Eton. He was in the same house as his brother and they shared the same tutor that William had for his first two years, Stuart-Clark. Some masters called him 'Wales'. Others referred to him simply as 'Harry'. Like William he joined the polo society and took a keen interest in football. 'He'd probably love to be playing soccer for England,' said his uncle, Charles Spencer. His talent with a ball was never that great, but like all schoolboys, he was entitled to his dreams. He also had a mischievous sense of humour, which he was quite willing to deploy at his brother's expense.

William was increasingly conscious of his position and disliked being reminded of it. When the Queen Mother held a tea party for Eton boys at the Guards Polo Club he arrived hidden on the floor of his bodyguard's car, and when he left he walked out backwards so that the waiting photographers could not get a shot of his face. And at school one day when William was striding through Eton High Street with his head bent in his customary posture so as to avoid eye contact with passers by, he was halted by a fellow pupil who then stood back to allow him to pass – giving him a sweeping mock bow as he did so. Without pausing or bothering to raise his eyes, William hissed angrily, 'Why don't you fuck off.'

Well aware of his brother's aversion to being recognised, Harry took advantage of it for his own amusement and on one occasion suddenly leapt out from behind a tree when William was taking part in a cross-country run to ask, 'Can I have your autograph?' That led to another flurry of expletives from William who complained that Harry's joke had cost him his place among the front runners.

'He was bit of a prankster when he first arrived at Eton and a lot more easy-going than his brother,' a contemporary in Gailey's house remembered. 'William was always aware of who he was. Harry didn't seem to care.'

It was an astute observation. Harry's devil-may-care attitude gave him a certain charm, but it was about to get him into the worst trouble of his life.

In his effort to merge into the background, William was always careful to avoid doing anything that was likely to attract attention. He was a studious pupil and he won the school cadet force's Sword of Honour, an excellent augur to the army career he was planning. For work experience he included a spell as an office junior with Spink and Co., the auction house a few minutes' walk from his home in St James's. He was appointed Eton's joint captain of swimming and wore a tracksuit bearing the initials WoW, which stood for William of Wales. In his last year he became a member of Pop, Eton's self-electing elite of prefects who are allowed to wear waistcoats of their own design. William had one made out of a Union Jack by the West End tailor Tom Gilbey with the message, 'Groovy Baby' written on it and another in purple with white spots. 'They made him look hoorayish but if you're that tall, with that build and have that youth you look good in any clothes,' said Old Etonian interior designer and style guru Nicky Haslam.

William enjoyed his five years at Eton 'very much'. Dr Gailey, he said, had been a 'tremendous support to me'. What he really liked, he said, was the anonymity the College had afforded him. As he admitted, 'I don't like attention. I feel uncomfortable with it.'

That wariness had not prevented him enjoying a varied social life. There was never any shortage of girls for him to choose from. In the argot of his contemporaries, he was 'fit', meaning handsome and desirable. On an official visit to Canada in 1998 he had been mobbed at every turn by screaming teenagers swearing undying love, and that enthusiasm for the good-looking prince carried over into the balls and clubs he visited in England. In his last year at Eton he was allowed to entertain and have what they called socials with girls from nearby schools such as Heathfield. He went to a number of dances and balls and ventured forth into the more louche environs of the K Bar Club in Soho, and to Jak's Club in Lower Sloane Street with his face daubed with gold paint for a 'Goldfinger' party. With his baggy trousers, hair jelled and self-conscious demeanour, he looked like any other teenager but his title gave him an immeasurable advantage when it came to chatting up the young women who circled around him like so many birds of prey. When he got fed up with their advances it amused him to round on them and say, 'Hi, I'm the future king. Wanna pull?'

Whatever tactic he used, he never suffered a shortage of girls and, proud of his fancy footwork, William would lure one then another young beauty on to the dance floor when techno music started playing. He usually outperformed them. Norwegian Annaliese Asbjornson, who William picked up at the bar in a nightclub in the Swiss resort of Crans Montana, gave a flattering account of her turn on the dance floor in which she compared the Prince to Patrick Swayze, star of the film *Dirty Dancing*.

He did some more picking up at the polo match in 1999 at the Guards Club hosted by Cartier the jewellers. He went with Edward van Cutsem and Viscount Bridport's Eton-educated son Peregrine Hood, a descendant of Admiral Nelson. The prince named the 'King of Cool' by America's *People* magazine was seated at a table at the back of the large marquee wearing what the fashion critics decreed was a pair of very uncool skiing sunglasses. That did not seem to detract from his appeal in any way. He was soon surrounded by a bevy of girls including Katherine Bearman, daughter of a Lloyd's insurance broker, and Lord Vestey's niece, Tamara, whose mother, Rosie, had once dated Prince Charles. In royal circles succeeding generations had liked to keep it in the family, but William was determined to cast his net wider and when he went for a cruise later that summer aboard the Latsis's yacht he insisted on inviting who he wanted. Among them were eighteen-year-old Emilia d'Erlanger, whose father worked for British Midlands Airways, sixteen-year-old Mary Forestier-Walker, the daughter of a former Guards officer, and Norfolk landowner's daughter Davina Duckworth-Chad, twenty-one, whose parents had frequently been shooting guests of his father's at Sandringham.

One young woman who wasn't aboard the yacht was the rich but erratic Tara Palmer-Tomkinson, who had known the boys since they were children and became a minor television personality after appearing in the programme *I'm a Celebrity . . . Get Me Out of Here*. Her mother, Patti, remained one of Charles's closest friends, but Tara's antics were deemed to make her a less than suitable influence on the princes. At a swimming party in the pool at Highgrove she discarded decorum along with her bikini top and then allegedly removed William's bathing trunks which she hid in the bushes. A rumour quickly spread that it had not ended there. She denied the story, saying, 'I've heard this stuff about sleeping with him. I have never even been to his rooms at the Palace. It's nonsense.'

In unabashed vein she continued, 'Kids are kids. People can make such an issue of things. It's so frustrating when things are taken out of context and it takes a fun situation and turns it into a serious thing.'

Of darker concern was Tara's taste for alcohol and cocaine. It was shared by Camilla's son, Tom. While studying English at Oxford University he became a leading light in the notoriously wild Assassins Club, whose members often drink themselves into a stupor, and the Piers Gaveston Society, named after the homosexual lover of the medieval King Edward II, where the emphasis was on sex. In 1995 he was cautioned by police for possessing cannabis and Ecstasy.

In 1999 Charles and Camilla entertained Patti Palmer-Tomkinson and her husband Charles to dinner at Highgrove. It was supposed to be a gesture of support for their guests, whose daughter Tara had just been admitted to a drug rehabilitation clinic in the United States. But that afternoon they received the news that Tom had been caught using cocaine.

The evening turned into a fraught discussion between three sets of parents. Charles was 'in despair' with concern over the dangers his sons were being exposed to and, although he was too polite to spell it out, their close association with two supposedly glamorous young people who they looked up to and admired but who happened to be beset with drug problems. He had always been frightened that his sons might go the way of the children of so many of his contemporaries and succumb to the lure of illegal substances. He once told me, 'Drugs are something that worries me a great deal, but I don't know what to do about it. They are so vulnerable, but how can you warn them off the dangers? They are so available, especially things like Ecstasy. Trying to talk to them from one's own experience is a little bit of help, but I don't have any first-hand knowledge of drugs. The only drug I ever took was cigarettes.'

Like any ordinary parent, the prince was caught between a desire to protect his children, while at the same time not wanting to be overly restrictive. He said, 'You can attempt to impose rules and regulations but those don't always work.' It was a delicate balancing act and there were occasions when he had got reason to be concerned about the company William was keeping in the clubs and bars of London's West End where drugs are readily available.

William managed to circumvent those pitfalls. His brother did not. The good fortune that had kept Harry out of trouble for so long finally deserted him in the summer of 2001. It arrived, not in a low dive in a big city, but in the seemingly innocent setting of the sixteenth-century Rattlebone Inn in the picturesque little village of Sherston, a short drive away from Highgrove in Wiltshire.

The pub had become a popular meeting place for the rich kids of the area. They arrived in Golf GTIs and Range Rovers for afternoons and evenings of drink and jollity. Harry was only sixteen, but he already had the

239

reputation for being what in his father's days at school had been called a 'bit of a shade'.

At the Duke of Westminster's grand dance in Cheshire the previous year he had drunk so much that he was sick in the bushes.

In Marbella in Spain a few weeks earlier he had made a nuisance of himself by turning the golf course into a mechanised polo field, tearing up and down the fairways on his buggy and hacking up the grass with his club.

On holiday at Rock in Cornwall he incurred the wrath of the well-connected mothers of several girls for treating their daughters with macho contempt. 'He seemed to think he could do whatever he liked because of who he is,' one complained.

Some of his exploits were exaggerated. He had been accused of being so drunk in a nightclub in Spain that he ended up crawling around the floor. 'That was rubbish,' he said. 'I had dropped my mobile phone and was looking for it. That was all.'

There was no denying what happened at the Rattlebone, however. He took part in several after-hours drinking sessions and got involved in a fight. When the French under-manager François Ortet banned him after being informed by the prince's protection officer that he was under age, Harry rounded on him and called him a 'fucking frog'.

It was the behaviour of a rich, spoilt brat and there was worse to follow. Even in sleepy West Country villages, drugs are available to those who want them and a number of dealers found a ready market for their wares among the well-heeled clientele of pubs like the Rattlebone. With cannabis in their pockets, Harry and his gang, including any available girls, would head back to Highgrove where part of the cellars, which run the length of the house, had been converted into a teenage den. Harry dubbed the area Club H. It was where he and William could play their techno and garage music as loud as they wanted without disturbing their father.

It was not the music that upset Charles. It was the revelation that Harry had abused his trust and smoked dope in the bushes outside.

Charles, often away on official business, had no inkling of what his younger son was getting up to. He only found out about home-alone

Harry's antics when he was alerted by a member of his Highgrove staff. He confronted his son, who had the honesty to admit what he had been up to. Rather than lose his temper, Charles sat him down and reasoned with him, explaining the dangers, pointing out that if it happened again he faced the catastrophe of being expelled from Eton and reminding him how upset Diana would have been.

What the Prince of Wales was hoping against hope was that Harry's misconduct would somehow escape notice. The Queen's uncle, the Duke of Kent, had suffered from serious problems with cocaine and morphine that had required treatment in a sanatorium. That did not become generally known until many years after he was killed in a military plane crash in 1942. The days when princely misdemeanours could be swept under a carpet of discretion were long past, however, as Charles was well aware. 'If they get into trouble everyone is going to know,' he told me and soon everyone did.

In January 2002, the story of 'Harry's drugs shame' was splashed across the front page of the *News of the World* and went on to make headlines around the world. Harry was pulled out of school for the day and driven to Highgrove where he was confronted by his father. In the effort to draw the sting, Charles revealed that he had taken Harry to a heroin clinic in Peckham in South London to listen to addicts describe their misery. 'Harry told me that he had definitely learned something,' the clinic's chief executive, Bill Puddicombe, said afterwards. He was contrite and apologised to his father, over and over, for what he had done.

That had been the intention. It also had the welcome spin-off of diverting attention from the future king. For William, too, had attended some of those late-night drinking sessions in the public houses around Highgrove. One night he had lined up thirty-six pints of 'snake bite', a brutal combination of lager and strong cider, and with the help of ten friends downed the lot. It was followed by a burping competition initiated by Emma Tomlinson, whose father Simon had started the Beaufort polo club, after one of the pints had proved too much for her digestive system. And William was there when Harry had called Ortet a 'frog'. William warned him, 'Careful – you know what happened to royalty in France,' and made the action of having his head cut off.

Ortet recalled, 'It did shut Harry up for a bit, but not for long. He wasn't really aggressive, just cocky. Sometimes when he was being loud William would say, "Hey, Harry, sit down, keep it cool." '

Significantly, William was on good terms with many of the people who had joined his brother on those late-night binges in Club H. But while William escaped censure, Guy Pelly did not.

The Stowe-educated son of a Kent landowner with a home in Gloucestershire, he was a paid-up member of the West Country set. His aunt Claire was once married to the Earl of Pembroke, who owns stately Wilton House near Salisbury where Charles and Camilla used to rendezvous while Diana was still alive. His father, John, said, 'Guy has spent a lot of time in Gloucestershire, involved in healthy country pursuits like the Beaufort Hunt. That is how they all met.'

One newspaper labelled him Harry's 'worst influence'. It was a damning condemnation for a family who had devoted over six pages in *Burke's Peerage* to their aristocratic lineage – a full two pages more than that given over to the Duke of Beaufort, a direct descendant of the medieval kingmaker John of Gaunt who numbers most of the royal houses of Europe among his relations. Guy, then aged nineteen and a student at Cirencester's Royal Agricultural College, issued a statement refuting the charge. It read, 'I should like to make it clear that I have never dealt in drugs at Highgrove, at the Rattlebone Inn pub or anywhere else. I have never taken drugs with Prince Harry or supplied any drugs to him.'

What he diplomatically declined to mention was the fact that he was best friends, not with Harry, but with William. In the horse trading between the *News of the World* and St James's Palace that took place before the story was published, William was conveniently air-brushed out. Someone was going to have to take the rap for this debacle, however, and Pelly made a convenient fall guy.

'William was furious about the whole business,' a friend recalled. 'He's very loyal and like Diana in that respect.'

Sandy Henney, who served as press secretary until her dismissal over the dispute between St James's Palace and the *Daily Telegraph* about the ownership of photographs taken to commemorate William's 18th birthday, told me, 'He doesn't like anyone saying things on his behalf.'

William felt he had done nothing wrong and believed that Harry had been unfairly pilloried. He also felt responsible, in part at least, for the ignominy that had been heaped on Pelly. A few weeks later he invited him and Harry to the England versus Ireland rugby match at Twickenham. It was a show of royal support to a beleaguered friend which Charles did not have the will to veto. Harry was still at school but William was now nineteen years old and legally of age to make his own decisions.

He had left Eton and the experiences of his gap year had taught him to stand on his own feet.

SIXTEEN

Gap Year Adventures

In his last term at Eton, after a game of football and some frantic last-minute revision for his looming 'A' level exams, William would slip out of his house and make his way to Tap. There, over a pint of lager drawn from behind the wooden bar, he would sit with friends on one of the red velveteen sofas and outline his plans for the year ahead.

Tap has been the setting for conversations of this sort for generations. Situated in an alleyway just off Eton's High Street, it is the drinking room reserved for the College's senior boys. William was a frequent visitor. On weekdays he would drop by during the mid-morning break known as Chambers for a quick cup of coffee and a hot sausage sandwich before rushing on to his next lecture. On Saturdays there was time to linger. It is the night when beer is served and it gave his conversation the animation of expectation. His schooldays were drawing to their close and, while he had thoroughly enjoyed the five years at the College, the future beckoned.

He was not quite as enthusiastic about that as most of his contemporaries. They could hardly wait to leave a college which, for all its privileges and kudos, was still a school with the rules and regulations that eighteen-year-olds find increasingly irksome. It was different for William. As he admitted, 'I've really enjoyed being able to go about Eton as just another student without the media attention. I have particularly appreciated being left alone at Eton, which has allowed me to concentrate on my school work and enjoy being with my friends without being followed by cameras.' The

College had given him the privacy he places such store in and which he knew was going to become ever more difficult to preserve.

However, with a couple of pints inside him (the maximum allowed), even this most self-conscious of young men could not help being caught up in the mood of excited expectation. Plans were outlined and endlessly mulled over – for touring Europe in camper vans, back-packing in South America or trekking in the Far East. None of those options was open to the prince, but that didn't stop him plotting his own schemes.

What he wanted to do, he told his friends in Tap, was go to Argentina and play polo. To his young mind it seemed a perfect way of spending the better part of his gap year, that twelve-month sabbatical between school and university that has come to be regarded as a right by boys and girls in Britain. William is an enthusiastic polo player and Argentina is to polo what neighbouring Brazil is to football. It produces both the best players and the best ponies, and William argued that a spell on the Pampas was vital if he was ever going to achieve his ambition and become a high-goal player. Argentina also has the advantage of being on the other side of the Atlantic, an ocean away from the destiny he wishes to postpone for as long as possible.

It was gross misreading of his position. The days when princes could behave like playboys and be applauded for it are long gone. His father was most emphatic on that point. Prince Charles rejected his son's suggestion out of hand, dismissing it as 'a decadent throwback'. Charles had hated his time at Gordonstoun but he had nonetheless been imbued with the school's tradition of community service, and was keen that his Eton-educated son should acquire some practical experience of helping those less fortunate. He told William that he had to use his time 'positively'. William can be very headstrong but on this occasion he had no choice but to fall in with his father's wishes.

In these disagreements between father and son it is Charles who usually backs down. Not this time. To William's surprise and annoyance Charles invited a meeting of worthies to lunch at St James's Palace to discuss his son's future. They included the Bishop of London, the Right Reverend

Two days before his seventeenth birthday in June 1999, William and Harry leave St George's Chapel in Windsor after the wedding of Prince Edward and Sophie Rhys-Jones (*PA Photos*)

Sibling rivalry: when William and Harry were younger they fought
with each other (above) but, although they now get on, the rivalry is still there on
the polo field (below) (*UK Press*; *PA Photos*)

Harry and William on opposing teams for bicycle polo at the Jockeys v Eventers
charity polo match at Tidworth Polo Club in Wiltshire (*PA Photos*)

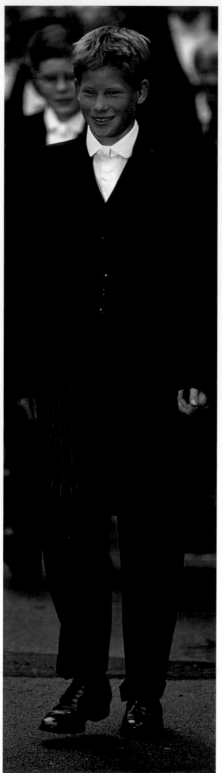

(Left) Harry in his Eton tails on his first day, 3 September 1998 (*Richard Gillard*); (above) William aged seventeen in Pop, Eton's group of twenty-one elected prefects in a school of 1,280 boys. They are allowed to wear fancy waistcoats and sponge bag trousers (*Alpha*)

Harry helps Prince Charles fasten his gloves on the steps of St Paul's cathedral for the Queen's Golden Jubilee service in June 2002 (*Alpha*)

William, an Aston Villa fan, shows off his skills with a ball while chatting to a friend on his mobile phone (*UK Press*)

Harry in his favourite Highgrove team polo shirt. He is a superb horseman and has the makings of a top-class polo player (*UK Press*)

William demonstrates his fancy footwork to one of his many female admirers during a break in a polo match in the summer of 2002 (*UK Press*)

Richard Chartres, who has been part of the prince's circle since their undergraduate days at Cambridge; former cabinet minister and governor of Hong Kong Chris Patten, who is now an EU commissioner; and William's Eton housemaster, Dr Andrew Gailey. Also at the lunch was Charles's private secretary, Stephen Lamport. Another influential voice was Dr Eric Anderson, former headmaster and now Provost of Eton, who had been Charles's tutor at Gordonstoun.

Just such a group of dignitaries had been summoned thirty-five years before to make a similar decision about Charles's own future. Led by his great-uncle Earl Mountbatten of Burma, they had decreed that he would attend university and then serve in the armed forces. The prince had hated what they did to him. He complained, 'You can't understand what it is like to have your whole life mapped out for you . . . it is so awful to be programmed.' He was determined that this would not happen to his son. He explained to his chosen advisers that while a year in Argentina was unacceptable, he wanted his son to travel and meet people from different lands and backgrounds in order to gain the worldly knowledge that would prepare him for the lifetime of responsibility that lay ahead.

Charles was proved right, for by the end of the his gap year William had formed clear views on a number of subjects ranging from the environment and the Third World to the plight of Britain's beleaguered farmers and, although he was too astute to speak about them openly, the policies of his grandmother's Labour government. In a constitutional monarchy, the sovereign must remain above politics. But that does not preclude them from having opinions and William's were becoming pronounced and, in many respects, notably conservative.

The time when William might be called upon to express his views to whoever happens to be his prime minister lies in the future, however. In the meantime, as William explained, 'My father wants me to finish full-time education before doing royal duties and so do I. It will be a few years before I do royal engagements, although I expect as in the past, I will sometimes accompany my father.' But that, as it turned out, was not very often – and hardly at all during his gap year when, on Charles's instance, his son was allowed to enjoy himself in a way as similar as possible to other boys of the same age.

That is exactly what his late mother would have wanted. She was adamant that William be allowed to grow up 'normally', and it was with the echo of Diana's wishes very much in mind that Charles asked his son to come up with a range of suggestions that would combine fun with worthy purpose. William had no choice but to fall in with his father's wishes. But if this was not quite what he had had in mind for his gap year, the promise that he would be given ample opportunity to enjoy himself was enough to keep William, who can be surly if he does not get his way, in reasonable spirits.

He was certainly in good humour during his last week at Eton. He was in his study packing his trunk and taking the posters down from the walls when a gaggle of fellow leavers burst in. A pillow fight erupted and William was overwhelmed and found himself beneath a mass of heaving boys. He tried to press the security bleeper he has to wear at all times to summon his Police Protection Officer to come to his aid, but the other boys were having none of that. This was the end of term and everyone was in party mood. They grabbed hold of the bleeper, rushed out of the room, down the staircase and out on to the lawn. With William in hot pursuit, they sprinted the 300 metres to the banks of the Thames. When they got to the river, they pressed the bleeper – and hurled it into the water. It sank without trace to great roars of laughter, with William joining in.

He was equally relaxed a few days later when he went to Rock, the resort on Cornwall's north coast that has become the summer magnet for thousands of public school-educated teenagers from all over Britain. It is a place the Famous Five would have enjoyed if Enid Blyton had allowed them to grow up, and William spent his days either lounging around on the beach (like his father he likes to keep up his suntan) or in a black rubber wet suit out on a surfboard catching the waves roaring in from the Atlantic (he is a good swimmer like his mother). He played tennis and spent a day on a smack fishing for mackerel.

At night he joined the other youngsters for pints of lager at the Oystercatcher pub before heading off into the dunes behind Daymer beach.

There he would sit around the campfires made out of driftwood, chatting, smoking the occasional cigarette and sipping beer out of a can. One night someone brought a ghetto blaster, which thundered out acid house music. William started dancing in the flickering firelight with first one girl then another. 'Well, sort of dancing, but in that light it looked more like prancing,' said Sherbourne-educated Richard Fox, who was there that night.

Unlike Tap there are no restrictions on how many beers he could drink, and after his spell at the Oystercatcher William's coordination was not all that it might have been. At one point he backed into a pretty blonde and stumbled in the sand. Another girl – a very pretty brunette – called Lally helped him to his feet and adjusted the sheepskin fleece he was wearing. The collar, she said, must not be worn down; it had to be turned up in the prescribed public school style. She turned it up for him. He wore it up for the rest of the summer.

On another evening on the beach a group of very pretty young girls had a bet among themselves to see which one of them could 'snog' William. The prince entered enthusiastically into the game. There were no losers. Asked how he coped with the attention of girls, he replied, 'In my own way.' At Rock, in the company of public school youngsters drawn from well-heeled backgrounds, his way seemed to work pretty well.

It wasn't long before the work his father had insisted should form an essential part of his year off came into play, however, and after his sojourn at Rock he flew to Belize to join the Welsh Guards on exercise in the jungles of Central America. It was a tough environment for a prince whose only trips abroad had been to expensive ski resorts and to St Tropez in the South of France as a guest of Harrods owner Mohamed Al Fayed, whose son Dodi romanced Diana.

Situated just to the north of what is aptly named the Mosquito Coast, Belize is undeveloped, hot, steamy and covered in thick jungle full of snakes, crocodiles and flesh-eating insects. The temperature rarely falls below 80 degrees even at night. It rains almost every day and when it isn't pouring down the humidity is in the high 90s. There is the danger of malaria and, even more threateningly, of leishmaniasis, an infection transmitted by insect bite which unless treated immediately has a 40 per cent death rate and results in as many as a dozen British soldiers a year being medi-vaced back to Britain for a month's in-patient treatment at the Hospital for Tropical Diseases.

When William was only four, in 1985, his uncle Prince Edward had spent a week there with 40 Commando and found it a daunting experience. So did William.

As he was being driven to the jungle by Winston Harris, a Belizean who had been awarded the MBE for his work in training the SAS in jungle tactics, he was told that if he was bitten by a poisonous snake he had to kill it with a machete so the doctors could measure it and assess the amount of anti-venom serum to administer.

He was taught how to kill and prepare his food. An exercise code-named Native Trail began with instructors slaughtering a pig, hanging it from a pole and butchering it. The soldiers, William included, were then given a live chicken to dispatch. They had to wring its neck and cut off its head and feet with a machete, pluck its feathers and gut it before cooking it over a fire, exactly as they would have to do if they were living off the land in a jungle war. They were shown how to make a termite stew – and then made to eat it. At night William tried to snatch what little sleep he could in the rain in a hammock strung between two trees.

It was very different from the 'What would you like for lunch and what time would you like it, sir?' pampered lifestyle he had been treated to at Balmoral and Sandringham (and, indeed, at Highgrove), but according to the Army he approached it 'with vigour'.

Corporal Claud Martinez of the Belizean defence force who took part in the exercises said afterwards, 'The prince would make a good soldier. He has the physical structure and mental strength. He was surrounded by men firing machine-guns and still he looked at ease. I never saw a moment of panic on his face.' That was not as surprising as Corporal Martinez made out. William, who had been an enthusiastic member of the Eton cadet corps, had handled firearms since he was a boy and is an excellent shot. Even so, he had found the Belize expedition tough going, and it was with a feeling of considerable relief that he flew back to Scotland to join his father grouse shooting on the moors of Balmoral.

It was a happy homecoming. While he was away his 'A' level results had come through. When his housemaster, Dr Gailey, failed to get through to the Welsh Guards barracks in Belize he had telephoned Charles who was with Camilla in Scotland to give him the news. The Prince then e-mailed them on to Belize. It was the first time he had ever succeeded in sending an electronic message, which made it something of a triumph for them both. 'Prince Charles was absolutely delighted,' recalled an aide. 'I have rarely seen him so happy.'

William had achieved an A in geography, a B in history of art and a C in biology, and although that did not single him out as an intellectual high-flier, it was enough to gain him admittance to St Andrews, his university of choice. 'I'm thrilled and relieved,' he said. So was his father, who gave him a motorcycle as a reward. William was delighted and somewhat surprised. As he told friends, 'I know the old man disapproves of motorbikes.' But in Charles's mind his son and heir had earned it and he was happy for him to use it on the private roads on Balmoral's 50,000-acre estate.

That still left the problem of what to do with the rest of his gap year, however. With the help of Mark Dyer, the former captain in the Welsh Guards and equerry to Prince Charles who had become William's confidant, he mapped out no fewer than five separate schedules. None met with the approval of Charles. He was concerned that William was still planning what the public would interpret as an unacceptable, year-long holiday.

There was talk of him taking a job at the art auctioneers Christie's, but this time it was William's turn to put his foot down. 'I didn't want to sit around and get a job back in London,' he explained. 'I wanted to get out and see a bit of the world.'

London would claim at least some of his time, however, and he took the opportunity to improve his dancing which had so noticeably failed to impress at Rock. One evening he learnt how to moonwalk in the style of Michael Jackson.

As a youngster, the Prince had always been a fan of the singer who no less an authority than Fred Astaire called 'the greatest dancer of the modern age'. At Kensington Palace he had tried to master some of Jackson's intricate footwork and he had practised the steps in his bedsitting room at Eton. But it was not until he attended the nineteenth-birthday get-together for his friend Guy Pelly at the Catch Bar on London's Old Brompton Road that he finally learnt how to give the appearance of movement while all the time standing still.

William arrived in the bar's private room downstairs wearing a baseball cap, a coat with the collar turned up and a scarf wrapped around his face. 'All you could see was his eyes,' one guest recalls. He looked like a celebrity trying to avoid attention, which of course is exactly what he was. Once he was safely among friends, he shed his disguise and drank a few glasses of champagne. Everyone was laughing and joking. When one of the guests started moonwalking to the music thundering in the background, William said, 'I'll have a go at that.' He put down his glass, stood up and with the other young man showing him the way, did his Jackson impersonation. After a few minutes he said, 'I've cracked it.'

Like both his parents, William is a good dancer but unlike his father he does not confine himself just to the waltz, quickstep and jive. When he gets out on to the dance floor he is more like his mother – unselfconscious and not frightened of letting his hair down.

He was able to do just that when, in September 2000 and accompanied by Dyer, he flew for a month-long visit to Rodrigues, a nine-mile-long island surrounded by coral reefs in the middle of the Indian Ocean. The trip was born out of William's interest in conservation. Diana had no interest in the hearty country pursuits the Royal Family is so addicted to. William, on the other hand, likes nothing better than crawling through the heather in pursuit of stag and bird and then talking about the day's activities afterwards with the gillies. Like his grandfather, Prince Philip, he sees no contradiction between shooting and conservation. In that sense he is very royal.

Away from the Highlands, however, he becomes a young man of his era. He is concerned about pollution and global warming, and it was the damage to the coral reefs caused by a rise in sea temperatures that took him to Rodrigues. His trip was organised by the Royal Geographic Society, which was running a programme to see what could be done to save that fragile, delicate marine life.

He arrived without fuss or protocol from Mauritius in a chartered light aircraft. He registered with immigration as plain 'Brian Woods' and stayed at Le Domaine de Decide, a £26-a-night corrugated iron-roofed lodge settled behind eucalyptus trees at the end of a pot-holed dirt track. The place suited him. He does not like the protocols of royalty and does what he can to avoid its trappings, including the titles that are part of his birthright. At the age of eighteen he should have become His Royal Highness Prince William of Wales. It is an honorific he declined to accept. 'Just call me William,' he insisted.

Everyone on Rodrigues was happy to do that. Most of them, in fact, had no idea who he was. Even the estates housekeeper Michelette Eduard, who served him his breakfast of ham, eggs, beans and coffee every morning, was unaware of his identity. 'It was only afterwards when people started talking about him being on the island that I realised who I had been looking after.'

He was able to drive around the rough roads unhindered on a Honda 125cc motorbike and go scuba diving off the reef looking for ancient wrecks without a camera in sight, to lounge in peace and solitude on the empty beaches of one of the world's remotest destinations. It was only by chance that a photographer took a snap of him teaching some youths on the beach how to play rugby.

It was not the only lesson he tried to give the local people. He went out with some fishermen and 'tried to stop them dynamiting for fish'. He had no more success at that than he had trying to explain the rules of rugby football to people who speak only a Creole patois. For William, fishing is a leisurely day's entertainment on the River Dee. For the people of Rodrigues it is a livelihood, and they did not take kindly to his suggestion that they should put in the hard labour of casting and hauling in nets for a fraction of the catch explosives bring them.

Yet despite that cultural conflict he was enchanted by the islands of the Indian Ocean, just as Camilla Parker Bowles had been when she holidayed there five months earlier and at whose suggestion William had visited the area. The following Easter he was there again, although this time he stayed at the altogether more salubrious five-star hotel St Geran on the tourist island of Mauritius.

It is not some distant isle the Prince was born to reign over, however. He is a future king of the United Kingdom of Great Britain and Northern Ireland and Head of the Commonwealth of which Mauritius is one of the smallest members. And once he was back home his anonymity was stripped away as quickly as he shed his shirt in the tropical sunshine. It was nearly four years since the tragic death of his mother, but she remained a subject of interest and controversy. There was a flurry of books about her, and for all her obvious attributes many were critical.

Her former private secretary Patrick Jephson wrote one of the most damning. He gave a harsh account of her mental state and what he regarded as her manipulative and at times hysterical personality. The author argued that it was a factual and therefore important examination of the princess who so dramatically reshaped the Royal Family. William saw it as a betrayal of trust.

On his return from Rodrigues he faced his first press conference. It was held at Highgrove and, in a show of parental support, Charles stood at his son's side as he faced a daunting phalanx of cameras and television lights and reporters armed with notebooks and pens. The difference between the two future kings was notable. Charles was dressed in a conservative double-breasted suit, his brown shoes polished to a parade-ground shine, a display handkerchief in his breast pocket, his hair neatly brushed and parted. William was in jeans, sweater and trainers with his blond locks tumbling over his forehead. But despite their sartorial differences there was an easy and affectionate bond between the two, underlined by Charles's presence at William's side for what both knew would be a difficult occasion.

The conference had been convened as a thank you to the media for respecting William's privacy while he was at Eton, but it was the Jephson book that excited everyone's attention. William knew exactly what was expected of him and in answer to a pre-prepared question he said, 'Harry and I are both quite upset about it, that our mother's trust has been betrayed and that, even now, she is still being exploited. But I don't want to say any more at the moment.'

Or ever, if he can get away with it. The prince is enough of a Windsor to grasp the fundamental rule of royalty that private matters must never be aired in public if regal dignity is to be maintained. Yet despite having to address a question he found too personal for comfort, William gave a confident performance in front of the cameras. This was his show, conducted on his terms, and it was clear that he liked being in charge. And when he wasn't, as with the direction his gap year was going to take, he still insisted on having a say in the details.

It had been his father's suggestion that he go on an Operation Raleigh expedition. It was William who decided on Chile. 'Some friends of mine said how nice the Chileans were, so I thought why not come and see how it is.' He said. 'I choose Chile because I had never been to South America before and I also wanted to go somewhere colder rather than hotter.'

He got what he wanted. The trip took him deep into Patagonia close to the southernmost tip of the continent. It is a wild, rugged region very like the Highlands of Scotland but on a grander scale where what passes for the summer sun never manages to melt the snows on the jagged peaks of the Andes. It rains with depressing frequency, and just getting to where he was going was a battle against the elements. There are no roads leading to the small logging town of Tortel in an isolated inlet. Even a horse could not make it. The only way in is by canoe or by light aircraft on one of the most dangerous flights in the world. William and eleven other fellow adventurers went by river.

It proved to be a perilous journey. The weather closed in without warning. William recalled, 'The wind whipped up into a storm. The tents were flapping so violently that we thought they were going to blow away. Everything was soaked through. I had never seen rain like it. It was so heavy and it just did not stop.'

They took refuge on a sandbank, where they were stranded for five days. 'It was quite demoralising even though we managed to keep ourselves going by singing and stuff like that.' He confessed, 'I don't think I have ever been as low as that. Everyone was thinking, "Why did I choose to come here?" '

Belize had been tough, but there he was with professional soldiers. In Chile he was with young people, many of them from deprived homes, and none of them trained in the art of wilderness survival.

As well the elements, he also had his own royal reserve to contend with. 'I found it very difficult myself to start with because I am a very private person,' he admitted. Later, in Tortel when the National Anthem struck up one night, he hid his head in his hands and groaned, 'Oh no, please no.' Wherever he was, his royal mantle went with him. There was no getting away from it even in the backwoods of Chile, a place that, if he had been allowed his own way, he would never have visited.

In a moment of candour, he admitted, 'I never thought I was going to like Raleigh,' he said. He certainly wasn't on a journey of self-discovery. 'I didn't really do it because I wanted to change myself, ' he insisted. Stranded on a sand spit, however, and surrounded by raging torrents, he had no alternative but to adapt. He had to get along with the people he was huddled with in a tent to escape the driving rain and the vicious wind. And the only way to do that, he discovered, was to be open and honest. 'You don't have any secrets,' he said. 'You share everything with everyone.'

Not quite everything. When fellow adventurer Claire Flood, a nineteen-year-old trainee hairdresser from Birkenhead, asked him point blank if he was still a virgin, 'he didn't answer my question and just went bright red'.

When William arrived in Chile the girls in the party surrounded him. Sensing his embarrassment, one of the young men decided to give him some streetwise support. Kevin Mullen, a former drug addict from Scotland who had spent several stints behind bars, recalled, 'He was surrounded there, absolutely surrounded by girls, so I decided to wander over and introduce myself. I said, "All right there, Will? I'm Kev. Are the lasses bothering you?" These girls were swarming all over him and he just laughed and said, "Yes, they are, actually." '

Gradually, however, the prince started to unbend. He joined the rest of the group for late-night drinking sessions of local wine and beer. And in a small town of some 400 souls, he had no alternative but to muck in with the locals.

There are no cars or motorbikes in Tortel. There aren't even any roads. The only link between the whitewashed, corrugated iron-roofed houses is narrow wooden walkways that thread their way through the hills tumbling down from the Andes into the coastal inlet. Life there is simple and the prince slept with the others in a makeshift dormitory in a wooden hut beside the river. His daily chores included taking his turn washing the dishes and cleaning the one communal loo, which did not have a seat and flushed only erratically.

There is an infant school next door where William went for the one photocall the press was afforded. It proved to be a painful experience. He was photographed with Alejandro Heredia on his shoulders. The unruly six-year-old took fiendish delight in pulling the prince's hair. Monica Barra, the twenty-two-year-old teacher who was pulling her own hair out trying to keep her young charges under control in front of the TV cameras, observed, 'The prince didn't look in very often. He only came here to have his picture taken.' William's wariness was understandable. As he diplomatically remarked after he had managed to extricate himself from Alejandro's clutches, 'The children are sort of different from English children because they don't hold back and they do whatever they want.'

They were better behaved at the high school where he taught English in between helping repair the narrow, rain-lashed walkways. There he was treated to a simple breakfast of coffee, toast and homemade papaya jam.

'He loved that jam,' recalled teacher Fresia Rios Vergare. 'He liked it so much that he started eating it straight off the spoon, without bothering with the toast. Just dipping his spoon into the jar and taking huge mouthfuls.'

They were not the table manners likely to impress his grandmother, the Queen, but then Tortel is a very long way from the refinements of Buckingham Palace. The entertainment served up at the Celes Salom was equally raw. The rough and ready restaurant perched on a hill ten minutes' walk from the dormitory doubles as the town nightclub. The red wine cost £3 a litre and the band that pounded away in the corner on weekend nights was composed of local loggers and port hands. The prince seemed to enjoy himself, though. The restaurant's owner Sara Quezada, recalled, 'He bought lots of drinks. He even took a turn as disc jockey when the band stopped for their beer break.'

What he refused to do when he first arrived in Tortel was dance. 'Too shy,' Sara said. It was the nursery teacher Monica Barra who broke through his reserve. One evening she boldly took him by the hand and led him out on to the tiny dance floor. He wasn't very good at following her Latin steps, but his efforts earned him a reward nonetheless.

Following local custom, Monica planted a kiss on his cheek when the tune finished. The prince duly reciprocated. The ice of aloofness broken, he invited other girls out on to the floor and by evening's end almost every girl in the tiny room had kissed William, thereby giving a new interpretation to the old song about knowing a guy who knew a girl who danced with the (future) Prince of Wales. Monica recalled, 'He was very charming.' As, indeed, a prince should be.

Not everyone was seduced by his royal charisma, however. A keen Aston Villa supporter, William had spent a lot of his spare time talking football with Kevin Mullen, a fan of Glasgow Celtic. Kevin proved a lot less friendly when the prince tried to move in on Sasha Hashim, a trainee beauty therapist from the Wirral who had teamed up with the tough Glaswegian at the start of the expedition.

'He was dirty dancing with a lot of the girls, but the lasses didn't mind because they liked him,' Kevin recalled. 'The next thing I knew he was trying to pull my girlfriend. Let's just say that words were exchanged. It was nothing nasty because he and I get on very well. But I don't care if you are the future king – you don't start messing about with other people's girlfriends.'

There was no stepping aside for royalty in Tortel and William backed away. It is not the kind of situation his father ever had to confront but

William dealt with it neatly enough. In his ability to respond to people's moods, he showed himself to be his mother's son. Even Kevin responded well to him, despite their spat. 'Will is good fun – a real joker and popular with everyone,' said the young man from the crime-hit View Park Estate outside Glasgow.

Sasha agreed. She admitted that she had been 'embarrassed' by the incident but added, 'Will was brilliant and actually much less stuck up than some of the other people, who I think looked down on us a bit.'

William responded, 'I was with a group of people I wouldn't normally be with and getting along with them was great fun – and educational. There were some real characters in the group who don't hold back any words at all.'

It had been a tough ten weeks that had rubbed off a lot of William's Etonian gloss. He had been forced to join in, pull his weight and stand up for himself and there had been occasions when he found it hard going. But in Patagonia's harsh environment he had learnt important lessons about compromise and adaptability. He had also come to value the spiritual release that is to be found in physical labour, as have other princes before him, and that turned out to be a good preparation for the next stage of his gap year.

On his return to England and after spending Christmas with his family at Sandringham, he went to work as a farm labourer. His day began before sunrise and the next twelve hours were spent shifting bales of silage, milking the ninety cows and washing down the milking sheds afterwards, with only a short break for a sandwich lunch. And all for the less-than-princely sum of £3.20 an hour.

The Prince of Wales's Duchy of Cornwall owns any number of farms where he could have picked up a pitchfork, but it had been William's own decision not to go to for work experience where, as he put it, 'I'd always be the boss's son.' By choosing to work for someone else, he was reaffirming his determination to break free from the protocols that so constricted his royal predecessors. 'I enjoyed the fact that I was put in as a hand and was paid and was just another guy on the farm.'

He was never 'just another guy', of course. Hill Court is an organic dairy farm belonging to Captain Simon Tomlinson and his wife, Claire, who owns the Beaufort Polo Club where Prince Charles is patron and William plays. While the other labourers were always careful to doff their caps whenever they were in the presence of the Tomlinsons, William treated them in the easy manner of lifelong friends. He has known their attractive daughter, Emma (who once appeared covered in nothing but slices of fruit for a cookbook, *In the Buff*, which raised money for a breast cancer charity), since childhood, and their son, Luke, was a good friend of William's at Eton. And at night, when the other workers retired to the pubs or their tied cottages, William drove the half-mile back to Highgrove.

However, the work left him too exhausted to do anything other than climb into his bed, and for four gruelling weeks his world was governed by the ancient dawn-to-dusk rhythms of the countryside. He recalled, 'I got my hands dirty, did all the chores and had to get up at 4 a.m.' It was, he later said, 'the best part of my gap year. I got to see a completely different lifestyle.'

His father was gratified. 'William likes the hugger mugger kind of life,' the Prince of Wales told me. That was just as well, considering the amount of sweat and toil his son was having to expend. But, as Charles had promised, it wasn't all work.

In the February of the new year William attended the Press Complaints Commission party held in his honour at London's Somerset House in the Strand. Among the 550 guests were hard-man footballer turned film actor Vinnie Jones, entrepreneur Sir Richard Branson and fashion designer Donatella Versace. So-called 'It girl' cum professional celebrity Lady Victoria Hervey, half-sister of the late drug-crazed Marquis of Bristol, exposed a bare midriff and spent ten minutes chatting to William.

It was the first time that the Prince of Wales was joined by Camilla Parker Bowles at an official function. It was also a first for William. Father and son arrived together but, as soon as the formal introductions had been made, William plunged off on his own to talk to as many people as possible.

It was a new experience for him in front of a demanding audience but he handled it reasonably well. He met John Savident, who plays Fred Butler in *Coronation Street*, and said, 'I recognise you – I watch *EastEnders*.' Charles kept glancing over anxiously to how his son was doing. 'It's not an ordeal,' William informed him.

This joining together of royalty and show business is a recent phenomenon. In 1912 William's great-great grandfather King George V had started the annual Royal Command Performance, better known as the Royal Variety Show, but he had always kept a suspicious distance from 'play actors', as he called them. He believed that royalty was a caste apart, illustrated by his wife Queen Mary's habit of referring to members of the Royal Family as 'dear so and so', and commoners as 'poor so and so', no matter how rich and healthy they were. Such condescension would now be regarded as offensive. It is not how Charles disports himself in the company of actors and singers. It is certainly not how William wishes to behave. Both are determined to create a new, more open style of monarchy and keen to hurry the process along.

Nevertheless, some old habits do linger. Charles and William are countrymen at heart. They are passionate about rural affairs and believe strongly in organically friendly farming methods. They both talk about what Charles calls 'stewardship – an important duty to be carried out with an eye to this and future generations'.

It is an attitude that brought Charles into conflict with Prime Minister Tony Blair's 'rural tsar', Lord Haskins, the Labour government's rural recovery coordinator. In 2002 Haskins told a conference on rural affairs, 'Too many people in the countryside look backwards and not forwards. The heir to the throne is a prime example of that, believing we should live in a feudal society and all pay more for our food.' Organic wheat, Haskins said, costs three times as much to grow as conventional wheat. Irked by the prince's hostility to genetically modified crops, he argued that the logical conclusion of Charles's pro-organic views would be Britain's withdrawal from the European Union. When the matter came up in conversation, Charles replied, 'So?'

That argument is likely to become more heated as William begins to take up more royal duties. Asked which part of his gap year he most enjoyed he replied, 'Working on a farm before the foot-and-mouth, which is partly why I have so much sympathy for the farmers who have suffered so much from it.' The foot-and-mouth outbreak in 2001 led to millions of sheep, cattle and pigs being slaughtered, and the government being accused in an official report of badly mishandling the crisis that caused such rural misery.

William also declared his support for fox hunting and made no attempt to hide his hostility to the government's plan to ban the sport. It was his own decision to venture out regularly on to the hunting field, fully aware that he was likely to be photographed. It was a barely disguised political gesture which indicted his willingness to stand up for issues he feels strongly about, regardless of the hostility this might generate among a public vehemently opposed to 'blood sports'.

He is just as keen on shooting. He enjoys the grouse shooting at Balmoral and regards going wild fowling with his grandfather, Prince Philip, on the mud flats around Sandringham as one of the high points of his year. His labrador Widgeon is named after one of the species of ducks they shoot together.

One guest at Balmoral recalled picnicking with Charles in a log cabin in the hills high above Balmoral. William and Harry came in late from stalking, dressed not in traditional tweed but in army combat kit. Charles pleaded with them to join the party, which included several teenage girls, at the long trestle table but they refused and insisted on heading off again in pursuit of their quarry. Charles was not pleased. 'But what can I do?' he asked. 'They have so little freedom. They must be allowed to enjoy it while they can.'

Both boys are expert marksmen, and as a reward Charles bought William a .243 rifle crafted by the Scottish gunsmith Michael Lingard in 2003. It has a Turkish walnut stock and gold inlay and cost £20,000. Charles offered to have it engraved with William's coat of arms but the prince, less ostentatious than his father, settled for a simple 'W'.

In Africa, however, the hunter turned gamekeeper. In March 2001, William embarked on a three-and-a-half-month visit to the game reserves of Kenya and Tanzania. It began in the Serengeti, the reserve in Tanzania famous for the great herds of migrating animals. His guide was Richard Leakey, the renowned palaeontologist and conservationist who explained the efforts being made to protect the wildlife of the savannahs, which are threatened by the encroachment of subsistence farmers desperate for land. The great herds of wildebeest and zebra are large enough to ensure their survival for several generations to come. The future of the elephants and rhinos, however, is more precarious. They are still being killed by poachers for their tusks and horns, and William joined a night patrol of park wardens on anti-poaching patrol.

This can be a very dangerous business. The poachers are heavily armed and have no compunction about killing either the animals or the men employed to protect them. In the early 1990s the situation had become so desperate that former SAS soldiers were enlisted to go into the bush and seek out the bands of desperadoes. In this clandestine war no quarter was asked or given and many of the poachers were shot dead. Things have improved somewhat since those dark days, but the threat remains and William's military fieldcraft acquired in the jungles of Belize was put to practical use.

At the Il Newesi in the Lewa downs he was given another practical, albeit more comfortable, demonstration of game conservancy in action. The 55,000-acre reserve, which is home to the world's largest rhino sanctuary, is owned by Emma and Ian Craig, whose grandparents arrived from England in 1924. Set in the wilderness of Samburu to the north of Mount Kenya, this game ranch provides luxurious accommodation for its visitors. Its facilities include a jogging trail for visiting Americans, a tennis court and a swimming pool built into the rocks overlooking the grasslands as well as en-suite bathrooms in the thatched and tented cottages where Prince William stayed. He was met at the airstrip by the Samburu warriors who accompanied him when he went out in an open-topped four-wheel-drive vehicle to view the game.

William set off each morning in time to see the spectacular African dawn. He saw herds of antelope grazing and lions moving in for the kill. He was also treated to the sight of giraffes and rare black and white rhinos, and followed a herd of elephants led by a forty-year-old matriarch. He went game viewing on the back of a camel. He also went on bush walks, seeking out the wildlife by following their spoor. He was told that if he came face to face with a lion he was to make no sudden movement but slowly back away, all the while relying on the lion's inherent fear of man to get him out of a potentially fatal situation.

At dusk he went out again before returning to the camp for open-air dinners of home-grown vegetables, spit-roast goat and wines of a better quality than he had drunk in Chile. In the evenings many of the men wore the traditional wrap-around kangas in the style made fashionable by footballer David Beckham.

William so enjoyed himself that he made three separate trips to the ranch. Keeping the ranch in tiptop working order was no easy task. Many Africans regard the game as 'white man's toys'. Ian Craig explained, 'There was an ingrained mistrust that wildlife protection inevitably led to the annexation of the land by the government for national parks. At my first meeting with the elders of the tribe I was clearly told to go home, as the Samburu were struggling to understand the concept.' Only by enlisting the local people as game guards and involving them in his conservancy projects had he been able to make a success of his ambitious project. As Craig pointed out to William, the cooperation of the people who lived there is vital for any scheme of this kind, which uses electrified fencing and short-wave radios to try to keep the poachers at bay. Even so, there is a limit to what even a reserve of this size can achieve, and the occasional elephant had to be shot to match the herd to the available food supply. William learnt how important these culls are.

It wasn't just the animals that occupied William's attention. Among the other guests at the lodge were three young children who had lost their mother in a car accident. Loo Mathews was killed in January in a head-on collision with a bus while on the school run in Nairobi. Her eight-year-old daughter Sharon died of her injuries shortly afterwards. Sharon's twin Justine survived, as did their brother Sean, thirteen, and sister Tanith, eleven. The surviving children came up to the lodge every weekend. William recalled spending long hours talking to them and giving them advice around the campfire.

It was advice drawn from his own experience, and in that he differs markedly from his father. When Charles was younger, he always sought the guidance of older men such as his great uncle Earl Mountbatten and the writer Laurens van der Post. William appears to be made of sterner stuff. It is he who, when occasion demands, gives advice rather than seeks it. Dyer was an exception. Despite having incurred Charles's displeasure by assisting in trying to organise an alternative programme, William insisted that he should accompany him on his travels. 'He had a very formative influence on William,' observed one St James's Palace official.

Dyer took time off from his work as a freelance consultant in the drinks and pub trade with a shareholding in bars in London's Fulham and Wandsworth to be with the prince in Belize, Mauritius, Chile and East Africa. He bought the beers in the Sports bar in the remote, tumbledown town of Maun when they travelled down to Botswana. And he was with William when the prince drove out across the red earth roads to see a few of Africa's remaining wild dogs at Wild Dog Camp.

These ugly canines have been shot to the point of extinction, and their method of killing puts them low on most tourists' checklist. Even Charles, who professes a great curiosity in the habits of African wild life, has no interest in them. On safari in Tanzania one year, he refused to join the rest of the party when they drove out early one morning in search of a pack, explaining that he much preferred to stay near the camp and do some sketching. The fates were not being kind to Charles's sensibilities. While the rest of the party, led by his then polo manager the late Major Ronald Ferguson, bounced through the bush in their four-wheel-drive trucks in a vain search, the pack came running into camp and, to Charles's considerable distress, disembowelled an antelope in front of him. William was spared that rare sight, rather to his regret. The years spent stalking deer across the hills of Scotland had hardened him to the ways of nature.

Altogether, William's year off had not left him short of memories. It had been hard work and there had been times when he was less than enamoured of the programme his father had insisted on. He had detested being stranded beside a raging river in Chile. And Harry's drug bust had been a chastening warning of the pitfalls that lay in wait for any prince who erred.

But that had been more than balanced by the good moments. The view of the African dawn rising over the great plains. Mixing with different people who turned out to be a lot nicer than he had imagined. And, most surprising of all, working as a labourer on the farm in Gloucestershire. 'I loved my gap year and I wish I could have another one,' he said.

That was not possible. The siren call of duty had to be answered. University now beckoned. And that would turn out to be a lot less enjoyable than he had hoped.

SEVENTEEN

University Days

WWilliam's declared intention when he went to St Andrews was to be
an 'ordinary student'. He said he wanted to broaden his intellectual
horizons and mix with people from different backgrounds to his own.

Good times were also part of the academic package. As he disclosed,
coyly dropping his head in a gesture Diana had made so familiar, 'I just
want to go to university and have fun.'

He got precious little of that in his first few weeks at the university. He
preferred to keep to himself, a decision based partly on shyness, partly on
his refusal to lower his regal guard. That made it all but impossible for him
to become properly integrated into the university.

William had been looking forward to 'going up' with the youthful
mixture of excitement and trepidation common to all students. He had left
behind the constrictions of school and was about to move away from home.
'Having independence is quite a big thing,' he said.

In his case it was always going to be severely limited. As he acknowledged,
'I've always got policemen around so I'm never completely independent.'

He was free enough to get himself nearly killed early in his second term,
though.

What he was never able to do was free himself from the burden of who
he was and the responsibilities and constraints and difficulties that imposed.
To protect his good name, he had foregone the students' pre-term parties,
an absence that would colour much of his first year.

Yet despite such precautions, within twenty-four hours of his arrival his royal status had involved him in a vicious internecine quarrel which embroiled his father Prince Charles, his grandfather Prince Philip, his uncle Prince Edward and the Queen herself. And when the dust finally settled, a new royal pecking order had been firmly established – with William's position ascendant.

It was not a fight of William's making. His fervent hope was to be treated like any one of the other 'freshers', as first-year students are called. There was never a chance of that happening. Like it or not (and he didn't), he was now a celebrity, and when he drew up at the ancient gates of St Salvator's College on Sunday, 23 September 2001, there were over 2,000 onlookers, plus an inevitable battery of photographers, waiting for him.

He arrived after lunching with his great-grandmother at Birkhall, her whitewashed holiday home on the Balmoral estate. It has been a jolly gathering around the polished Georgian mahogany dining table. Even that redoubtable lady had been forced to bow before the advance of age, and in the final months of her life the Queen Mother had sometimes found it hard to maintain her zest. That afternoon, however, she was her old jovial self, full of good humour given added effervescence by the glasses of champagne she continued to consume in defiance of the advice of doctors, most of whom she had long outlived. The food was served by white-gloved members of her staff – the Queen Mother always lived in an imperial splendour that took little account of cost-cutting economies – and included fresh wild salmon from the River Dee. There was also a chicken dish, cooked without so much as a hint of garlic which the Royal Family are always careful to avoid.

By her standards it was nonetheless an 'informal' occasion and William, according to his standards, was dressed accordingly. The Queen Mother was wearing an immaculate tweed skirt and toning jacket. The Prince of Wales was dressed in chinos, a double-breasted tweed jacket and a collar and tie. Prince William was in faded jeans, sloppy blue jumper and trainers, with a copper bracelet around his right wrist.

Queen Victoria would not have been amused. She recognised how much importance people attached to first impressions. 'Dress,' as she wrote to her son, the future King Edward VII, 'is the outward sign from which people in general can and often do judge upon the *inward* state of mind and feeling of a person. On that account it is of some importance particularly in persons of high rank.' Edward VIII, who became the Duke of Windsor after his abdication in 1936, summed up the royal attitude when he said, 'Clothes make the prince.'

It is a maxim that continues to apply through to the present day, and the Queen Mother abided by it. She always dressed in a manner that she maintained befitted a queen; when she went to visit the bombed-out ruins of London's East End during the Blitz she arrived draped in furs. Charles is equally fastidious and employs four valets to make sure that he is correctly attired. Diana was independent enough to wear more casual clothes when the mood or the occasion suited, but even when she was wearing jeans she always took great care to look like a princess.

William, on the other hand, shied away from flaunting his royal rank and made a point of dressing down as much as possible. At nineteen, he was signalling his wilful intention to dress as he saw fit, not as tradition dictated. With his father unwilling to take his son to task and without a mother to chivvy him, that often resulted in him looking decidedly scruffy. He certainly did that day. But if the Queen Mother noticed William's departure from royalty's sartorial norm, she didn't let on. William is the heir in line to the throne and that, as far as the Queen Mother was concerned, is a position that gives him rights and privileges denied to others.

Besides, she was enjoying herself. And that meant that she took no account of the time.

There were eleven long-case 'grandfather' clocks in the dining room but they served no practical purpose and the lunch, as William recalled, went on 'longer than normal'. Prince Charles, who lives his life on the run, in constant dread of being late, kept glancing at his watch but the Queen Mother sailed blithely on, passing comments, dispensing droll witticisms, revelling in the company of two men born to be king.

'We talked about me going to university and what I was studying,' William recalled. 'She always took a great interest in all her great-grandchildren.' And most especially in the young man who bore on his young shoulders the ambitions for the Royal Family she had done so much to shape.

There came the moment, though, when even William, whose time-keeping is often typical of his age group, was anxious to leave. It was his first day, he was nervous, he was already running a week behind the other students and he did not want to be later still. His great-grandmother tried to allay his fears. William recounted, 'As she said goodbye, she said, "Any good parties, invite me down." I said yes, but there was no way. I knew full well that if I invited her down she would dance me under the table.'

It is a two-and-a-half hour drive from Birkhall to St Andrews along winding country roads, and the Prince of Wales pushed hard on the accelerator of the green Vauxhall Omega estate car. He was flustered enough to miss the entrance to the halls of residence as he drove down North Street and had to reverse back, much to the amusement of the crowd. William looked apprehensive when he stepped out of the car to face the multitude.

'It will be easier as time goes on,' he said, after spending a few minutes doing his royal duty and pressing the flesh of outstretched hands. 'Everyone will get bored of me, which they do.'

It was a remark made more in dull hope than realistic anticipation. He had been spared the excesses of screaming teenagers and near-riot of over-excited bystanders that had greeted his father's arrival at Cambridge thirty-five years earlier, but his welcome had still been hyperbolic enough to put William on his back foot.

At Eton he had been able to disappear into the throng to become just another schoolboy in an archaic morning coat. St Andrews could offer no such anonymity. The outside world could to an extent be kept at bay (the Press Complaints Commission had persuaded Britain's newspapers to continue their hands-off approach to his time at university in exchange for the occasional photocall and interview), but the attitude of his fellow students was bound to be more ambivalent. He was going to have to make his own way in the rough and tumble of university life and without meaning to, and through no fault of his own, he had already attracted exactly the sort of attention he had been anxious to avoid.

In an interview in January with the independent student newspaper, *The Saint*, the principal, Dr Brian Lang, had declared his determination to protect the prince's privacy and warned that any student found guilty of passing on information would face expulsion. He added, 'I would take a very dim view of information of an inappropriate nature about any member of the university being passed on. At worst, a perpetrator might find him- or herself having to find another university. I have responsibility for the rights of every member of the university, and the implications of taking care of every member of the university, with Prince William's arrival, will take on a very new meaning.'

It was a threat that some took as a strike against the core of the university's time-cherished liberties. St Andrews had played a prominent role in the Scottish reformation of the sixteenth century, and there are many memorials around the town to those who died for their beliefs and their right to express them. Professor Ian Wilcock of the law department at nearby Dundee University said any such action might well be a violation of human rights, and several students raised vocal concern that Lang's caution was an attack on free speech. Marcus Booth, president of the Students' Association, tried to give a light-hearted definition of what would and would not be tolerated. 'This is not an attempt to gag students in the pub, but if someone smuggles a member of the European paparazzi into a changing room where the prince is getting changed, that is a different issue.' But he went on to add, 'Of course, we do not want to live in a police state.'

The Prince of Wales's office was at pains to point out that it had asked for no rules to be applied during William's time there. However, in a small and intellectually vibrant community where many of the students hold radical anti-monarchist views, even the suspicion that the Royal Family was interfering with their liberties was certain to provoke an unfavourable reaction. As one student leader put it, 'This is Scotland's oldest university and we place great store in our freedoms.'

What not even the most fervent republican could have predicted, however, is that the first person to be accused of prying into William's life was not a tabloid newspaper or the European paparazzi but his own uncle.

William had spent his first night settling into St Salvator's College, known as Sally's. There, first-year students are usually required to share, but for security reasons he had been allocated his own room on the first floor of a heavy stone building overlooking the fifteenth-century quadrangle. A new electronic lock had been installed on the front door to the building in readiness for his arrival. As an added safety measure his personal bodyguard, conspicuous in baggy brown corduroy trousers of the kind favoured by undergraduates half a century earlier, was assigned the room next door.

He ate his evening meal sitting on one of the benches drawn up alongside the refectory table in the wood-panelled dining room. The choice that evening from the self-service bar was pasta or a cut of roast meat with either vegetables or salad, followed by fruit. The food, he remarked to a fellow student, was better than it had been at Eton. Afterwards he took a brief look around the Common Room, which has a full-size snooker table and television set linked to the satellite channels. He then retired to his room, sparsely furnished with a sink, shelves, wooden wardrobe and desk. On his bedside table there was a copy of the Bible provided by the Gideon Society, with specific psalms helpfully indicated for students who might be depressed or lonely.

Monday had dawned damp and gusty with the first hint of winter bearing in on the wind blowing off the North Sea. It was the day William had designated for finding his way around and going to the lecture room to sign on for his course in the History of Art.

Instead, he found himself at the centre of an unseemly royal row which was to effectively end Prince Edward's career as a television producer and demonstrate to William just how careful he had to be to prevent himself being used as a pawn in a game which was beyond his control.

As William was making his way from his hall of residence to the History of Art department on the other side of the road overlooking the sea, he

272

caught sight of a television crew. All media had been 'requested' to leave the university after the Sunday photocall and the prince was surprised by what he regarded as a clear breach of the agreement struck between the Palace and the press.

Two days later it became clear that this had been no one-off incident. As he set off for his first lecture on Wednesday his protection officer told him there was a film crew in the town. It was reported to the university who sent someone to investigate and then dutifully reported the matter to the Prince of Wales's office at St James's Palace.

According to the St James's Palace version, the crew at first refused to identify themselves. Only after a heated exchange of words did they reluctantly admit to being freelancers working on a documentary commissioned by Prince Edward's production company, Ardent. Prince Charles was said to be 'disappointed' when he was informed of what had happened.

Ardent executives gave a different account of what took place over those two days. They firmly denied that they had a crew there on the Monday and that if William did see one, it was not employed by them. They did own up, though, to the Wednesday incident, but insisted that they had permission from the student union to film students in an Indian restaurant, in the streets of the town, in a shop, in the student union offices and in one of the many pubs where undergraduates at this most sociable of universities spend so much of their time. They adamantly denied that they had tried to film the prince.

What both sides agreed on was that Charles's so-called 'disappointment' was in fact 'incandescent' rage. His ire was shared by William, who had spoken to his father on the matter several times on the telephone. He was suspicious that his good name was being used as a way of getting at Prince Edward and he didn't like it.

'There is a lot of Spencer in William and a lot of his mother,' one of Diana's friends said. 'And, like the Princess, if he finds out he is being used he will dump that person and go mad. If Diana thought she was being used she'd go off like a rocket. He is the same.'

At the heart of this quarrel lay a fundamental dispute about the job of the Royal Family and, more particularly, who should be doing what as an institution increasingly unsure of its position tries to adjust to changing demands.

After Edward quit the Royal Marines he had chosen to go into the theatre, first with Lord Lloyd-Webber's Really Useful Company, then with Biddy Hayward's Theatre Division. When that folded he elected to form his own television production company. His family were uneasy. The House of Windsor is wary of involving itself in anything that smacks of 'commercialisation', and Prince Philip warned Edward that 'any member of the family who has been anywhere near a commercial activity is always criticised'. He wanted his youngest son to learn accountancy instead.

Prince Charles also expressed his misgivings. The Royal Family, he argued, must never be seen to be trading off its royal name.

To ease their concerns, Edward's adviser, film accountant Malcolm Cockren, suggested some sort of trust funding 'to distance himself personally from the company should it run into trouble'.

Edward was having none of that. He argued that the loss of the Queen's tax immunity, which had resulted in him losing his £96,000 Civil List allowance, meant that within royal reason he was free to pursue any career he liked. He had decided on television and said that he had no intention of hiding himself away behind a trust. As he explained, 'You've got to put your money where your mouth is.' Ardent was duly formed in 1993 with Prince Philip's hesitant approval, Cockren as chairman and the financial backing of the oil-rich Sultan of Brunei. Edward's declared ambition was to make Ardent one of the twelve top independent production companies in Britain by the end of the twentieth century.

It hadn't worked out like that. The company's productions proved to be lacklustre, Edward's on-screen presenting was wooden, and by the end of the century it was only just managing to keep itself ticking over by turning out documentaries about the one subject Edward knew something about – the Royal Family. By the time it sent a two-man crew to St Andrews to make a documentary series entitled *The A–Z of Royalty* for the American cable company E!TV, Ardent was £1.9 million in debt.

From his headquarters at Bagshot Park in Surrey, Edward seemed sublimely unaware of the furore generated by the decision to film at St Andrews. In business he calls himself plain Edward Windsor, but his royal upbringing can sometimes cloud him to the repercussions of his own actions.

Bagshot is a case in point. Built in 1877 in the florid Gothic style for Prince Arthur, Duke of Connaught – like Edward, the third son of a reigning monarch – its fifty rooms and seventy-eight acres reflect a grandiose pomposity out of keeping with the modern age. In the attempt to justify his extravagance, which saw him spend upwards of £2 million on refurbishment, he said, 'I will be able to use the house for formal entertaining.' However, by giving the newly decorated rooms names such as 'Balmoral' and 'Sandringham', he was courting the distinct impression that he was going into the corporate entertainment business – and using his princely status as a blatant sales pitch.

When he moved Ardent's offices out of central London and into the house's converted stable block, he tried to argue that he was rationalising his operations. 'I will be able to maintain my production work – the house is within easy reach of the major studios – and my public duties,' he said. 'The house will help me balance my two roles.' But that division, between prince and television producer, was by then perilously blurred.

Shortly before William went up to St Andrews, Edward's wife, Sophie, had been tricked by a phoney Arab sheikh working for a Sunday newspaper into making indiscreet remarks about the Royal Family in what seemed like a naive attempt to drum up business for her public relations company. The unsavoury episode had called into question the wisdom of even minor members of the Royal Family engaging in activities likely to call their integrity into question, and Sophie had been forced to resign from her own business. An internal review was set up at Buckingham Palace under the Lord Chamberlain, Lord Luce, to review the rules for 'working royals'. Lord Luce had concluded that they should be allowed to continue their careers.

Prince Charles disagreed. He believes in a 'slimmed-down' monarchy. He argued that it was beholden to princes and their wives to maintain their dignity at all times and that if they wished to go in pursuit of commercial gain they should retire from public duties.

As the future head of the family, Charles's opinion carried weight. What he had never been able to do, however, was face down his father. And Philip, for all his initial misgivings, came down firmly on the side of Edward, the favourite of his three sons. They enjoyed a rapport Charles could only envy: while he was frequently reduced to communicating with their father by handwritten note, even when they were both under the same roof, Edward enjoyed an easy, informal intimacy. 'They are always talking,' observed Paul Arengo-Jones, the former colonel in the Gloucestershire Regiment who became the General-Secretary of the Duke of Edinburgh's International Award.

Edward enthusiastically explained to his father what he hoped to achieve with Ardent, and won Philip round. Charles had been outmanoeuvred. He could huff and puff all he liked but Philip made it clear that he was not going to countenance Edward being sidelined and effectively stripped of his royal standing on the say-so of his elder brother.

The argument generated a great deal of bad feeling within the Royal Family and left Charles fuming with frustrated anger. He was badly rankled, as he always is when he does not get his way. But if it is overstating the case to suggest that his response to his brother's indiscretion at St Andrews was an act of spite, he was nonetheless quick to take advantage of the situation to reassert his authority.

At first Edward had appeared oblivious to the trouble he was in. His wife, on the other hand, was not. Still smarting over the way she had been treated over the incident of the phoney sheikh (badly, in her opinion), Sophie burst into Edward's office at Bagshot and, in front of his staff, told him, 'Now you are going to have to apologise. Now you are going to have to eat humble pie – as I had to do!'

Edward tried to make light of the situation, informing his production team that it was 'a storm in a teacup'. The Prince of Wales quickly disabused him of that idea. It was alleged that the crew had been buying dinners for students at the local Indian restaurant and plying them with drinks in the pubs, all the while urging them to pretend that William had already been at the university for six months. One of the questions they were asked to answer was, 'Has Prince William been able to get on with his life without media intrusion?' When Edward finally got his brother on the telephone, Charles was in a thundering rage.

According to his staff, Edward was 'very abashed'. He tried to explain that the film crew had not been there to film Prince William but Charles refused to accept his apology.

By then the argument between the brothers was out in the public domain – with Charles's side occupying the public relations high ground. His private secretary, Sir Michael Peat, tried to dampen down the controversy by declaring, 'There was a muddle – these things happen.' That did not stem the leaks from St James's Palace, however. Charles was said to be 'apoplectic' and 'barely on speaking terms' with Prince Edward. Ardent eventually handed the film over to Buckingham Palace for scrutiny and insisted that it contained no footage of William. But as a St James's Palace aide tartly observed, 'We presume it took them five days to hand it over because they were so busy editing it.' When Edward tried to telephone Charles again, the Prince of Wales refused to take his call.

The Queen, for whom rows are anathema, tried to remain impartial. But eventually she too got drawn in, as she was bound to be. She had wholeheartedly backed Prince Charles's decision to protect his son and heir's privacy. Now one of her own children was being accused of 'stalking' the student prince – the very thing her courtiers had asked the newspapers and television news companies not to do. A senior Buckingham Palace aide summed up her dismay when he said, 'There are ethical questions here for Prince Edward to answer, not about his role as a royal, but the way his company behaves.'

Ardent again attempted to defuse the situation. Cockren stated, 'Clearly, we were at fault by continuing to do anything in the town. Our people were in public areas and felt that was acceptable. We have been misguided and at fault and must take responsibility.' The statement had been written by Ardent's production producer Robin Baxter and rewritten by Edward. It should have been read by Edward but he refused and the apology, if that was what it was, was grudging at best.

Even so, that might still have been the end of the matter had Sophie not reignited the controversy the following day by trying to shift the blame on to the freelance crew who, she said, owed Edward an apology. She said, 'Bigger things are at issue here – Edward, after all, is a member of the Royal Family.' The clear implication was that Edward knew nothing about their ill-advised filming expedition to St Andrews and was therefore innocent of any wrongdoing. But that, as the rector Andrew Neil brusquely observed, 'beggars belief'.

With no other excuses to offer, Ardent had little alternative but to announce that henceforth it would not be making any more royal programmes. With no other shows in the pipeline, however, the company had no option but to place itself in mothballs. By the actions of his company, Edward had trespassed into commercial quicksand of the kind that threatened to swallow his reputation, taking another chunk of the Royal Family's good name down with it.

He could hardly excuse himself by claiming ignorance. As he told me himself just before he started Ardent, changing public perceptions had created 'a total lack of confidence and understanding of certain members of the Royal Family's activities'. And the member whose activities inspired the least confidence was clearly Edward.

Prince Philip found himself in a corner of his own making. He had always been vocal in his condemnation of unwarranted press intrusion. But when he was accused of backing Edward and condemning William for 'over-reacting', his press secretary, Penny Russell-Smith, went to the extraordinary length of issuing a statement on his behalf emphasising that he fully supported the efforts being made to ensure that Prince William's privacy was respected at St Andrews.

Whatever his private feelings may have been – and the row only served to emphasise the differences between Prince Philip and Prince Charles – the situation had moved beyond Philip's control. There was nothing he could do now to help Edward without laying himself open to the double charge of hypocrisy and favouritism. Without his father's backing, Edward was forced to back away from the confrontation with his brother and future king.

In the opinion of one soon-to-be unemployed senior Ardent executive, 'It hailed the end of Edward's TV career.' The prince who had hoped to become one of the most powerful producers in British television announced that henceforth he would be concentrating on royal duties. Like the Duke of Connaught, the long-forgotten son of another queen, Edward was being pushed off centre stage to become a mere bit player in a royal production where the starring roles are always reserved for those who will inherit the throne.

If William felt any sympathy for his embattled uncle, he did a very good job of hiding it. Like his father, he had deeply irritated by Edward's behaviour ('crass stupidity' was one barb directed at the prince who is known as 'IE', which stands for instant expert). William felt badly let down, and with justification. One of the prime reasons behind his choice of St Andrews, a remote university town on the far coast of Fife, was that it appeared to offer him the best chance of escaping the attention of the media which, like his mother before him but in his case even more so, he regarded as both intrusive and offensive. To then discover that a close relation, someone he should have been able to depend on, had joined forces with the opposition was profoundly disturbing. Many families have their differences and the Royal Family is no exception. But this had gone well beyond the personal to become a matter of royal principle.

Nonetheless, the personal did play a significant part in shaping William's reaction. Relations between his uncle and his mother had once been of the friendliest and in the early days of her marriage Diana had sought out Edward's company. He was, she said, the nicest and most sympathetic of her in-laws. When Diana started rebelling against the constraints of royal life, however, Edward had distanced himself from his sister-in-law. Diana, in turn, came to look on Edward's wife, Sophie, with envy that bordered on dislike.

'She got a lot more help than I ever did,' she complained to me. '*They*' (she was referring to her in-laws) 'did all they could for *her*. *I* was simply left to get on with it.' It was not said in a friendly way.

The detachment of Diana from Edward (and, indeed, from the rest of the Royal Family) reached its unpleasant denouement with her interview on the BBC's *Panorama* in the autumn of 1995. It was the moment the Queen came off the fence and ordered Charles and Diana to finally bring to an end a marriage that was ruining the reputation of the Royal Family and in the process causing untold damage to their sons.

Edward had watched the programme with friends. As Diana poured out her heart, Edward kept interjecting, 'She's barking . . . no one is going to believe this twaddle.'

William had been embarrassed by his mother's extraordinary outburst. But she was his mother and his affection for her never wavered. And when the battle lines of recrimination were drawn up in the bitter aftermath of the broadcast, he took his mother's side. That produced a lingering estrangement between William, reticent but loyal, and Edward, who regarded Diana as 'bonkers'.

The rupture was compounded by Edward's insensitive reaction to Diana's death. 'It was the only way it was going to end,' he said shortly after the news came through of the car crash in Paris. 'It was amazing it took that long for it to happen.' It was not a remark that was ever going to endear him to Diana's elder son.

There was nothing he could do about it then, but time was certain to give William the upper hand in this unseemly dispute. As the first-born of the first-born, he occupied a crucial position in the hierarchical structure of the Royal Family. As a thirteen-year-old he had been too young to throw his weight around. As a nineteen-year-old, however, his views carried mounting authority. And what he was not prepared to tolerate, as the Ardent affair made plain, was having his privacy compromised – and most certainly not by a member of his own family. He told his father precisely that, in words explicit and unequivocal. Now, with the Ardent film crew withdrawn (and Edward to all intents and purposes out of television),

William could justifiably claim to have established his pre-eminence within the Royal Family.

That was not going to help him as he set about making his way at St Andrews. The battle for the high ground within the Royal Family had been fought out in meetings at Buckingham Palace and in fraught telephone conversations between St Andrews, Bagshot Park and St James's Palace. But while the outcome was of immense importance to William, it was of no consequence to his fellow undergraduates. The obsequiousness that had once greeted members of the Royal Family wherever they went was long gone and he was met, not with deference, but with either feigned indifference or the starry-eyed curiosity usually reserved for pop singers and soap stars.

After it was announced that he would be attending the university, entry applications increased by 44 per cent, with a large proportion of the enquiries coming from North America. 'I hope that people have not applied to come here because of him but I suppose it is human nature,' said the then Students' Association president Dana Green, daughter of a New Hampshire surgeon.

But despite the sudden interest, St Andrews was nonetheless determined to retain its traditional character. 'This really is a sort of haven from the world,' Green said. It was beholden to the university authorities, she added, 'to protect our rights'. William, she insisted, must not be singled out for exceptional treatment. The underlying warning was that if William was going to make a success of his time at university, he was going to have to do so on merit.

He did not get off to the best of starts. The other first-year students had all arrived a week earlier to enjoy a seven-day, non-stop round of parties and drinking organised by the senior undergraduates by way of a welcome. Most emerge at the end at the end of Freshers' Week, as it is called, nursing crippling hangovers. There is purpose to the excess, however. This is when everyone gets to know each other. A contemporary of William's at St Salvator's explained, 'It is a great opportunity to get to meet everyone. Everyone makes an effort and everyone says hello.'

New students are greeted with five classic questions: 'What hall are you in? Where do you live? What "A" levels did you take? What degree are you studying for? Where did you go to school?'

That last is indicative of St Andrews social traditions. Nearly 60 per cent of the undergraduates come from state schools, but the university still remains a popular choice for public school-educated students who failed to get into Oxford or Cambridge, and Eton is always well represented in each year's new intake. In the excitement of Freshers' Week, however, the barriers of school and background are quickly broken down. As William's contemporary observed, 'It's fun to meet new people,' which was precisely what William said he was looking forward to doing.

But William did not attend Freshers' Week. Ever wary of the attention he draws, he was anxious to avoid being the focus of attention. He explained, 'It would have been a media frenzy and that's not fair to the other new students. Plus, I thought I would probably end up in a gutter completely wrecked and the people I met that week wouldn't end up being my friends anyway. It also meant I would have another week's holiday.'

His brother, Harry, never harboured such concerns and spent a good part of his later teenage years gulping back Alcopops and sipping pints of lager through a straw in public view. William, increasingly mindful of his responsibilities, had learnt to be more circumspect, but in a small community like St Andrews it was inevitable that some would draw the conclusion that he was being just a mite stand-offish.

He did nothing to dispel that image in the weeks to come. Just before he arrived at St Andrews he said, 'People who try to take advantage of me and get a piece of me, I spot it quickly and soon go off them.' It was a defensive approach to university life, but it was symptomatic of the barriers of reserve the prince is wrapped in. Despite his declared intention to be as 'ordinary' as possible, he preferred to keep to himself, mixing only with a few chosen friends, mostly Etonians, who call him 'Wales'. While his contemporaries were out roistering (like many modern university students, the under-graduates of St Andrews are inclined to spend more of their first year partying than they do studying), William was usually to be found cloistered either in his single room in his hall of residence or in the library a few minutes' walk away on the far side of the quadrangle.

The library especially afforded him the seclusion he craved. On the third floor of the 1970s building, which stands in stark contrast to the 500-year-old quad, there are six lines of books dealing with the history of art, and the students work in private booths. The view of the coastline is hidden behind smoke-tinted windows. On occasion he would retreat even further by asking for a key and retiring into one of the library's small windowless cubicles.

He joined the water polo team, but in his effort to maintain his fitness he chose not to go to the university gymnasium. Instead he enrolled in the private gym at the St Andrews Bay Hotel, a fifteen-minute drive outside the town. The decor there would find no place in his study of the history of art. On a wet winter's day it can look like the setting for the Jack Nicholson film, *The Shining*, with walls painted a pale bluey grey, purple carpet and plastic flowers. The equipment, however, is up-to-date but, at £450 per year, the membership charge is beyond the means of most undergraduates.

St Andrews is home to the Royal and Ancient Golf Club, the world headquarters of the sport, and as a member of the university William was entitled to play on its prestigious links course. It is an opportunity his uncle Prince Andrew would have jumped at. He is a dedicated golfer (sometimes to the point of tedium: he often spends entire evenings curled up on a sofa watching endless old golf videos).

William, however, was slow to show an interest in the game, and it was not until the end of his first year that he first ventured out on to the practice range. Other than water polo and the gym, his preferred exercise was water-skiing or, if it was too rough, riding through the choppy North Sea astride an inflated yellow rubber tube called a banana in the nearby seaside resort of Elie, half an hour's drive away.

His contemporaries were rather taken aback by his boyish enthusiasm for bouncing around on a yellow banana, a pastime favoured more by children than undergraduates of a distinguished university. When asked why he wasn't taking part in other, more customary, sporting activities, he replied, 'I want a bit of space.'

He did make an appearance at Raisin Weekend, however. Unique to St Andrews and dating back several hundred years, it is held in November and it is when the first-year students are inducted into the university by the senior students. It begins on Sunday, often with a champagne breakfast, and turns into a marathon drinking session hosted by the third- and fourth-year undergraduates who have taken the newcomers under their wings. William was not observed stumbling drunk. He avoided the photographers (the published pictures that were supposed to be of the prince turned out to be of someone else).

The next day the students converge on St Salvator's quad dressed in a selection of outrageous costumes and cover each other in shaving foam, which has replaced the flour and eggs deployed in olden days. At the end of the proceedings, the first-year students traditionally handed their older minders a pound of raisins, but these days the gift is more likely to be a bottle of booze. Clive Pelbrough-Power, who was studying History of Art on the same course as Prince William, said, 'It is so much fun and although it isn't essential, everyone should come. They miss out on a lot of fun if they don't. And because it is so cold, it really helps to cure your hangover.' William joined in the throng in the quadrangle, but he was careful not to become involved in the foaming excess and by the time the revellers disgorged on to the streets of the town, William had already slipped away.

He was equally reticent when it came to joining the clubs that proliferate at St Andrews. Indeed, so reluctant was he in his first year to involve himself in its societies and associations that he became a virtual bystander to university life.

The first club he refused to join was the all-male Kate Kennedy club, the most active of the university's myriad institutions. Supposedly named in honour of the beautiful niece of Bishop Kennedy, who founded the university in 1411, but quite possibly derived from an ancient Gallic festival with a name that sounds vaguely similar, the KK club organises a procession in the first week of the Easter term. The highlight is the sight of one of the club's first-year members dressed up as Kate Kennedy, surrounded by eight shield bearers and preceded by 200 students in costumes depicting the history of St Andrews. 'Kate' is dragged through the cobbled streets on a horse-drawn carriage to deliver a speech of thanks outside the Holy Trinity Church to the 15,000 people who regularly gather for the event. It is the town's biggest event other than the British Open when it is held at the Royal and Ancient.

It is followed in May by the KK charity ball which is the biggest in the whole of Scotland. Over 2,000 people, a third of the entire university population, pay £50 a head to dance and dine in three giant marquees pitched on council land at Craigtoun Park.

The revelry continues until six in the morning, but it is carousing in the name of an altruistic purpose. Every year the KK club raises upwards of £8,000 for charity. Some of the cash goes to such established causes as cancer research but smaller, more parochial, needs are also addressed: in William's first year an old lady of the town was given money to buy her granddaughter a computer.

The KK would have welcomed William. There are forty members and any first-year male student can apply to join. The club is self-selecting and anyone who comes across as pushy or snobbish (any mention of the school they attended is regarded as 'naff') is unlikely to progress past the interview. Those who do must promise to uphold the traditions of the university, to sponsor good relations between 'town and gown', and to raise money for charity. Only nine new members are elected every year but, as that year's president Marcus Booth said, 'The qualities it looks for are people who are best able to promote our interest and I am sure Prince William will be a very strong candidate should he apply.'

William never did. For all its good works, the KK club remains an all-male bastion. That has invited inevitable criticism, not least from the university's own principal, Dr Brian Lang, who pointedly refused to attend the procession (though it was wryly noted by *The Saint* newspaper that his stance on equal rights did not prevent him accepting the membership of the all-male Royal and Ancient Golf Club that comes automatically with his post). And while most of the female students are happy to join enthusiastically in the events that the KK organises, there is always a hard cadre who take vocal exception to the club and its ethos.

That was enough to put William off. Politically sensitive, he was anxious 'not to generate any news that might be marked against me', as he explained to a friend.

It was for that reason that he refused to take part in the dawn swim on the first of May in the sea pool in the shadow of the castle. Upwards of 400 students, including all of his friends, gathered at 5 o'clock in the morning to plunge, often naked, into the bitterly cold water for a quick dip, followed by a barbecued breakfast on the beach.

He didn't take part in the tradition of the Sunday Pier Walk when the undergraduates parade down the pier wearing their red gowns. He also turned down the invitation to join the Breakfast Club, which meets on certain days on the pier at 10 o'clock in the morning wearing full evening dress for a fry-up washed down with champagne.

Even the newly formed Jazz Club failed to draw him in. Co-founded by Fergus Boyd, his friend from Eton, he initially said he would like to join and was awarded the membership number 0001. Before the club had got properly going, however, he had dropped out. He explained, 'I don't want to commit to anything regular. I want to do things spontaneously.'

William admitted, 'I am hugely disorganised.' It is an assessment his contemporaries had ample cause to agree with. Said one, 'He lacks commitment. He is inclined to tag along at the last minute but doesn't want to organise anything himself. He prefers to do things on the spur of the moment.'

The trouble with that approach was that the 'fun' he said he was keen to participate in was certain to pass him by. 'He's missing out,' was the harsh judgement of a committee member of one of the clubs he was invited to join, indicated he would, only to back out at the last moment.

He turned up to watch the fashion show featuring his friend Kate Middleton, but he was careful to keep a straight face for the cameras when the scantily dressed student models paraded by. The real reason he was there was to give support to his friend Fergus, who was also in the show.

He sometimes stopped by the Westport pub, and he was an occasional visitor to Ma Bell's, a pub 200 yards from the Royal and Ancient club house, especially when a football match was being screened on the television next to the bar. If Aston Villa was playing, he would leave his favoured seat in the banquette beside the window and draw up one of the modern wooden chairs to down pints of lager and cheer on the team he has supported since childhood. 'He is always very animated when Villa are playing,' observed a fellow football fan.

It was a rare exception to his self-imposed rule of reticence which seemed to exclude anything that might conceivably draw any unwelcome attention.

In the winter term he attended the Reel Ball upstairs from Ma Bell's in the Golf Hotel. St Andrews is a Scottish university, reeling is Scotland's national dance and everyone else uses the occasion to show off their Scottish connections, regardless of how remote or spurious they might be. The men wear kilts or tartan trews, while the women sport tartan sashes.

No family has made more of their Scottish links than the ruling house. Since Queen Victoria's reign they have had an attachment to the rituals and castles and tartans of the Highlands that borders on the theatrical. Even Prince Philip, who has not a discernible drop of Scottish blood coursing through his royal veins, often dons a kilt. Only William seems immune to the lure of the glens.

'They are welcoming people, the Scots,' he said, but the remark bears the resonance of a passing tourist. He makes no obvious effort to immerse himself in Scottish culture and never dresses in anything overtly Scottish. It was not a kilt or a pair of trews in Royal Stewart tartan he wore to the ball, but a plain black dinner jacket which, as one of his fellow reelers observed, 'was at least one size too big for him. He looked out of place.' If clothing has its own language, as many psychologists believe, this is another visible example of the prince's single-minded determination to conduct himself as he sees fit.

At the Reel Ball he spent the better part of the evening at his table beside the bandstand with a small group of Etonian and aristocratic friends. They included fellow undergraduate and his distant cousin, the very attractive

Princess Alexandra Romanov, who is a member of the family that once ruled Russia. Other good-looking girls whirled by, hoping to catch his eye, but the prince paid them scant attention. 'He seemed happiest with his own set,' remarked another guest.

'The prince put himself in a tricky situation,' one student said. 'Because he kept turning down invitations, people stopped inviting him in case he said no. But if you don't join in it is hard to make friends.'

William found it hard to join in. In his first seventeen weeks he only spent four weekends at St Andrews, preferring to drive to Edinburgh for quiet dinner parties with friends from Eton like William Rickards who was at university there, or retreating to his cottage on the Balmoral estate. Highgrove provided another bolt hole for the prince and he often spent his weekends at Charles's home in Gloucestershire in the company of friends like Guy Pelly.

By the end of his second term he was unsettled enough to suggest to his father that it might be better if he pursued his higher education at another university. He said he was 'bored'. He was also very lonely. It came to be known as 'William's wobble'.

Prince Charles is the most compliant of fathers. Indecisive himself, he finds it difficult to impose firm discipline on others. He prefers to reason with his sons. 'I like to talk things through with them, to explain the pros and cons of the situation,' he explained to me. William had told his friend Rickards that he would much prefer to be at Edinburgh. He said the same to his father. Charles responded by pointing out that Edinburgh presented enormous security problems, that St Andrews had been William's own choice and that he should stick by his decision, and that the homesickness that often besets students away from home for the first time would soon pass.

'Lots of people take a while to settle in,' agreed one of William's Etonian friends at St Andrews.

There was also the cautionary tale of William's out-of-favour uncle to be borne in mind. Edward's decision to leave the Royal Marines had done immense damage to his public image. At the Royal Tournament that year the 100-odd members of Yankee Company 45 Commando wore T-shirts bearing the legend, 'You can turn a frog into a prince – but you can't turn a prince into a Marine'. Another T-shirt read, 'NOT by Royal Appointment'. They were wounding insults.

The Royal Family had closed ranks around Edward. Even the irascible Prince Philip who, as Captain General of the Royal Marines, had good reason to be angered, was surprisingly sympathetic to his son's plight. However, in private the Queen took a more calculated line. She viewed the matter from the perspective of royal duty and the good name of her family. She felt that Edward had done himself no favours by walking out, and she was right – by quitting, Edward had, albeit unfairly, saddled himself with the reputation for being something of a 'wimp', a perception he has never been able to dispel.

This was not a reputation a future king would wish for himself and William was persuaded, albeit grudgingly, to stay on at St Andrews.

In fact, he was lucky to have made it that far. William keeps his car at St Andrews but like most of the students he uses a bicycle to get around the campus. Cycling with head down and eyes hidden under a baseball cap is not the safest way to travel, however, and part-way through his second term his university career almost came to an abrupt end.

As he pedalled out of St Salvator's one morning he hit a passing car. He was thrown across the bonnet, to land in a painful heap on the cobbled street. He survived with just a few scratches and a dent to his pride. He was lucky and it proved to be a portent for the months ahead. In his second year he settled down, as his father had predicted he would. He moved into his own flat in a converted Victorian house with large rooms. He shares it with Fergus Boyd, his contemporary in Gailey's house at Eton, and Kate Middleton, but it is William who prepares many of the evening meals, putting to practical use the skills he acquired in his cookery course at Eton. He also started mixing in more and even found the confidence to attend a jazz night organised by the Kate Kennedy Club.

He had finally come to appreciate what the university offered and that was anonymity. To the world at large he is Prince William, heir to the British throne. At St Andrews he was plain 'William Wales'. That is how he signed his cheques. That is what he wants to remain for as long as possible.

Postscript

The British monarchy has an infinite capacity to reinvent itself. It needs that talent now as never before and the future is very much in William's hands.

He is the prince who will one day be king, and it will be his task to give a new and more vital definition to the institution he was born to head. It is not an obligation he relishes. He refuses to use the title 'His Royal Highness' and shuns the limelight, undertaking very few royal duties and then only reluctantly.

Harry is different. He enjoys his princely status and the perks that go with it. He is the second son. And that, as he tells everyone, has given him the licence to do what he likes with his life.

Yet he, too, will have his part to play in supporting his brother as the Royal Family sets about redefining itself to satisfy the demands of a new social era in which awe has been replaced by quizzical scepticism, and the splendours of pageantry no longer disguise faults of behaviour. If the monarchy is to move forward it must rediscover the stability it forfeited to the scandals of the recent past. Sybaritic excess cannot be part of that agenda.

Diana's example is one course for the brothers to follow. They have come to recognise her faults but that has served to highlight her extraordinary ability to empathise with the problems of others. She took royalty out of the ivory tower and in among the people. After her, there can be no return to the old ways, and in that William is very much his mother's son. He makes no attempt to disguise his dislike of pomp and protocol, and has questioned the need for so many royal homes and palaces.

Nor does he share his father's nostalgic attachment to the kind of pampered luxury exemplified by the Queen Mother. Charles likes to dress for dinner. William is much happier wearing jeans and a woolly Aston Villa hat. He is more New World casual than English country squire. So is Harry. That is how Diana would have wanted it. 'My sons are my legacy,' she said. Her friend, Vivienne Parry observed, 'Diana gave them a sense of their value as people rather than princes.'

Charles's influence is not to be discounted. He, too, wanted his sons to show concern for people's feelings. That is a lesson Harry is still learning, but his brother grasped it at an early age. Diana called William 'sensitive'. Charles viewed that as a strength, not a weakness. He said, 'Sensitivity to others which, by any definition, is actually called good manners, I think a lot of people have forgotten. And also, to do to others as you would have them do to you.'

He also refused to allow his sons to be poured into a straitjacket of royal tradition. He said, 'I feel very strongly that they should be protected as much as possible from being dragged from pillar to post. I don't want them to do too many official things until they absolutely have to, because it's very important to develop in as private an atmosphere as possible.'

There is a limit to how much privacy they will be afforded, however. Being royal is a life sentence without the possibility of parole. George V's estimable private secretary Lord Wigram summed it up when he informed Edward VIII shortly before the Abdication, 'Sir, you have *no* private life. The king has *no* private life. You are mistaken if you believe otherwise.'

In a celebrity-orientated age, that rule applies equally to princes and their consorts. It consumed Diana and drove her to the edge of distraction. It is a problem that the women who marry William and Harry will have to contend with. For that reason, both have been careful to shield their girlfriends from the ruthless spotlight of public attention. They had seen what it did to their mother. William said, 'No one is going to know who I'm really going out with until I am ready to let them know.'

That does not preclude them from engaging in a little test-marketing. Their social life away from school and university revolves around polo and hunting. To help them in their organisation they have the services of a personal secretary, Helen Asprey, a member of the jewellery family, while Mark Dyer, back in the royal fold on William's insistence, coordinates their sporting activities. Both are friends as well as employees, and there is never a dearth of attractive young ladies on the outings they arrange. One who caught William's eye was Arabella, the daughter of the manager of the Cirencester Park polo club, Major Nicholas Musgrave. They enjoyed a companionable relationship that continued well into William's first year at St Andrews. Harry, meanwhile, has preferred to play the field, at one point showing a particular penchant for the girls at Westonbirt, the girls' public school near Cirencester.

It will be some time yet before these flirtations develop into anything more serious. They have to establish themselves first. Harry has jokingly said that he would like to be a professional polo player and, according to model Jodie Kidd's brother Jack, who is one, he has the talent to become a fully fledged international. 'That idea was mainly put out to wind up my father,' Harry later admitted. 'We had not discussed my gap year until then, so I casually mentioned spending the year playing polo to him to see what the reaction would be.'

Charles was suitably taken aback. He was concerned that Harry, who had struggled to pass his GCSEs and failed in two out of three of his first AS levels, should concentrate on completing his full-time education. Only then would the matter of his career be decided on, with the armed forces the likely choice.

It is his mother, however, whose example he intends to follow. He plans to take on charitable work in areas reflecting the type of causes Diana was interested in. It would be the fulfilment of the promise he made in the days following his mother's death.

He said, 'I always wanted to do it, but especially after my mother died.

The fifth anniversary was important because she wasn't remembered the way I would have liked. She had more guts than anybody else. The way she got close to people and went for the sort of charities and organisations that everybody else was scared to go near, such as landmines in the Third World. She got involved in things that nobody had done before.

'I want to carry on the things she didn't quite finish.'

In psychiatric terms, this is seen as a process of unconscious identification with the dead person and a way of keeping his memory of her alive.

William's future is more prescribed. He is also giving serious consideration to taking a commission in the armed forces. 'I'd like him to go into the Navy,' said Charles, who had served in the Royal Navy, as his father, grandfather and great-grandfather had done before him. William, however, has expressed a greater enthusiasm for the Army. Charles would be happy with that.

'A period in the armed forces is of enormous value and benefit,' he said. 'It certainly was for me. Apart from anything else, I think the question of man management, human relations, of being responsible for other people's welfare, which is what happens when you go into the armed forces, is very important. You are given responsibility and I learned an enormous amount from that.'

An ability to deal with responsibility will be vital in the years ahead. The power of the monarchy may have been whittled away but it remains central to the British constitution. It will be up to William to keep it there. His father has told him to 'make sure that he's got advisers around him, to choose the right people to help him do the job'.

Charles has not always followed his own advice. He is inclined to ignore the counsel he is given, preferring to follow his own intuition, often with calamitous results. That has led to a fast turnover of staff, which is hardly the finest of examples.

In other areas, however, Charles has proved himself more adept at being what his former press secretary Sandy Henney called a 'fine role model'. She was referring to his good works, particularly with the Prince's Trust, rather than his domestic arrangements. Explaining his approach, Charles said, 'To me the object of life is not to pursue personal happiness. It sounds ridiculously self-righteous and trite, but I would rather pursue other people's happiness.'

William has indicated that he wishes to do the same. The manner in which he sets about it will be his own, however. As his father acknowledges, 'He will no doubt have his own outlook and his own way of doing things, which wouldn't be exactly the same as mine by any means.'

That independence to make his own choices does not allow William to discard completely what has gone before. Continuity is fundamental to the Royal Family's role. Diana never fully appreciated that. William does.

He was at Buckingham Palace to see the outpouring of national pride that marked the Queen's Golden Jubilee. And he witnessed at first hand the emotion that attended the death of his great-grandmother, the Queen Mother. She had pulled the monarchy through the disaster of the Abdication and exemplified Britain's fighting spirit in the Second World War. William recalled, 'It was a pleasure to sit next to her at lunch. She always had some great war stories and to hear them from her really brought it all to life, something that happened long before we were born.'

She was an example to him. 'Whenever I felt ill I always used to remember that in the same circumstances she would battle on, no matter how she felt,' he said. 'She never gave up. I remember her as being a huge inspiration to me, someone to really look up to and admire. She was an historic link.'

William, with Harry at his side, walked behind her coffin when it was borne on a horse-drawn gun carriage from the Queen's Chapel opposite St James's Palace to Westminster Hall. They walked behind it again four days later as it was carried from Westminster Hall to the ancient Abbey for the funeral. William had conquered the reluctance that had made him so unwilling to accompany his mother's cortège five years earlier.

It was the Queen Mother's turn to take her place in the annals of the past. For William it was another step on the steady march into the future.

Bibliography

Anderson, Christopher, *Diana's Boys* (HarperCollins 2001)

Barry, Stephen, *Royal Secrets* (Villard Books 1985); *Royal Service* (Macmillan Publishers Ltd 1993)

Bedell Smith, Sally, *Diana in Search of Herself* (Times Books 1999)

Benson, Ross, *Charles: The Untold Story* (Victor Gollancz Ltd 1993)

Berry, Wendy, *The Housekeeper's Diary* (Barricade Books 1995)

Dimbleby, Jonathan, *The Prince of Wales* (Little Brown 1994)

Edwards, Arthur, *I'll Tell The Jokes* (Blake 1993)

Figes, Kate, *The Terrible Teens* (Viking 2002)

Fontana, Dr David, *Your Growing Child* (Fontana 1990)

Friedman, Dennis, *Inheritance* (Sidgwick & Jackson 1993)

Garthorne-Hardy, Jonathan, *The Rise and Fall of the British Nanny* (Hodder & Stoughton 1972)

Gregory, Martin, *Diana: The Last Days* (Virgin 1999)

Hewitt, James, *Love & War* (Blake Publishing 1999)

Jephson, Patrick, *Diana Princess of Wales* (HarperCollins 2000)

Junor, Penny, *Charles: Victim or Villain* (HarperCollins 1998)

Kay, Richard and Levy, Geoffrey, *Diana: The Untold Story* (Daily Mail 1998)

Menkes, Suzy, *Queen and Country* (Grafton Books 1992)

Morton, Andrew, *Diana: Her True Story – In her own Words* (Michael O'Mara Books 1997)

Parsons, Betty, *The Expectant Father* (Paperfronts 2001)

Rees-Jones, Trevor, *The Bodyguard's Story* (Little Brown 2002)

Rose, Kenneth, *King George V* (Macmillan Publishers 1983)

Seward, Ingrid, *Diana Portrait of a Princess* (Weidenfeld & Nicolson 1987); *By Royal Invitation* (Sidgwick & Jackson 1988); *Royalty Revealed* (Sidgwick & Jackson 1989)

Sarah H.R.H. Duchess of York (HarperCollins 1991); *Royal Children of the Twentieth Century* (HarperCollins 1993); *Prince Edward: A Biography* (Century 1995); *The Last Great Edwardian Lady: The Life and Times of Queen Elizabeth the Queen Mother* 1999); *The Queen & Di* (HarperCollins 2000)

Simmons, Simone, *Diana: The Secret Years* (Michael O'Mara Books 1998)

Snell, Kate, *Diana: Her Last Love* (Grenada Media 2000)

Spencer, Charles, *Althorp* (Viking 1998)

Wharfe, Ken, *Diana: A Closely Guarded Secret* (Michael O'Mara Books 2002)

Index

Note: The following abbreviations are used in the index: C for Charles, Prince of Wales; CPB for Camilla Parker Bowles; D for Diana, Princess of Wales; H for Prince Henry (Harry); W for Prince William